The Development of the American Public Accountancy Profession

This book presents a unique series of researched biographies of professional accountants who immigrated to the United States and developed their careers there in the late nineteenth, and early twentieth, century. Until now, little has been written about the positive impact of immigrant professionals on American life.

These accountants greatly influenced the public accountancy profession, and this volume is a tribute to the efforts of a relatively small group of Scots who helped to establish and nurture American public accountancy at a time when demand for its services greatly exceeded the ability of native-born accountants to provide them. And their impact on public accountancy in the US was disproportionate to their size as a group.

This book will interest accounting historians and social historians, particularly those whose focus is on the development of professions from a historical point of view. It should also be fascinating reading to the partners and staff in the large public accountancy firms as these have been built in part on foundations laid by the skills and efforts of a relatively few Scottish immigrants.

T. A. Lee is Emeritus Professor of Accountancy at the University of Alabama. He is one of the most published accounting researchers of the last 50 years, publishing extensively in accounting history. He has worked in Scottish universities for twenty-five years, and in US universities for twelve. In 2005, Professor Lee received the Lifetime Achievement Award of the British Accounting Association and was inducted into its Accounting Hall of Fame.

Routledge New Works in Accounting History
Edited by

Garry Carnegie
Melbourne University Private, Australia

John Richard Edwards
Cardiff University, UK

Salvador Carmona
Instituto de Empresa, Spain

Dick Fleischman
John Carroll University, USA

The Development of the American Public Accountancy Profession

Scottish chartered accountants and the early American public accountancy profession

T. A. Lee

R Routledge
Taylor & Francis Group

LONDON AND NEW YORK

First published 2006
by Routledge
2 Park Square, Milton Park, Abingdon, Oxon, OX14 4RN

Simultaneously published in the USA and Canada
by Routledge
270 Madison Avenue, New York, NY 10016

Routledge is an imprint of the Taylor & Francis Group, an informa group

© 2006 T. A. Lee

Typeset in Times by Keyword Group Ltd
Printed and bound in Great Britain by Biddles Ltd, King's Lynn

British Library Cataloguing in Publication Data
A catalogue record for this book is available
from the British Library

Library of Congress Cataloging in Publication Data
A catalogue record for this book has been requested

ISBN10: 0-415-40394-4 (hbk)
ISBN13: 978-0-415-40394-8 (hbk)

This book is dedicated to all Scottish Chartered Accountancy immigrants to the United States who have and continue to contribute so much over the decades to American public accountancy.

Contents

List of tables

The author

Tom Lee was born and educated in Edinburgh. He qualified as a Chartered Accountant (CA) in 1964 with the Albert J. Watson Prize in 1963 and the award of Distinction and Institute of Chartered Accountants of Scotland (ICAS) Gold Medal in 1964. The Prize and Gold Medal were funded by a gift to ICAS from one of the immigrants in this study, Albert John Watson. Tom Lee was placed first nationally in the Associateship examination of the Chartered Institute of Taxation in 1966. Following post-qualifying experience as an auditor with Peat, Marwick, Mitchell & Company (PMMC), he pursued an academic career until his retirement in 2001 as Professor Emeritus of Accountancy at the University of Alabama. Previously, Tom Lee had held chairs in accountancy at the Universities of Liverpool (1973–6) and Edinburgh (1976–90), and was the Culverhouse Chair of Accountancy and a State of Alabama Eminent Scholar at the University of Alabama (1990–2001). He was awarded that University's Burnum Award for scholarship in 1997. Professor Lee has served on numerous ICAS committees, including the Scottish Committee on Accounting History (SCAH) and the ICAS Council (1989–90), and was ICAS Director of Accounting and Auditing in 1983 and 1984. His research specialties include corporate audit theory, income and capital theory, shareholder use and understanding of accounting information, cash flow accounting and reporting, the sociology of the accountancy profession and academic accountancy, and accounting and auditing history. Professor Lee has published in all of these areas in major journals throughout the world and authored and co-authored numerous books. He is a past President of the Academy of Accounting Historians (1997) and, respectively, an Honorary and Visiting Professor of Accounting at the Universities of Dundee and Newcastle-Upon-Tyne. In 2005, Professor Lee received the Lifetime Achievement Award of the British Accounting Association and was inducted into its Accounting Hall of Fame. He lives in the village of Haddington in the County of East Lothian in Scotland.

Preface

This book celebrates the 150th anniversary of the formation of a professional accountancy body whose members have influenced not only accountancy in Scotland but also that of many countries throughout the world. ICAS was formed in 1951 by the union of the Society of Accountants in Edinburgh (SAE) (formed originally as the Institute of Accountants in Edinburgh in 1853), the Institute of Accountants & Actuaries in Glasgow (IAAG) (1854), and the Society of Accountants in Aberdeen (SAA) (1867). The charter founders of these bodies totalled 125 men. The initial membership of ICAS in 1951 was 5,181 and, by the end of 2004, after 150 years of Scottish CAs, there were in excess of 15,500 ICAS members – 121 times the foundation level of 100 years previously. More than 2,000 of the 2004 members were located in 98 countries other than the United Kingdom (UK). Sixty-one per cent worked in Scotland and 27 per cent were in public accountancy practice. In 1854, all members of the SAE and the IAAG worked in, respectively, Edinburgh and Glasgow. All were listed as public accountants although several SAE members were insurance company managers and many IAAG members were also stockbrokers.

This book presents a series of researched biographies of 161 SAE, IAAG, and SAA members who immigrated to the United States (US) and developed their careers there from 1875 to 1914. Some returned to Scotland or moved elsewhere (e.g. to Canada), but the large majority lived and died in the US and many greatly influenced the development of its public accountancy profession through its firms and institutions. Most appear to have immigrated for economic reasons, although one left Scotland with criminal charges pending. The book also examines the lives of 16 Scots accountants who immigrated to the US prior to 1914 as unqualified accountants (UQ) and about whom there is archival material available. Most of the UQ men were associated with the IAAG and had incomplete apprenticeships in that body. The remainder trained in other related areas such as business or law. The UQ immigrants are included in the text because of their typically significant contribution to US public accountancy and to compare with the CA migrants. For example, the UQ men include Arthur Young, the founder of Arthur Young & Company (AYC) (now Ernst & Young), and Simpson Rodger Mitchell, the co-founder of Marwick, Mitchell & Company (MMC) (later PMMC and now KPMG).

The book is a tribute to the efforts of a relatively small group of Scots who helped to establish and nurture American public accountancy at a time when demand for its services greatly exceeded the capacity of native-born accountants to provide them. As such, the biographies represent a history of well-known contributions to public accountancy as well as less well-known influences. They also reveal insights into the rich variety of experiences enjoyed by Scots immigrants to the US at the end of the nineteenth century and beginning of the twentieth century. These insights should be of interest to historians of migrations generally and migrations to the US particularly. However, the text is also intended for CAs in the UK and Certified Public Accountants (CPA) in the US who wish to understand the heritage and foundation of their profession.

There are several limitations to this text. The first constraint is that the book has been prepared from archival material discovered by the writer in the UK and the US. Numerous libraries and national archives were visited in these countries. However, this should not be regarded as an exhaustive archival search. There may well be archival material that has yet to be accessed by accounting historians. A second constraint relates to the UQ accountants. A relative few were discovered during the archival searches for biographical material for the Scots CAs. This means that there may well be other UQ individuals from Scotland who practised in the US but who left no trace discovered by the writer. Finally, all of the biographies are of male subjects. This is not because of a deliberate bias on the part of the writer – merely that female public accountants in Scotland began to appear for the first time in the early 1920s following the First World War and are therefore outside the scope of this study.

Acknowledgments

Funding for the research on which this book has been based came initially from a grant from SCAH, the history committee of ICAS. Further funding was received from the Culverhouse Endowment of the University of Alabama until the writer's retirement in 2001. Funding for research since 2001 has come from personal savings. Students at the Universities of Edinburgh and Alabama provided research assistance in the early stages of the project and several publications reported various statistical analyses of the migration. These papers were presented at various research seminars and conferences and are cited in the bibliography. The author wishes to express his grateful thanks to all funding agencies, host institutions and organisations, research assistants, and reviewers and editors who contributed to the completion of this book. Particular thanks go to members of SCAH in the early 1990s for their encouragement of this type of research and to Isobel Webber of the Research Department of ICAS for administering the first stage of the project.

Abbreviations

In order to assist the reader with the text, the following abbreviations appear throughout. When they first appear in the text, the full text and abbreviation are stated. Thereafter, only the abbreviation appears.

AAM: Association of Accountants in Montreal
AAPA: American Association of Public Accountants
AIA: American Institute of Accountants
AICPA: American Institute of Certified Public Accountants
AASCPA: Arizona Society of Certified Public Accountants
ASCPA: American Society of Certified Public Accountants
AYC: Arthur Young & Company
BBAP: Bookkeepers' Beneficial Association of Philadelphia
BCICA: British Columbia Institute of Chartered Accountants
BWGC: Barrow, Wade, Guthrie & Company
CA: Chartered Accountant or Chartered Accountancy
CBC: Cooper Brothers & Company
CICA: Canadian Institute of Chartered Accountants
CPA: Certified Public Accountant or Certified Public Accountancy
CSCPA: California Society of Certified Public Accountants
DDGC: Deloitte, Dever, Griffiths & Company
FSPAUS: Federation of Societies of Public Accountants in the United States
HS: Haskins & Sells
IA: Institute of Accounts
IAAG: Institute of Accountants & Actuaries in Glasgow
IABCNY: Institute of Accountants and Bookkeepers of the City of New York
IAL: Institute of Accountants in London
IAPA: Illinois Association of Public Accountants
ICAA: Institute of Chartered Accountants of Alberta
ICAEW: Institute of Chartered Accountants in England and Wales
ICAS: Institute of Chartered Accountants of Scotland
ISCPA: Illinois Society of Certified Public Accountants
IASCPA: Iowa Society of Certified Public Accountants
JCC: Jones, Caesar & Company

LBC: Leslie, Banks & Company
LBD: Lingley, Baird & Dixon
LRBM: Lybrand, Ross Brothers & Montgomery
MIC: Mackay, Irons & Company
MICA: Manitoba Institute of Chartered Accountants
MISCPA: Michigan Society of Certified Public Accountants
MMC: Marwick, Mitchell & Company
MMPC: Marwick, Mitchell, Peat & Company
MNSCPA: Minnesota Society of Certified Public Accountants
MRC: Menzies, Robertson & Company
MSCPA: Missouri Society of Certified Public Accountants
NJSCPA: New Jersey Society of Certified Public Accountants
NYSSCPA: New York State Society of Certified Public Accountants
PMMC: Peat, Marwick, Mitchell & Company
PPC: Pogson, Peloubet & Company
PTD: Paterson, Teale & Dennis
PWC: Price, Waterhouse & Company
QICA: Quebec Institute of Chartered Accountants
SAA: Society of Accountants in Aberdeen
SAE: Society of Accountants in Edinburgh
SAIE: Society of Accountants in England
SCAH: Scottish Committee on Accounting History
SEC: Securities Exchange Commission
SIAA: Society of Incorporated Accountants & Auditors
SSC: Solicitor Before the Supreme Courts
TNBS: Touche, Niven, Bailey & Smart
TNC, Touche, Niven & Company
TSCPA: Texas Society of Certified Public Accountants
TWGC: Thomas, Wade, Guthrie & Company
UK: United Kingdom
UQ: Unqualified accountants
US: United States of America
VSCPA: Virginia Society of Certified Public Accountants
WS: Writer to the Signet
WSCPA: Wisconsin Society of Certified Public Accountants

1   The first migrant

Eric Mackay Noble was twenty-eight years old when, in 1875, he journeyed from Edinburgh to board ship at the port of Greenock near Glasgow and sail to New York. Little is known about Noble and there does not appear to be a physical description of him in the public record. On arrival at the Manhattan Island reception point, he appears to have proceeded immediately from New York to Washington in the District of Columbia and practised there as a public accountant until his death in 1892 at the age of forty-five. He was unmarried and the first of the Scots accounting immigrants in this book to die in the US. In Washington, Noble's professional services included the duties of a commissioner in the Court of Claims.[1] This meant that he was approved to present property claims of clients to the Court and therefore continued the court-related practise he probably experienced in Scotland. Noble's place in accounting history, however, is as the first CA to emigrate from the UK to the US and develop a career there as a resident rather than as a public accountant visiting that country for purposes of providing an audit or investigatory service for a UK-based client.

Eight men qualified with Noble as members of the SAE in 1871. They all had fathers of either independent means or professional backgrounds. However, despite this homogeneity, their professional careers took distinctly different routes. One man, who was part of a well-known Edinburgh family associated with the Scottish medical profession and the insurance industry, died soon after qualification. Another disappeared from the SAE records in the 1880s and nothing can be found about his career. A third man whose father was a medical doctor with the Honorable East India Company in India practised accountancy in Edinburgh for a short time before immigrating to New Zealand to pursue a career in farming. The fourth member of Noble's class became the manager of a major Scottish life insurance company based in London. This means that only three of the nine members of the 1871 intake to the SAE membership practised as public accountants in Edinburgh and only two achieved office in the SAE. These features were relatively typical of the early history of the SAE membership.

Noble was the son of a Free Church of Scotland minister in Fife. He was born in the village of Stobbo in Peebles-shire. However, his family roots were in at least three other Scottish counties – Ayrshire, Lanarkshire, and Linlithgowshire – and reflect the migratory character of eighteenth and nineteenth century Scots. He resigned from the SAE in 1875 when he entered the US, but became a member of the newly formed American Association of Public Accountants (AAPA) in 1888. Noble does not appear to have been active in the AAPA. However, he was followed to the US by 160 other Scottish CAs by the end of 1914 and many became active and influential in American public accountancy affairs. Their lives before and after their migration are the subject of this book, as are the careers of 16 other Scots who were not professionally qualified (UQ) prior to immigration.

2 The mobile Scot

The history of the Scottish people demonstrates a national propensity to move from one location to another and there has always been a steady haemorrhaging of Scots to other parts of the UK and overseas. This phenomenon started as a trickle in the seventeenth century and grew to upwards of 100,000 individuals during the eighteenth century. However, it was in the nineteenth century that the migration of Scots accelerated. Quantifying this development accurately is impossible until 1851 because of the paucity of earlier records. However, nineteenth century data generally suggest a period of massive European immigration to the US particularly. Estimates suggest that more than 50 million Europeans immigrated mainly to the US between 1815 and 1914, including 22 million from the UK. From 1825 to 1914, nearly two million Scots left their native land for non-European destinations. Approximately 800,000 went to the US and a further 600,000 arrived in Canada. The total population loss during this period represents approximately 42 per cent of Scotland's population by the beginning of the First World War in 1914. This compares with an equivalent figure for England and Wales of 25 per cent. Migration was therefore a significant influence on the economic and social life of Scotland and recipient countries such as the US.

Underlying the migration statistics for Scotland is a history of persistent economic and social upheaval as, first, agriculture commercialised, and, second, industrial processes expanded and matured within urban centres. These events resulted in a steady internal migration from country to town, with more and more of the population residing in towns and cities until Scotland in the nineteenth century was one of the most urbanised nations in the world. Unsurprisingly, such migrations spilled overland to England and overseas to developing industrial countries such as the US. They were predominantly economic in nature and had long ago surpassed the earlier movements made for penal or religious reasons. The evicted tenant farmer and skilled artisan had replaced earlier immigrants such as the persecuted Catholic, jailed Covenanter, or habitual criminal. The economic model at work was one in which immigrants compared economic conditions at home and economic prospects abroad, and decided that prospects looked brighter in foreign parts. They were therefore more often than not pushed to relocate overseas because of poor conditions at home. These men and women included farm labourers and domestic servants and, increasingly, skilled workers unemployed during frequent economic recessions in Scotland. There were others, however, who were pulled to countries such as the US by opportunities created by new industries and shortages of skills, or by the prospect of better opportunities (as in farming). In the eighteenth century, these immigrants included managers needed by entrepreneurs such as the Glasgow tobacco merchants. Later immigrants took skills in mining, steel making, and engineering and then professional competencies that were in short supply such as in medicine, law, religion, and teaching. The prospect of cheap and abundant land also fuelled much of the early migrations from Scotland.

The movement of Scots to the US reached its peak in the last half of the nineteenth century, with Glasgow as one of the two main UK ports for embarkation to North America (the other being Liverpool). Indeed, between 1865 and 1910, the US became the most popular overseas destination for Scots immigrants. This was a period in which there was a marked disparity in economic performance between the UK and the US. For example, between 1870 and 1913, US total and industrial outputs increased at average annual rates more than double those of the UK. In the early 1870s, the UK had in excess of one-third of world manufacturing output, compared to less than one-quarter for the US. By 1914, however, these proportions had reversed to 36 per cent for the US and 14 per cent for the UK. In addition, the US was changing from a predominantly agricultural economy (53 per cent of value added in 1880) to one dependent on industry (62 per cent of value added in 1909). However, over much of the same period (i.e. 1875 to 1914), the UK was the world's leading exporter of capital. By 1914, for example, it had almost one-quarter of its national wealth invested overseas, and of this proportion, one-quarter was in the US (predominantly in industries such as breweries, railways, and steel making). This investment triggered the need for public accountancy services to protect individual investors residing in the UK from fraudulent or incompetent management in the US. The first British public accountants to visit the UK were therefore conducting audits or investigations on behalf of British shareholders with commercial operations in the US.

Scots immigrants came from mainly lower middle and working class backgrounds during most of the period of the overall migration to the US. As previously mentioned, the evolution of migrant backgrounds started with low skill occupations with an agricultural focus and gradually included craft and trade skills in areas such as mining, moving to a full range of industrial skills from the early nineteenth century onwards. By mid century, 59 per cent of Scots immigrants to the US were from industrial communities, and by 1885, this figure had increased to 80 per cent. During the latter period, immigrants with appropriate skills were attracted to industrial developments in the US where there was a lack of local expertise. The translation of skills between Scotland and the US increasingly included professional competencies and, during much of the period from 1875 to 1914, Scots immigrants in the US included, first, members of the traditional professions such as medicine and law, and, second, those from the newer professions such as accountancy. The Scottish CAs in this study formed an important subset of the skilled professional immigrants who were essential to this expansion.

3   Propensity to migrate

Although the large majority of Scots immigrants to the US were from lower middle and working class backgrounds, there were also many men (predominantly) from the upper and upper middle classes who decided to leave Scotland for foreign parts. These included several of the accounting immigrants in this study. Because of their family backgrounds, it is difficult to argue economic necessity as a major reason for their migration. The phenomenon of upper and upper middle class men migrating from Scotland in the late nineteenth century is illustrated by a case study analysis of students at the Edinburgh Academy who were at school there with nine of the accounting migrants to the US. The Academy was founded in the New Town of Edinburgh in 1824 at a cost of £12,000 in order to provide a traditional education in the classical subjects of Latin and Greek. Its founders included leading Edinburgh professionals such as Henry Cockburn, an Advocate who was to become one of Scotland's most famous judges, and Sir Walter Scott, the lawyer and novelist. The driving force behind the foundation of the Edinburgh Academy was a belief held by its founders that the only Edinburgh school then providing a classical education, the Royal High School of Edinburgh, was incapable of doing so to a high standard because of its management by the Edinburgh Town Council. In turn, this lack of quality was perceived by Cockburn and his associates as preventing Edinburgh men from obtaining positions as senior government officials in the Scottish civil service. Once founded, the Academy rapidly became and remains a leading private school in the Scottish educational system.

Nine Scottish accounting migrants in this study were educated at the Edinburgh Academy. A further four migrants had siblings educated there. A characteristic of education at the Edinburgh Academy was and remains that parents of students have to be well-off to be able to afford the fees charged. For this reason, migration by Edinburgh Academy students to the US for economic reasons is less probable than for other immigrants in this study. The following analysis in Table 3.1, however, reveals a surprisingly high incidence of migration among members of Edinburgh Academy classes attended by the nine accounting migrants who were educated there. Data for the analysis were taken from *The Edinburgh Academy Register: A Record of All Those Who Have Entered the School Since Its Foundation in 1824* (1914, T & A Constable: Edinburgh) and supplemented from

Table 3.1 Immigration and Edinburgh Academy students

Migrant	School Entry	Class Size	Total Migrants	England	India/ Far East	North America	Africa	Australia/ New Zealand	Other
Blaikie	1860	89	46	11	14	6	2	8	5
Caesar	1871	15	5	1	1	2	0	1	0
Marwick	1872	55	32	9	6	4	6	5	2
McEwan	1877	25	12	4	2	2	2	2	0
Fraser	1888	113	67	14	19	12	19	3	0
Cuthbert/									
Rettie	1889	87	49	13	14	9	8	4	1
McGregor	1891	95	50	16	12	7	9	2	4
Duncan	1892	101	56	15	16	9	4	7	5
Total		**580**	**317**	**83**	**84**	**51**	**50**	**32**	**17**
Percentage			**55**	**26**	**27**	**16**	**16**	**10**	**5**

other sources (migrant = immigrant Scottish accountant educated at Edinburgh Academy; school entry = year in which immigrant Scottish accountant entered Edinburgh Academy; class size = total number of students in Edinburgh Academy class entered by immigrant Scottish accountant; total migrants = number of students in class known to have subsequently immigrated from Scotland; England = immigrants from Scotland to England, Wales, or Ireland; India and Far East = immigrants from Scotland to India, Ceylon, China, Malaysia, Burmah, etc; North America = immigrants from Scotland to the US and Canada; Africa = immigrants from Scotland to all parts of Africa (including South Africa); Australia and New Zealand = immigrants from Scotland to these countries; and other = immigrants from Scotland to European and South American countries).

The analysis in Table 3.1 reveals the popularity of migration among students at the Edinburgh Academy who entered it between 1860 and 1892. Restricting the analysis to those students who entered the Academy at the same time as the nine accounting migrants, a total of 580 students can be observed. All of these students came from upper and upper middle class backgrounds that suggest immigration ought not to have been for economic reasons when leaving school. Yet, 55 per cent of students migrated on a permanent basis to various parts of the world. More than one-quarter (26 per cent) of this group moved within the UK and Ireland in a form of internal migration (typically to England as merchants or medical practitioners). A further one-quarter (27 per cent) moved to India and the Far East (mainly to various colonies then comprising the British Empire). The remainder arrived in parts of North America, Africa, and Australasia (42 per cent) (usually to countries in the British Empire), as well as Europe and South America (5 per cent). The migration factor was present in all nine classes of the Edinburgh Academy represented in Table 3.1 and it was therefore not an unusual occurrence. Indeed, overall, more Edinburgh Academy students in these classes migrated than remained in Scotland.

Table 3.2 Occupations of Edinburgh Academy migrants

Occupation	1860	1871	1872	1877	1888	1889	1891	1892	Total	%
Military	8	0	5	2	18	11	8	11	63	27
Professions	4	1	4	3	9	6	6	11	44	19
Commerce	5	1	4	1	10	5	9	4	39	17
Agriculture	8	2	7	2	8	9	4	10	50	21
Other	4	0	1	0	4	2	3	2	16	7
Unknown	6	0	2	0	4	3	4	3	22	9
Total	**35**	**4**	**23**	**8**	**53**	**36**	**34**	**41**	**234**	**100**

Table 3.2 reports the occupations of the Edinburgh Academy migrants moving outside the UK and Ireland on a permanent basis – i.e. a total of 234 students (including the nine accounting migrants) (military = army and navy commissions; professions = accountants, engineers, medical practitioners, and lawyers; commerce = merchants, bankers, factors, and insurance managers; agriculture = farmers, planters, and ranchers; other = government officials and teachers; per cent = percentage of total comprised of each stated occupation).

According to Table 3.2, the largest proportion of the Edinburgh Academy school leavers who migrated overseas where either army or naval officers (27 per cent). Many served in various wars in South Africa and China as well as in British colonies such as India and remained there when they retired. The next largest group worked in agriculture, again predominantly in British colonies (21 per cent). Many were tea and coffee planters and several had trained professionally before employment as planters. For example, two SAE members switched from public accountancy to planting as did a lawyer who qualified as a Writer to the Signet (WS). These agricultural occupations created trading opportunities between the UK and the British colonies and 17 per cent of the migrants worked as merchants, agents, bankers, and factors in countries such as India, Canada, and Australia. A small proportion of the immigrants were professionally-qualified men (19 per cent) spread over several professions, including 14 CAs. The remaining migrants were government civil servants and teachers.

The above figures reveal that late nineteenth century migration to the US by Scottish accountants was a very small part of a greater migration that appears to have been stimulated not only by economic and social conditions at home but also by economic and social opportunities overseas. What appears to have been central to the overall migration was the expansion of the British Empire and the trading opportunities, government administration, military activity that this created. In other words, trading resulted in military presences to fight and police, and civil servants to administer the colonies. Within this general development, there also started to appear a need for specialist professional services such as accountancy. Most interestingly, however, this need was most pronounced in the developing industrial state of the US rather than in the under-developed agricultural states of the British Empire such as India. The Scots accounting immigrants were therefore attempting to satisfy a need for specialist professional services associated with an advancing industrial economy.

4   Departure and arrival cities

The accounting migrants to the US described in this study came predominantly from four Scottish cities or towns – i.e. Aberdeen, Dundee, Edinburgh, and Glasgow. These were the major Scottish commercial or professional centres of the time and Aberdeen, Dundee, and Glasgow were major Scottish ports. Even Edinburgh had an adjacent port link of Leith. Most of the migrants arrived in the US at the Manhattan reception point in the port of New York, with the remainder entering at ports such as Chicago and Minneapolis. The following notes provide a brief background to these cities.

Aberdeen

Aberdeen was first settled on the banks of the River Don in the north-east of Scotland prior to the twelfth century. The town received a royal charter to manage its affairs in 1124 and became a religious and educational centre in the region. The University of Aberdeen had its origins in the town by 1494. Occupations of early Aberdonians included agriculture and fishing, and the development of port facilities established a merchant community and later industries such as shipbuilding. The arrival of the railway in the second half of the nineteenth century further assisted Aberdeen's growth as a commercial centre. It particularly improved communication between the town and other main centres of commerce in Scotland. By 1871, Aberdeen's population was 88,000 and, forty years later, this had grown to 151,000. It became a city in 1899. By the time of the migration of Aberdeen CAs to the US, Aberdeen had several banks and insurance companies formed there in the late eighteenth and early nineteenth centuries. It also had a well-established legal profession with the Faculty of Advocates in Aberdeen chartered in 1774. There was a small community of CA firms. The SAA was formed in 1867 with twelve members. By 1884, it had twenty members and two apprentices. Thirty years later, in 1914, there were 75 members and five apprentices. Aberdeen was therefore not a large producer of CAs between 1875 and 1914. Its links to the US, however, were strongest during the North Sea oil boom of the 1970s and 1980s when the city became the port base for off-shore oil rigs, many owned by US companies.

Dundee

As with Aberdeen, Dundee was a small port settlement formed in the eleventh century. Situated on the north bank of the River Tay on the east coast of the central lowlands of Scotland, the town became a royal burgh in 1191 and a city in 1894. By the fourteenth century, it had a population of approximately 4,000 and its major activities were the importing of wines from France and Spain, as well as grain, hides, and wool. Woollen weaving was a main industry from the fifteenth century. However, this died away by the eighteenth century to be replaced with the manufacturing of linen, thread, and leather goods. The population in 1801 was 26,000. Sixty years later, it had increased to 90,000 largely due to an Irish immigration because of the potato famine. In the nineteenth century, a whaling industry developed and linen manufacturing gave way to the production of jute products such as sacks. In 1871, the population of the town was 119,000 and, in 1911, 629,000. There were relatively few CA firms in Dundee and most of the migrants trained with firms in Glasgow. They all became members of the IAAG. It is interesting and unexplained why Dundee accountants did not train either with SAA or SAE members despite their relative proximity. Dundee remains today as a major commercial centre in the east of Scotland.

Glasgow

Glasgow started as a religious settlement on the banks of the River Clyde on the west coast of the central region of Scotland. The date for this foundation was about 543 and the town's population by the late twelfth century has been estimated at 1,500. In 1175, the town received a royal charter and, by the end of the fifteenth century, it was a major academic and religious centre in Scotland. The University of Glasgow was founded in 1450. The town became a major trading centre from the early 1500s with crafts such as metalwork, weaving and brewing. By 1670, it was the second largest Scottish burgh after Edinburgh. The tobacco trade with the American colonies began in the early 1670s and Glasgow became the main tobacco importing centre in Europe by the 1730s. By then, a major trade in sugar and rum had also been established with the West Indies. Dredging the River Clyde in 1772 allowed large vessels to dock in Glasgow and this became the catalyst for shipbuilding and other heavy industries. By the nineteenth century, Glasgow was described after London as the Second City of the British Empire and was famous for industries such as soap, distilling, glass, sugar, and textiles. Proximity to raw materials such as iron ore and coal enabled major industries to develop such as locomotives and shipbuilding. The city benefited in this regard by mass urban migrations from the Highlands of Scotland and Ireland. In 1871, Glasgow had a population of 477,000 and this grew to 1,055,000 by 1911. As well as its merchant and industrial heritage, the city had a substantial professional community. In 1867, for example, there were 210 members of the Faculty of Procurators in Glasgow. This was the main legal body in the city and was chartered in 1796. The Glasgow Stock Exchange was formed in 1844. The IAAG had been founded in 1854 with 49 members. In 1884, it had 118 members and, thirty years later, 826 members with 102 apprentices. Glasgow remains today as a major commercial, financial, and industrial city in Europe.

Edinburgh

Edinburgh is the capital city of Scotland and achieved that status in 1437. Its foundation was a fortress built by an English invader, King Edwin of Northumbria in 626. A castle was built on a high rock by King Malcolm III at the end of the eleventh century and a town grew around it. It was chartered in 1329. By the sixteenth century, Edinburgh was a centre for publishing and printing and, by the eighteenth century, was the focal point of a European-wide development in education, arts, and science that became known as the Scottish Enlightenment. The University of Edinburgh was founded in 1582 and several professional bodies emerged at about the same time – e.g. the Royal College of Surgeons in Edinburgh (1505), Faculty of Advocates (1532), and Society of Writers to the Signet (1600). The city was the headquarters for the national church (the Church of Scotland) and, from 1842, the break-away Free Church of Scotland. It also housed the national courts of law and became a major European financial centre with the Bank of Scotland (1695), Royal Bank of Scotland (1727), and insurance companies such as the Caledonian Insurance Company (1805). Leading Scottish schools were established in Edinburgh – e.g. the Royal High School of Edinburgh (early twelfth century) and Edinburgh Academy (1824). So, too, were numerous national clubs and associations. Railways from 1842 and the Union Canal to Glasgow linked Edinburgh not only to the other major cities in Scotland but also to those of England. By the mid nineteenth century, Edinburgh comprised two parts – the Edinburgh Old Town (largely abandoned to the working class) around the Castle and the Georgian New Town (established in 1767) for the upper and middle classes. These included members of the SAE formed in 1853 with 61 founders. By 1884, the SAE had 179 members and 21 apprentices. By 1914, these numbers were 580 and 36, respectively. The population of Edinburgh in 1871 was 196,000 and, by 1911, 322,000. Edinburgh today is a major financial and cultural centre in Europe.

Chicago

In 1880, Chicago was an American city with a population of 503,000. By 1910, this had quadrupled to 2,185,000 and the city had become the second largest city in the US. It is situated on the Chicago River on Lake Michigan in northeast Illinois. Its principal importance from its foundation in the 1670s to the time of the Scottish accountancy migration was as transportation centre for trade and commerce (e.g. grain and livestock) and eventually as a location for manufacturing industry. Chicago's origins are a settlement by explorers from Canada in 1673 that traded in products such as fur. A religious mission was set up in 1696 but abandoned in 1700. In 1779, the first permanent settlement was made by an African-American, Jean Baptiste Du Sable, and Fort Dearborn was built in 1803.

Chicago was part of the Indiana and Illinois Territories from 1801 to 1818 when it became part of the State of Illinois and, from 1831, part of Cook County. 1830 was, in fact, the first time Chicago was given a definite geographical location. It was incorporated in 1833 with a population of 350 and became a city in 1837. Its population has risen steadily over the decades – from 299,000 in 1870 to 1,100,000 in 1890 and 2,185,000 in 1910. During that time, Chicago developed its reputation as a major transportation, industrial and financial centre. Starting with the fur trade, it developed into shipping, grain, and meat packing. Its financial services community grew into the second largest in the US after New York. In 1848, the Illinois and Michigan Canal was opened and linked the Great Lakes to the Mississippi River and the Gulf of Mexico. Also in 1848, the Galena & Chicago Union Railroad established Chicago not only as a major US port but also as a main railway hub. By 1857, Chicago was the largest city in the north-west of the US.

A major fire in 1871 paradoxically facilitated the rebuilding of Chicago with modern buildings and roads. Given its trading, industrial, and financial importance within the US economy of the late nineteenth century, it is unsurprising that so many Scottish CA and UQ migrants worked in public accountancy in Chicago and set up firms there. For example, Arthur Young started his first firm there in 1893 with a fellow migrant Charles Stuart. This was at a time when Chicago was being rebuilt after the fire of 1871. Skyscraper buildings appeared and cable cars operated in the main streets as did an elevated railway. British investors in the US had been hard hit by a financial panic in 1893 and Young's initial work in Chicago was on corporate liquidations. English CA Lewis Davies Jones and Edinburgh CA William James Caesar opened a Price Waterhouse & Company (PWC) agency called Jones Caesar & Company (JCC) in Chicago in 1892. JCC had previously operated out of New York and, in 1890, acted in the $25 million capitalisation of the Chicago Junction Railway and Union Stockyards Companies. It acquired the audit of six Chicago milk companies in 1899. Other JCC services focused on companies in which there was considerable British investment – e.g. breweries, meat packing, railways and stockyards. One of the earliest American public accountancy institutions, the Illinois Association of Public Accountants (IAPA), was founded in 1897 with several CA members from the UK. The IAPA was later renamed the Illinois Society of Certified Public Accountants (ISCPA).

Minneapolis

Minneapolis is today one of the largest cities in the US and centred in the state of Minnesota at the confluence of the Mississippi River to the south, the Red River to Hudson's Bay, and the Great Lakes to the Atlantic Ocean. It is a major port and railroad centre with the grain industry as its primary economic focus. Minneapolis appears to have formed in the early 1800s, originally as the settlement of St Anthony's Falls on the Mississippi River. In 1838, it was part of the land east of the Mississippi that was ceded under the Treaty of Dakota. A sawmill was built in 1848 and, three years later, the land to the west of the Mississippi was bought from the Dakotas. In 1856, Minneapolis was named as a town and during the 1850s and 1860s it grew as settlers migrated there – particularly from Scandinavia. These migrants included timber speculators and the town's main commercial activities were lumber and the milling of wheat. In 1872, St Anthony and Minneapolis merged.

The largest influx of migrants to Minneapolis from Scandinavia, Ireland, and Germany occurred at the end of the nineteenth century. By 1890, the population of the city was 163,000, of which nearly 37 per cent was of non-US origin. It was the world's largest flour producer from 1882 to 1930. It also became the primary US wheat receiving market from 1885. Minneapolis emerged from the nineteenth century as a growing financial centre and developed industries from its original timber and grain origins – e.g. food retailing and furniture manufacturing. In 1903, the City of Minneapolis employed PWC to review and reorganise its entire accounting and financial system. Several of the CA immigrants from Glasgow appear to have started their US careers in Minneapolis, and at least two firms were founded there by IAAG members.

New York

New York City is the largest American city and situated at the mouth of the Hudson River. The area was first explored by Henry Hudson in 1609 and formed as New Amsterdam in 1624 by the Dutch. It was seized by the British in 1664 and renamed New York. It remained in British hands until the end of the American Revolutionary War in 1783. From 1788 to 1790, it was the temporary capital of America. Over several centuries, New York developed as a major commercial centre and port, starting in 1825 with the opening of the Erie Canal. The city comprised five boroughs from 1898 – Manhattan, Brooklyn, Queens, Bronx, and Staten Island. Lower Manhattan became the financial centre of the city based on Wall Street and the New York Stock Exchange, and rapidly developed into the main financial centre of the US. By 1880, New York City had a population of 1,912,000 and by 1900 it had reached 3,347,000, having become the main entry point for immigrants and a focal point for careers in commerce, finance, and the arts. In 1920, the population was 5,621,000.

Most of the Scottish accountancy immigrants started their American careers in New York. This is unsurprising as all the major public accountancy firms founded in the US by British immigrants had their origins or quickly opened a branch office there. The city also witnessed the start of organised institutional public accountancy – e.g. the Institute of Accountants & Bookkeepers of the City of New York (IABCNY) in 1882 (renamed the Institute of Accounts [IA] in 1886 (based on a similar Philadelphia body in 1874), the AAPA in 1887, and the New York State Society of Certified Public Accountants (NYSSCPA) in 1897 following the first CPA law in 1896.

5   The US public accountancy profession

Despite the rapid expansion of US industry in the last half of the nineteenth century, there was little attempt to organise an American public accountancy profession until the 1880s. For example, in 1870, there were less than 30 public accountants in the three major cities of New York, Chicago, and Philadelphia with a combined population of 2,451,000. Indeed, the first US organisation of accounting-related professionals, the Bookkeepers' Beneficial Association of Philadelphia (BBAP), was founded in that city in 1874 by 25 bookkeepers whose primary purpose was the provision of death benefits for their families and gaining employment. Philadelphia had a population of nearly 700,000 at that time. Public accountancy was therefore not then a mainstream occupation. Indeed, by 1880, the number of public accountants in New York, Chicago, and Philadelphia had increased by 19 to 49, and by 1890 by 76 to 125. In contrast, the population of New York City in 1880 was 1,912,000, Chicago 503,000, and Philadelphia 847,000 – a total of 3,262,000.

The next significant organisation of professional accountants, the IA, was based on the BBAP and appeared in New York in 1882 as the IABCNY. It changed its name to the IA in 1886. The IA had 37 founding members, of whom nine are known to have been public accountants in practise. Two founding members appear to have been English accounting immigrants. The aim of the IA was educational as well as professional, and the emphasis was on a scientific approach to accounting. Membership numbers were never disclosed, although it is reasonable to suggest they were not large. Despite numerous meetings and lectures in the 1880s and 1890s, the life of the IA was short-lived and it appears to have stopped functioning effectively in the early 1900s. However, its members were active in later professional developments such as the CPA law, and it preceded the forerunner of the present American Institute of Certified Public Accountants (AICPA), the AAPA founded in 1886 with 28 members – 13 of whom were British accounting migrants, including two founding members of the Institute of Chartered Accountants in England and Wales (ICAEW) in 1880.[1] There was no Scottish accounting immigrant associated with the formation of the IA although James Roderick Robertson (UQ) was a founding member of the AAPA.

The AAPA membership grew to 1,100 by 1914 and several of the Scottish accounting migrants in this study joined it (e.g. Robert Bayne [SAE] in 1899,

William James Caesar [SAE] 1897, James Craig Kerr [UQ] 1896, John Leith [UQ] 1899, Duncan MacInnes [UQ] 1902, Robert Nelson [IAAG] 1899, John Ballantine Niven [SAE] 1904, Eric Mackay Noble [SAE] 1888, and David Rollo [UQ] 1893). The first CPA law appeared in New York in 1896. None of the Scottish accounting migrants was involved in the process of obtaining it, although Robert Lancelot Cuthbert (SAE) received Certificate 16 in 1896. Many of the immigrants received CPA certification in New York. By 1913, there were 33 state boards administering CPA legislation – e.g. Pennsylvania in 1899, Illinois in 1903, Ohio in 1907, and Missouri in 1910. A further 16 appeared by 1923 when a law was passed in the District of Columbia. The first state bodies of CPAs appeared in 1897 – the IAPA in Chicago and the NYSSCPA in New York. The Federation of Societies of Public Accountants in the United States (FSPAUS) was formed in 1902 to promote the establishment of CPA laws in each state of the Union. Due to internal disputes with the NYSSCPA about its role, however, the FSPAUS was absorbed into the AAPA in 1905. Scottish accounting immigrants were active in most of the major boards and societies created at this time, particularly at the state level, and details are contained in their biographies.

During the 1870s and 1880s, public accountancy in the US included numerous visits from UK accountants contracted to protect British investments in America. These temporary engagements led eventually to the location of permanent offices of UK public accountants in the US. Immigrants managed and staffed these offices in the first instance. For example, PWC sent auditors from London to Tennessee in 1873 to examine the accounts of an ironworks owned by a company in the north of England and, in 1891, the firm had several brewery audits as well as that of the Union Stockyards Company. Although the firm suffered from economic downturns in the 1890s, it founded a US agency in New York in 1897 – JCC whose two partners were immigrant CAs from, respectively, England (Lewis Davies Jones [ICAEW]) and Scotland (William James Caesar [SAE]). The JCC practise gradually developed an American client list including various railway companies as well as the newly merged American Steel & Wire Company. It also worked for banks such as J. P. Morgan and Rothschild. The London-based PWC, on the other hand, provided services in the US for UK interests there.[2]

In 1883, BWGC formed in New York as the American agency for Thomas, Wade, Guthrie & Company (TWGC), CAs of London and Manchester. Edwin Guthrie, a TWGC partner and a founder Council member of the ICAEW in 1880, was a major influence in the formation of the AAPA in 1886, having first come to New York in 1883 on behalf of TWGC to investigate US assets of bankrupt UK companies and develop its US client base. Because he found no suitable local firms to undertake the investigations required, he formed BWGC in 1883 with a New York partner, John Wylie Barrow. Guthrie was never permanently resident in New York. Barrow was a cousin of the well-known novelist Charles Dickens and had developed a considerable diplomatic career in Europe before the age of 25 when he received the Freedom of the City of London for his governmental services. He travelled to New York in 1853 as a commissioner for the London Crystal Palace Exhibition and then worked for a lace merchant for twenty years before practicing as a public accountant. His professional practise was solely the provision of actuarial services to insurance companies. Unsurprisingly, therefore, BWGC's clients included the English insurance companies Royal Insurance Company of Liverpool and the Sun Insurance Company. The firm expanded over the decades to include 14 city offices in the US and, by 1950, it was larger than rivals AYC and Touche, Niven & Company (TNC). The adverse effects of client litigation in 1950, however, resulted in its absorption into PMMC.

London-based Deloitte, Dever, Griffiths & Company (DDGC) opened an office in 1889 in New York that was managed by English CAs Edward Adams and Percival Davis Griffiths.[3] By 1888, it had the largest fee income of the UK firms in the US. Its clients included Westinghouse Electric & Manufacturing Company and National Cordage Company. However, economic conditions in 1894 forced it to reduce staff. By the early 1900s, it was beginning to expand its business again. Other national public accountancy practises specifically founded by Scottish immigrant accountants included AYC (in 1894 by Arthur Young [UQ]), MMC (1897, James Marwick [IAAG] and Simpson Rodger Mitchell [UQ]), and TNC (1900, John Ballantine Niven [SAE]).[4] All of these firms exist today as part of the organisational structures of the four largest public accountancy firms in the world (Deloitte & Touche, Ernst & Young, KPMG and PricewaterhouseCoopers). There were also other local public accountancy firms founded by UK accounting immigrants during the early part of the nineteenth century. Several partnerships included Scottish CAs. For example, Mackay, Irons & Company (MIC) was a New York agency of the Dundee firm of the same name. Menzies, Robertson & Company (MRC) (1900), Lingley, Baird & Dixon (LBD) (1907) and Leslie, Banks & Company (LBC) (1910) were all formed in New York.

The formation and expansion of all these firms at a time when the local supply of American public accountants was limited inevitably led to recruitment drives focused on the UK where there was a clear oversupply of CAs. One of the best known of these recruitment efforts is that of the Glasgow immigrant James Marwick (IAAG) of MMC who advertised regularly in the Thursday edition of the *Glasgow Herald* newspaper. The effect of these drives appears in the expansion of the total number of British CAs in the US in the period between 1875 (when Eric Mackay Noble arrived) and the outbreak of the First World War in 1914. For example, in 1889, there were seven UK CAs permanently resident in the US. However, by 1899, this number had increased to 46. Ten years later, it was 162 and, at the end of 1914, 281.[5] These may appear to be small numbers but put in the context of the overall size of the American public accountancy profession of the times, they are a very significant element. The AAPA membership, for example, was 70 in 1899 and 214 in 1905. By the latter year, there had been more than 600 CPA certificates issued nationally and, by 1913, there were approximately 2,300 CPAs in the US with a population of approximately 92,000,000. In contrast, the SAE, IAAG, and SAA had a combined membership of 1,432 in 1913 with a Scottish population of approximately 4,800,000.

It is difficult to determine accurately the condition and quality of US public accountancy during the period of this study as there are relatively few authoritative sources. Two that are occasionally cited in this context are the personal memoirs of James Thornley Anyon, an English CA immigrant who became the senior partner of BWGC (Anyon, J. T., *Recollections of the Early Days of American Accountancy 1883–1893*, New York, NY: privately published, 1925) and the recorded memories of Arthur Young (UQ), founder of AYC (Burton, J. C., *Arthur Young and the Business he Founded*, New York, NY: privately published, 1948). There is also a personal account by another English UQ accounting immigrant, Ernest Reckitt, who formed various public accountancy firms in Chicago in the late nineteenth and early twentieth centuries (Reckitt, E. (1953), *Reminiscences of Early Days of the Accounting Profession in Illinois*, Chicago: IL, Illinois Society of Certified Public Accountants). The following comments are an overview taken from these sources.

The first notable feature of professional accountancy life in the late nineteenth and early twentieth century is that American business was not used to employing public accountants on a regular and routine basis (e.g. for audits). Instead, public accountants were typically hired on an ad hoc basis to provide accounting services or fraud investigations. It therefore took time for immigrant firms such as AYC and BWGC to establish themselves as providers of audit services. The public accountancy operations of immigrant accountants were typically small in terms of office accommodation, accounting staff, and non-accounting staff. The telephone had appeared for the first time (one instrument per office) as had the typewriter. There were difficulties in recruiting accounting staff because of the lack of men of suitable quality. Even qualified immigrants from the UK were treated with suspicion as so many had left there with various problems such as alcoholism. There were few public accountancy firms and they had few clients. The total fee income of AYC in 1906 was $100,000 and $125,000 six years later. Many public accountants practised on their own from a home address. Anyon, Reckitt, and Young were agreed that American-born practitioners lacked personality and impressiveness, and therefore did not inspire confidence. They typically provided bookkeeping services, supplemented by occasional investigations. The accounting immigrants, on the other hand, brought a range of public accountancy skills, but within a context of anti-English feeling in many parts of the US. They were willing to travel far to obtain clients but found travelling difficult and time-consuming in a vast country. It therefore took time to establish practises and gain the confidence of American business, and recruitment tended to involve UK CAs. However, the immigrant firms eventually abandoned this policy of recruitment in favour of American-born CPAs as local education and training standards improved. Indeed, firms such as PWC were explicit in this change and encouraged staff and partners to become US citizens.

6   Overview of the Scottish chartered accountancy migrants

There were 48 SAE immigrants, 99 from the IAAG, and 14 from the SAA – a total of 161 men. In addition, two of the SAE founders, Henry Callender and Donald Smith Peddie, fled Scotland in the 1870s as a result of criminal activities in their professional practises.[1] They probably immigrated to the US although no trace of this appears in American public records and they are therefore not included in this book. As previously mentioned, 16 UQ men are included, giving a total of 177 individuals.[2] This overview examines the Scots immigrants from a variety of perspectives. The first analysis describes the group as a whole and its subsets, and establishes the size of the immigrant population from 1875 to 1914. The second analysis provides various observations of the immigrants' background on entering the US (i.e. age, social class, birthplace, prior migration experience, and qualifications and experience. The third analysis looks at the residency of the immigrants in terms of permanence, length, marriage and family, and death. The final analysis contains various insights into the American experience of the immigrants (i.e. arrival cities, initial employment, subsequent careers, involvement with institutions, and examples of success in the US.

Population of Scots accountants

The population of Scots accountants resident in the US grew steadily between 1875 and 1914 and reflected a growing demand for public accountancy skills absent in that country. As Table 6.1 implies, there were no qualified immigrants prior to 1875.

Table 6.1 reveals the evolution of the accounting migration prior to 1915. In total, 177 men left Scotland for the US and, prior to 1890, most of the migrants were in the UQ category. However, from 1890 onwards, the predominant entry comprised CAs – with 144 men arriving between 1900 and 1914. Of this number, 142 were CAs and, of these, 36 were from the SAE, 93 from the IAAG, and 13 from the SAA. As a result, and allowing for return migrations and deaths, the overall US population of Scottish accountants expanded more than four-fold from 1899 to 1914. The most significant change in this period concerned IAAG migrants who increased from five in 1899 to 76 in 1914. These population move-

Table 6.1 Scots Public Accountants in US: 1875–1914

Movements	1875–9	1880–9	1890–9	1900–9	1910–14	Total
Population	0	2	10	31	88	0
Arrivals	2	9	22	72	72	177
Exits	0	0	0	–12	–21	–33
Deaths	0	–1	–1	–3	–7	–12
Population	*2*	*10*	*31*	*88*	*132*	*132*
Comprising						
SAE	1	3	11	27	35	35
IAAG	0	0	5	42	76	76
SAA	0	0	1	4	9	9
UQ	1	7	14	15	12	12

ments coincided with the previously mentioned establishment and expansion of specific firms of public accountants founded by Scottish accountants. For example, AYC, JCC, MMC, and TNC appeared between 1894 and 1900. The earliest CA migrants appear to have been predominantly SAE members. There were 11 Edinburgh CAs resident in the US at the end of 1899 compared to six from the IAAG and SAA combined. The median year of arrival for SAE migrants is 1905 compared to 1910 for IAAG and SAA men. These data suggest an over-supply of CAs in Scotland that affected Edinburgh before Glasgow or Aberdeen – or, perhaps, a greater sense of adventure or risk-taking by Edinburgh men compared to their counterparts in the west and north of Scotland. The SAE, IAAG, and SAA residency numbers by 1914 represent respectively, 6 per cent, 9 per cent, and 12 per cent of these bodies' membership totals – suggesting oversupply of CAs was greatest in Glasgow by the beginning of the First World War.

Age of immigrants

Eighty-two of the 177 Scots accountants immigrating to the US were born between 1880 and 1899 and only 28 were born prior to 1870. The oldest subset was the UQ men with 11 of the 16 born prior to 1870 and a median date of birth of 1866. The SAE group had an older age profile than that of its IAAG and SAA counterparts. The SAE median date of birth was 1877 compared to 1881 for the IAAG and 1884 for the SAA. Thirty-three of the 48 SAE migrants were born prior to 1880. Eighty-six of the 177 immigrants arrived in the US between the ages of twenty-four and twenty-seven and a further 24 were under the age of twenty-four on arrival. There were relatively insignificant differences between the sub-sets. The median ages on arrival for the SAE, IAAG, SAA, and UQ men were, respectively, 28, 28, 27 and 28 years. The overall pattern, therefore, was of relatively young and therefore relatively inexperienced accountants leaving Scotland for professional careers in the US.

Backgrounds of immigrants

Measured by the characteristic of economic class, the social origins of the founders and the early members of the SAE, IAAG, and SAA reflect the communities of which they were a part. Early SAE members were typically from paternal backgrounds of independent means or professions. For comparable IAAG and SAA members, the economic backgrounds were predominantly those of merchant or manufacturer. However, social class reproduction in these terms became impossible from the 1880s onwards. Increasing demand for public accountancy services resulted in the expansion of public accountancy firms and this expansion could not be met largely from recruits from the upper class (i.e. landowners and independent means) and upper middle class (i.e. professionals, manufacturers and merchants, and farmers). Instead, men from the lower middle class (e.g. shopkeepers and clerks) and working class (e.g. tradesmen and labourers) were increasingly recruited to satisfy growing demand for public accountancy services. The Scots immigrants to the US reflect these changes as seen in Table 6.2 (F = fathers, GF = grandfathers, middle 1 = upper middle class, and middle 2 = lower middle class).

Fifty-one per cent (91 of 177) of the total group came from lower middle and working class parental backgrounds, with the remainder predominantly in the upper middle class grouping (83). Two migrants had fathers of independent means. This configuration changes little when examining the occupations of migrants' grandfathers. Thirteen of the latter were landowners or had independent means and 170 of 354 (48 per cent) were lower middle or working class in origin. The latter categories were most evident with respect to the fathers of IAAG (59 or 60 per cent) and UQ (8 or 50 per cent) men and least evident for the SAE (18 or 38 per cent) and SAA (6 or 43 per cent). There are fewer differences between subgroups when examining grandfathers' occupations, although SAE accountants had 44 per cent (42) of grandfathers in the highest classes compared to 28 per cent (9) of UQ migrants. These data confirm the sociological changes occurring within the Scottish CA community during the last decades of the nineteenth century and the first decades of the twentieth century.[3]

Table 6.2 Economic class origins of Scots Public Accountants in US: 1875–1914

| Class | SAE | | IAAG | | SAA | | UQ | | Total | |
	F	GF	F	GF	F	GF	F	GF	F	GF
Upper	2	7	0	5	0	0	0	1	2	13
Middle 1	28	35	40	68	8	9	7	8	83	120
Middle 2	13	18	38	38	3	7	4	5	58	68
Working	5	30	21	54	3	7	4	11	33	102
Unknown	0	6	0	33	0	5	1	7	1	51
Totals	**48**	**96**	**99**	**198**	**14**	**28**	**16**	**32**	**177**	**354**

Birthplaces

The birthplaces of the immigrant accountants were widespread and varied. One man was born at sea, another in India, and five in different areas of London. In total, of the 176 men for whom there is a known birthplace, 12 (7 per cent) were born outside Scotland. Of the 164 with a Scottish birthplace, 59 per cent were born in the four major cities of Aberdeen (11), Dundee (14), Edinburgh (including Leith) (31), and Glasgow (40). This leaves 68 immigrants who were born in 53 small towns and villages throughout Scotland. In other words, approximately four of every ten Scottish-born immigrant accountants were born in a predominantly rural environment. Most of the 53 non-city locations contained farming or fishing communities of various sizes (e.g. Arbroath, Haddington and Perth), although several were small towns with manufacturing facilities for products such as textiles (e.g. Forfar, Kilmarnock, Paisley and Renfrew). There were no major differences between the four groups of immigrants – the majority of each group were born in one of the four main cities of Scotland (56 per cent of SAE men; 55 per cent of IAAG men, and 50 per cent of SAA and UQ men). The one difference concerned IAAG migrants born in Glasgow (36 per cent) compared to 54 per cent of SAE migrants born in Edinburgh or Leith and 50 per cent of SAA migrants born in Aberdeen.

Prior migrations

The nineteenth century witnessed an enormous migration of population in Scotland from rural to urban communities as a result of farming efficiencies, land clearances, decline of rural industries, and expansion into factory-based industrial manufacturing. For this reason, the immigration of Scots accountants to the US may well have been a further step in a longer journey of dislocation for the families concerned. The available data support this presumption. Only 41 or 23 per cent of the total migrant group came from families where there had been no previous local or national migration in the previous two generations. In fact, 115 of the 177 (65 per cent) immigrants had families with at least one major regional migration involving parents or grandparents within Scotland. The remaining 21 immigrants had families with either migrations by grandparents or parents to or from Scotland. In terms of the individual subgroups, there were relatively few differences, with SAA families arguably the least migratory and SAE families the most migratory (only seven Edinburgh men had no previous migration from their grandparents onwards).

Qualifications of immigrants

All of the SAE, IAAG and SAA migrants were fully qualified CAs and therefore had completed the training and examination requirements for membership of these bodies. These requirements varied between the three bodies for many years during the 1860s, 1870s and 1880s – particularly with respect to the IAAG and

admission of experienced UQ accountants. However, it is reasonable to gener-
alise that most of the 161 CA migrants brought with them a four- or five-year
training with a public accountancy practitioner and success in prescribed professional examinations. For those CAs who started their apprenticeship after 1892,
these examinations were identical for all three bodies due to the formation of the
national General Examination Board in that year. Seven of the 16 UQ men completed at least part of a CA apprenticeship or worked for several years for CAs
prior to migration. Of the remaining nine UQ immigrants, three were university
law graduates and a fourth was an experienced London stockbroker at the time of
his migration.

Experience of immigrants

Regulations for apprenticeship, examination, and admission were not uniform
until the late 1890s with respect to the SAE, IAAG and SAA. For example, as
mentioned previously, examinations became uniform in 1892 when a general
examination system was introduced for all Scottish CA apprentices. In addition,
until 1898, the apprenticeship period for the SAE and SAA was five years compared to four years for the IAAG. In 1898, it was standardised at five years for all
three bodies. Given birthdates and dates of admission to membership, it is reasonable to suggest that, during the period 1875 to 1914, the typical age of entry to a
Scottish CA apprenticeship was between 16 and 18 years. With the apprenticeship period varying between four or five years, and assuming the passing of
exams at the first or second attempt, this means that most Scottish CA apprentices
qualified for membership of their respective bodies in their early to mid twenties.
However, this did not mean that they applied for membership at this point.
Several of the CA migrants delayed admission for several years. One reason for
doing so was the affordability of the membership fee – many qualified accountants did not have the savings to pay for membership. Table 6.3 provides a summary of the years of professional experience brought to the US by the Scottish
accounting migrants. Averages have been rounded up or down to the nearest
whole number.

Table 6.3 Professional experience of Scottish accounting migrants: 1875–1914

Post-qualifying experience (years)	SAE	IAAG	SAA	UQ
	%	%	%	%
0–1	40	59	64	6
2–4	35	23	36	6
5+	25	18	0	88
Total migrants	**48**	**99**	**14**	**16**
Average post-qualifying experience (years)	3	3	1	NA
Average apprenticeship experience (years)	5	4	5	NA
Average total experience prior to migration (years)	**8**	**7**	**6**	**11**

Overall, for each of the SAE, IAAG and SAA, the largest proportion of migrants left Scotland for the US immediately or within a year of qualifying as CAs. The largest proportion was for SAA members (64 per cent) and the smallest proportion for SAE members (40 per cent). In total, 86 of the 161 (53 per cent) CA migrants left shortly after qualification. This statistic reflects a probable lack of post-qualification employment opportunity due to oversupplies of CAs during the period. A smaller proportion of each group delayed immigration for between two and four years post-qualification. This ranged from approximately one-third of SAE and SAA men to less than one-quarter of IAAG men. Many of these migrants remained with their apprenticeship firm before moving on or had no employment after qualifying. The remaining CA migrants from the SAE and IAAG remained in the UK for between five and 20 years (25 per cent and 18 per cent respectively). Most attempted to establish a professional practise as a CA. Thus, the CA migrants were split into three groups – those that recognised the need to migrate immediately, those that took a little longer to come to the same conclusion, and the remainder who tried and failed to establish themselves as CA practitioners in Scotland.

In contrast, almost nine of every ten (88 per cent) UQ migrants spent several years in practise as accountants before leaving for the US. The average practise experience they brought to the US is estimated at 11 years, compared to eight years for SAE migrants, seven years for IAAG migrants, and six years for SAA migrants. These estimates include approximate apprenticeship periods served by the CAs in order to provide comparability. Overall, the migrant group as a whole brought a small yet significant level of public accountancy experience to the US. Most of the immigrants brought not only needed public accountancy skills but also, in many cases, practise experience beyond training. However, the single greatest benefit to US public accountancy was the formal apprenticeship training and examination experiences of all CA migrants and several of the UQ men.

Permanent residency

All of the CAs described in this text intimated their residency in the US for a period of at least a year and none of the UQ immigrants left the US. Thirty-seven per cent of the 161 CA migrants returned to the UK (38) or moved to another foreign country (21) such as Canada. As reported in Table 6.1, 33 of these men left the US permanently by the end of 1914. These exit statistics are consistent with more general reverse migration patterns of the times. Returns were typically because of homesickness or relative success that permitted homecoming without the connotation of failure. In this study, most of the exiting immigrants prospered later in Canada or the UK, although some returned home because of injuries sustained during army service in the First World War. Approximately eight of every 10 (48 of 59) exits were during the period 1901 to 1920. Twenty-four men returned to Scotland and many practised as public accountants there. Eighteen men continued their careers in Canada. The lowest exit rate was for SAE members at 25 per cent. The equivalent IAAG and SAA data were, respectively, 40 per cent and 50 per cent. Forty per cent of IAAG returns went to Canada. Overall, therefore, the qualified immigrants appear to have had more options available to them because of their qualification as CAs in the sense of being able to use this as a basis for future employment in Canada or the UK.

Length of residency and marriage

One hundred and eleven of the 177 migrants (63 per cent) remained in the US for more than 19 years and 67 (38 per cent) were resident for 40 years or more. The average residency in years varied between groups – 41 for UQ, 31 for SAE, 26 for IAAG, and 24 for SAA. These data suggest that the earliest immigrants to the US (i.e. SAE members and UQ men) stayed the longest and were least likely to return to the UK or move on to another country. Overall, therefore, the large majority of the immigrants moved to the US on a permanent basis and many married there and had children. More specifically, of the 177 migrants, 77 per cent remained permanently either in the US (118) or Canada (18). Of these 136 men, there is information about the marital status of 116. Eighty-one (70 per cent) married and 50 (62 per cent) of these had children. A curiosity of the marriages is that 26 (32 per cent) were to women born in Scotland. In a few of these cases, the marriage took place in Scotland prior to migration. Overall, 35 men are known not to have married – a not unusual feature of Victorian times when men married typically when they felt sufficiently secure financially to support a family.

Death of immigrants

There were four UQ immigrants whose death cannot be determined. Of the remaining 173, two died before the turn of the twentieth century, a further 53 died prior to the outbreak of the Second World War in 1939, and 118 died between 1939 and 1980. Within the group as a whole, the first death was that of Eric Mackay Noble, the first immigrant CA, in 1892. The last death was in 1980 when IAAG member Gladstone Cherry died. Seventy-one per cent of IAAG immigrants died after 1941, compared to 63 per cent of the SAE group, 50 per cent of the SAA group, and 44 per cent of the UQ group. Deaths took place in a large number of locations. The largest single number (38) were in New York, followed by Scotland (28), Illinois and England (17 each), and California (15).

Arrival city

Fifty-eight per cent (103) of the 177 immigrants began their careers in the US in the city of New York. A further 14 per cent opted for Chicago and 7 per cent for Minneapolis. These locations were where Scots founded major public account-ancy firms such as AYC, MMC, TNC and JCC/PWC, and each city had a major financial services community. The remaining immigrants appear to have travelled to a variety of locations in California, Colorado, Massachusetts, Montana and Pennsylvania. There were no significant differences in these matters between the various subsets of immigrants. The overall impression, therefore, is of a typical Scottish immigrant accountant arriving in New York and either staying there or moving on to a variety of locations within the US.

Initial employment

The typical starting employment for 177 immigrants was in public accountancy as audit staff (163 or 92 per cent) and the initial employers were primarily a small group of public accountancy firms. Very often, these staff positions were seasonal and therefore no long-term contract was offered to the migrant (e.g. as in PWC). The remaining 14 immigrants started their American careers in industry or local government. Table 6.4 provides a summary of the public accountancy employers of the migrants. The first five columns refer to the initial employment in the UK. The six named firms (termed here the "Big 6") refer to nationally-based US firms. "Local" refers to city-based firms, and "industry" includes industrial and local government positions. The remaining five columns refer to secondary employment positions in the "Big 6" firms only.

For most of the period studied, there were six national firms (MMC, PWC, BWG, AYC, TNC and DDG) primarily associated with the Scots immigrants. The most popular firm was MMC with 57 initial recruits and a further 8 migrant employees, representing 37 per cent of the total group of 177. Most of these employees (49) were IAAG members and constitute approximately one-half of the IAAG group, reflecting the deliberate policy by co-founder James Marwick to recruit from his home city of Glasgow. JCC/PWC was the next largest recruiter with 26 initial immigrants and 11 others later in their careers. One-half of the 37 JCC/PWC employees were SAE men. The English CA firm BWGC employed 18 immigrants, with a preference for IAAG immigrants (13). Glaswegians founded AYC. It employed 20 of the immigrants and favoured the IAAG source (10). Edinburgh CAs, on the other hand, formed TNC, but its employment of 12 immigrants did not favour SAE men – the firm recruited relatively evenly from Edinburgh and Glasgow immigrants but never from the SAA.

Table 6.4 Initial employment and subsequent national firm employment

	Initial employment					Subsequent employment				
Firms	*SAE*	*IAAG*	*SAA*	*UQ*	*Total*	*SAE*	*IAAG*	*SAA*	*UQ*	*Total*
MMC	7	44	6	0	**57**	2	5	0	1	**65**
PWC	14	11	0	1	**26**	4	5	1	1	**37**
BWGC	2	10	0	0	**12**	3	3	0	0	**18**
AYC	0	5	1	4	**10**	4	5	1	0	**20**
TNC	3	3	0	0	**6**	2	4	0	0	**12**
DDGC	1	1	1	0	**3**	5	4	1	0	**13**
Big 6	**27**	**74**	**8**	**5**	**114**	**20**	**26**	**3**	**2**	**165**
Local	15	21	3	8	**47**					
Industry	6	4	3	3	**16**					
Total	**48**	**99**	**14**	**16**	**177**					

In total, MMC, JCC/PWC, BWG, AYC and TNC account for 114 (64 per cent) of the initial employment of the 177 immigrants. This influence extended further with post-immigration employment. The five firms at one time or another employed 165 of the 177 migrants (93 per cent). This reflects the importance of the Scots immigrants to the development and growth of these firms and particularly to MMC and JCC/PWC. Exactly one-half of the 48 SAE migrants and 58 of the 99 IAAG migrants remained in the city of their initial employment, revealing an underlying stability in the migration as a whole. Six of the 14 SAA members moved three or more times during their US residency. UQ immigrants tended to remain in their initial location, again reflecting stability.

American careers

The careers of the Scots immigrants in the US followed four distinct types, three of which were variants of public accountancy. Exactly one-third, or 59 of 177 men, worked solely as audit staff (i.e. non-partners) throughout their residency in the US. A further 41 of 177 (23 per cent) became partners in national and local firms. An additional 45 either immediately or eventually formed small public practises. The remaining 32 immigrants developed a career in industry or local government as accountants, internal auditors, and comptrollers. There were variations in this distribution between members of the three bodies and the UQ men. SAE and UQ immigrants had the largest proportion of sole practitioner practises (22 of 64 or approximately one in every three). There was only one SAA immigrant who formed a public practise. Audit partnerships were highest with IAAG immigrants (24 of 99 men or nearly one-quarter). Audit staff positions, however, formed the highest category for all three qualified subsets of immigrants – ranging from 40 per cent of IAAG members to 29 per cent of SAE members.

Involvement in American bodies

Arguably because so many of the immigrants were members of one of the three bodies of Scottish CAs, and believed in the high reputation of these bodies, 74 of 161 (46 per cent) did not become involved with any American national or state society or board. Indeed, many of these men continued to describe themselves as CAs in their professional practise. However, 64 of the 161 (40 per cent) CA migrants joined at least a national and state society, eight a national body only, and 15 a state society only. The largest proportion with no involvement with American bodies was 64 per cent of the SAA immigrants. Fifteen of the 16 UQ men were involved with American bodies and 10 joined both national and state organisations. For SAE and IAAG members, each group split between those who joined at both national and state levels and those who were uninvolved (approximately four of every 10 in each case). There were 77 immigrants who became members of the AAPA or its successor body, the American Institute of Accountants (AIA).[4] Thirty-one immigrants were New York CPAs, followed by 26 in Illinois, 24 in Minnesota, 17 in Ohio, 12 in each of Missouri and Michigan,

11 in Louisiana, and 10 in California. There were CPA licences held by immigrants in 17 other states.

There were no CA immigrants involved in the formation of national bodies, although eight CAs were founder members of state societies (mostly from the SAE). Four of the 16 UQ immigrants were state founder members. Part of the explanation for the lack of involvement in national formations by the immigrants is undoubtedly due to most of them arriving in the US after the formations. CA migrants also had their loyalty to their Scottish bodies. Almost all CAs in this study remained members of these bodies until their death. In contrast, state societies appeared throughout the early decades of the twentieth century, coinciding with the initial arrival and settling in of most CA immigrants. Immigrants, however, were active in the formation of major national and large city firms. For example, 32 of the 161 (20 per cent) CA immigrants helped to form such firms (e.g. JCC, MMC and TNC) and two of the UQ men were founders of the national firms AYC and MMC.

Professional success

Most of the Scots immigrants succeeded in some way or another during their residency in the US. Of course, there were exceptions to this general rule. For example, James Affleck (IAAG) fled Glasgow as a result of criminal investigations and does not appear to have prospered in New York. He became a photographer and his wife kept a boarding house. Andrew Connor (IAAG) developed tuberculosis, was deported from the US for this reason, and received financial support from the IAAG until his death in 1912. Robert Cuthbert (SAE) and Ronald McOnie (IAAG) died in action during the First World War – Cuthbert at the age of 47 on hazardous scouting action in France. James Fraser (SAE) drowned while bathing in New Orleans soon after immigrating. Matthew McEwan, who captained Scotland at rugby, died of pneumonia during a Chicago winter in 1899. Robert Nelson (IAAG) was refused re-admission to the IAAG in 1915 on the grounds of his poor financial situation. William Skinner (SAE), the son of a lawyer and former Town Clerk of Edinburgh, ended his days as a clerk in the local tax office of Glasgow Town Council.

There were several successes in industry by immigrants. For example, Thomas Drever (SAE) became President of American Steel Foundries. Alexander Houston (IAAG) was Treasurer of the Asiatic Petroleum Company, the American joint venture of Shell Transport & Trading Company and Royal Dutch Shell. John Laurie was the Comptroller of the US Smelting, Refining & Mining Company, later asset-stripped by Victor Posner and Saul Steinberg in the 1970s. Duncan McInnes, a teenage railway ticket seller in Edinburgh, became the Deputy Comptroller of the City of New York. Thomas McLaren (IAAG) was the Treasurer and a Vice-President of the Crown Zellerbach Corporation, one of the world's largest paper makers, later asset-stripped by the British financier, James Goldsmith, in the mid 1980s. Ralph Main was Secretary and Treasurer of the Minnesota & Ontario Paper Company. William Ogg (SAA) was the President of the American Zinc, Lead & Smelting Company. John Pirie (IAAG) became the Secretary and Treasurer of American Bakeries.

Other immigrants succeeded on their return to the UK. George Barr (IAAG) was the trustee for the estate of Viscount Furness and managed the latter's large shipbuilding and coalmining interests. Stephen Forsyth (SAA) became a Church of Scotland minister. Steven Hardie (IAAG) was a well-known non-executive director in Scotland as well as a leading practitioner in the west of Scotland. Several other immigrants succeeded in Canada. For example, Alexander Brodie (SAE) was a leader in the development of Canadian public accountancy, both as a PWC partner and as President of the Quebec Institute of Chartered Accountants (QICA), a body founded in 1880 as the Association of Accountants of Montreal (AAM) and therefore the oldest body of public accountants in North America. George Burden (IAAG) also held the latter office. Douglas Dewar (IAAG) was deputy senior partner of MMC in the US before leaving for Canada where he worked for the UK government and was honoured for this service. Alexander Fairnie (IAAG) was President of the British Columbia Institute of Chartered Accountants (BCICA). David Kerr (IAAG), a partner in MMC in Canada, was also a regular writer there on technical accounting matters. David Young (SAE) was a PWC partner in Canada and a Council member of the Canadian Institute of Chartered Accountants (CICA).

The majority of the migrant success stories in the US, however, were in public accountancy. In some cases, this was at the state level of administration. For example, Donald Arthur, a UQ migrant, became the first CPA in Montana and, later, an international tax expert with PWC. Alexander Banks (IAAG) was the NYSSCPA representative on the Council of the American Society of Certified Public Accountants (ASCPA).[5] He also represented the ASCPA in London at the 1933 International Congress of Accountants. Harry Boyack (IAAG), an AYC partner, was Secretary and Treasurer of the IAPA as well as active in the AIA. Gladstone Cherry (IAAG) became President of the Wisconsin Society of Certified Public Accountants (WSCPA). Hugh Cuthbert (SAE) held the same office with the Arizona Society of Certified Public Accountants (AASCPA) and John Dawson (UQ), a PWC partner, with the Illinois body, the IAPA. Edward Fraser (SAE) was a mainstay of the Missouri Society of Certified Public Accountants (MSCPA) and became its President in 1920 in addition to being active in the AIA. David Grey (SAE) was also President of the MSCPA, on the AIA Council, and represented Missouri at the 1933 International Congress. William Guthrie (IAAG) was a charter member of the Iowa Society of Certified Public Accountants (IASCPA) and chaired the Iowa State Board of Accountancy. James Hall (IAAG), senior partner of MMC from 1930, chaired the Illinois State Board of Accountancy in addition to memberships of various AIA committees. John Hurst (SAE) was involved in the formation of the Texas Society of Certified Public Accountants (TSCPA) but never became a CPA. James McGregor (IAAG) was an AYC partner who was Secretary and Treasurer of the IAPA and chaired the State Board. He was also on the Council of the AIA. John Medlock (IAAG), a PWC partner, chaired the Illinois State Board and was active in the AIA.

Gordon Steele (IAAG), Comptroller-General of Manitoba and a partner in AYC before founding his own practise, was a Vice-President of the MSCPA. Angus Steven (IAAG) held the same office with the IAPA. UQ immigrant William Tolleth was a charter member of the Virginia Society of Certified Public Accountants (VSCPA) and became its President in 1916 as well as joining the AIA Council. Albert Watson (IAAG), a PWC partner, became President of the California Society of Certified Public Accountants (CSCPA) and had several AIA responsibilities. Stanley Young (UQ), brother of Arthur Young, was the first President of the MSCPA in 1909.

Other immigrants focused mainly on administering public accountancy at a national level. Archibald Bowman (IAAG) was the senior partner in MMC from 1925 to 1930 and active in the AIA. James Burton (IAAG) was senior partner in AYC but did not become involved in state or federal bodies. The same can be said for William James Caesar (SAE), the co-founder of JCC. Frank Lowson (SAE) was a partner in Patterson, Teale & Dennis (PTD) and a Vice-President of the AIA. William McGregor (IAAG), an AYC partner, was an AIA Council member. James Marwick (IAAG), co-founder of MMC, preferred to concentrate his attentions on his firm, as did his partner Simpson Mitchell (UQ). John Niven (SAE), however, was involved in many matters. He was the co-founder of TNC, President of the New Jersey Society of Certified Public Accountants (NJSCPA), and President of the AIA in 1924. UQ immigrant David Rollo from Edinburgh became AAPA President in 1899. John Scobie (SAE), senior partner of PWC, was active in the AIA. Andrew Stewart (IAAG), a partner with MMC and Haskins & Sells (HS), was President of the NYSSCPA and an AIA Council member in 1941. He was also AIA Auditor in 1924 and Treasurer in 1928. Arthur Young (UQ) held office in state and national bodies. He was President of the IAPA, Vice-President of the AAPA, and a Council member of the AIA.

This is a considerable record of achievement, given the relatively small number of accounting immigrants to the US in the crucial four decades of public accountancy development at the end of the nineteenth and beginning of the twentieth centuries. Scottish public accountants not only provided their professional skills and experience in accounting and auditing matters, they also founded public accountancy firms to provide needed services. They also had time to be involved in the formation and administration of institutionalised public accountancy in the US – both at the state and national levels. All of these institutions thrive today and many of the firms continue to exist, albeit within larger and merged organisations. The evidence is clear. Scottish immigrant accountants influenced US public accountancy disproportionately to the size of their community. Many of these men revealed strengths in professional leadership that benefited the US economy as well as its accountancy profession. It is an unanswerable question as to whether the UK profession generally, and the Scottish one particularly, would have similarly benefited. Suffice to say that American conditions were conducive to the developments enhanced by the presence of Scottish public accountants.

7   The immigrants

ABERNETHY, William Gray (1890–1966)   **IAAG (1913)**

William Gray Abernethy (*WGA*) was born in 1890 at Paisley in Renfrewshire. Paisley is a town situated directly west of the city of Glasgow and was famous in the early nineteenth century for cotton spinning and later for its textile industry, including the weaving of shawls and thread manufacturing (particularly with the firm of J. & P. Coats). Paisley's population in 1881 was approximately 56,000. *WGA*'s father, John Adamson Abernethy, was ordained in 1880 and became the Church of Scotland minister for the Linwood parish. His mother was Margaret Arneil Gray, the daughter of William Gray and Margaret Arneil of the village of Kilbarchan on the western outskirts of Paisley. William Gray was a farmer of 115 acres and had six employees on his farm at the time of *WGA*'s birth. His son, *WGA*'s uncle, was a factory worker in Paisley. The paternal grandparents were Peter Abernethy, a Glasgow woollen and wincey manufacturer, and Marion Adamson. *WGA* had another uncle, also Peter Abernethy, who was a medical practitioner in Glasgow.

  WGA was educated in Paisley Grammar School and Academy, apprenticed to Glasgow CAs Gourlay & Deas, and joined the IAAG in 1913. He also immigrated in that year to work for CAs MMC in New Orleans in Louisiana. His employment there continued until 1920 when he started to practise on his own in New Orleans. No further information is available about *WGA* until 1937 when he is recorded as the senior staff member in charge of training with the national firm of AYC in New York. He does not appear to have been a member of any American public accountancy body, did not marry, and was a lodger at Brooklyn in New York in 1930. He ceased to be a member of the IAAG in Glasgow in 1925 and died in New York in 1966.

AFFLECK, James (1853–?)   **IAAG (1877)**

James Affleck (*JA*) was born in 1853 at Paisley in Renfrewshire. He was the son of John Affleck, an English-born assistant manager of the Union Bank of Scotland in Glasgow and a Justice of the Peace for Lanarkshire. *JA*'s mother was Ann Dow (Taylor) from the farming village of Methven a short distance from

Perth in Perthshire and he had two brothers and a sister. His younger brother, William Affleck, was educated at the Edinburgh Academy in 1875 before starting a legal apprenticeship in Edinburgh. The youngest brother, Edward Gordon Affleck was born in Govan in Lanarkshire in 1876. No information can be found concerning the life or career of Edward Affleck after 1880. The paternal grandparents were James Affleck, a landowner in Renfrewshire, and Agnes Copland, and John Taylor, a farmer, and Catherine Millar. Uncle William Affleck was a graduate in divinity from the University of Glasgow and a minister of the Free Church of Scotland in the farming village of Auchtermuchtie in Fife. Nephews of *JA* included James Ormiston Affleck who, following education at Edinburgh Academy, became an engineer in the Public Works Department of the British administration in India. He was also a Lieutenant in the Royal Engineers during the First World War and was discharged in 1918 as an acting Major.

JA was apprenticed to CAs McClelland, MacKinnon & Blyth in Glasgow and joined the IAAG in 1877. He became a partner in the CA firm of Bird & Affleck in Glasgow and was a Lieutenant in the 3rd Battalion of the Lanarkshire Rifle Volunteer Brigade. His partner was David Bird, an IAAG member in 1877 and the son and brother of Glasgow solicitors. By 1887, *JA* was residing in New York and, in 1888, was struck off the membership records of the IAAG because of court actions against him. He is not listed in New York directories as an accountant, and was never a member of an American public accountancy body. In the 1900 US Census, *JA* is recorded as a photographer at Brooklyn in New York. His Scottish wife was a boarding house keeper with two lodgers. The couple had no children and arrived in New York in 1886. There is no sign of *JA* or his wife in the US Census of 1910 and the date of his death is unknown.

ALLAN, Peter McKerchar (1882–1941)   SAE (1911)

Peter McKerchar Allan (*PMA*) was born in South Leith near Edinburgh in 1882. Leith was a separate town and port to Edinburgh and had a population of 58,000 in 1881. *PMA*'s father was George Allan, a printer's compositor from Edinburgh, and his mother, Margaret McKerchar, a domestic servant, was from the fishing village of Dunbar in East Lothian. He had one brother, Henry Allan, named after his grandfather, Henry Allan, who was a bookbinder employing six individuals in Edinburgh and married to Agnes McBain. Peter McKerchar was the maternal grandfather and from the village of Kenmore in Perthshire. He was a merchant draper and husband of Ann Galbraith. There were numerous uncles and cousins of *PMA* in Edinburgh, Perthshire, and elsewhere. Edinburgh occupations for these family members included bookbinder, compositor, pocketbook maker, and lithographer and printer. Two uncles also worked in South Leith as, respectively, a hairdresser and a sanitary inspector. A Glasgow uncle was an engine fitter and there was a general merchant in Logierait in Perthshire. A further uncle, Donald McKerchar, was the minister at the Free Church of Scotland in the port of Dunoon in Argyllshire, and his brother, Duncan McKerchar, was a draper in the fishing village of Arbroath in Forfarshire.

PMA was educated at the Royal High School in Edinburgh and later served an apprenticeship with the firm of CAs Whitson & Methuen. He became a member of the SAE in 1911 and continued to work for Whitson & Methuen for a further two years until immigrating to New York in 1913. He was employed there as an audit assistant with CAs BWGC for a year before serving in the British Army in the First World War from 1914 until 1919. On discharge, he returned to BWGC and continued to work there for several years as an audit assistant. He was next employed from 1923 as an accountant with the Federal Sugar Refining Corporation in Wall Street in New York and remained with this company until his death in New York in 1941. He was not a member of any American public accountancy body. *PMA*'s wife was from New Jersey and they had a son and two daughters. He owned his home in New York and it had a value in 1930 of $15,000 ($167,000 in 2004 terms using the Consumer Price Index).

ANDERSON, James (1854–?) UQ

James Anderson (*JA*) was born in 1854 at Liff and Benvie, a small farming village to the west of Dundee in Forfarshire. His father was James Anderson, the Registrar of Births and Deaths in Dundee, and his mother, Catherine M. Anderson, was from the village of Longforgen in Perthshire. He had a sister, Catherina Anderson, who was a dressmaker in Dundee. *JL* was educated in Dundee, and apprenticed and employed there from 1880 to 1887 with CAs Moody, Stuart & Robertson. He became an associate member of the IAAG in 1883 after three years of service but failed to achieve full membership. In 1888, he immigrated to San Ontario in California and ceased his associate membership of the IAAG in 1889. No further trace can be found of him in the US.

ARTHUR, Donald Angus McIntosh (1879–1956) UQ

Donald Angus McIntosh Arthur (*DAMA*) was born in 1879 at Bo'ness in Linlithgowshire and died in 1956 in New York. Bo'ness was a small port on the south bank of the River Forth and its harbour was built originally by the Duke of Hamilton in the early nineteenth century for coal exporting. *DAMA*'s parents were Lachlan Fraser Arthur, a Glasgow insurance company secretary or manager, and Mary Learmonth Fraser. Grandfather Alexander Arthur was an iron works manager near Bo'ness and married to Agnes Laurie Cunningham, the daughter of Robert Cunningham and Margaret Gowans. Grandfather Robert Fraser was a gardener and married to Mary Wilson. *DAMA* had two brothers, Lachlan and John T. Arthur, and a sister. There is no information available about any of these siblings beyond 1881.

DAMA was educated in Glasgow and apprenticed from 1895 to 1897 with CA John Munn Ross. In 1897, he became an associate member of the IAAG but failed to qualify as a full member. By 1899, *DAMA* was an accountant with a mining company in South Africa. From there he immigrated to the US and New York. Then, in 1901, he was working for public accountants Pogson, Peloubet &

Company (PPC) in Montana (the firm merged with PWC in 1963). He remained with this firm until 1909 when he started to practise on his own and was largely responsible for obtaining legislation for public accountants in Montana. He was the first Montana CPA. His practise in Montana lasted until 1918. During this time, he was appointed Secretary to the Montana State Board of Accountancy (1914–17) and was an assistant to Commissioner Daniel Roper of the Internal Revenue Service in Washington from 1914 to 1918. In the latter year, he became the manager in Montana for PWC. This was because of his friendship with fellow Scot and CA, George Rae Webster, with whom he had shared lodgings in New York.

In 1919, *DAMA* went to PWC in New York and also renewed his assistantship with the Commissioner of the Internal Revenue Service in Washington. He was admitted to the PWC partnership in 1924 and specialised in taxation, particularly with respect to inter-company transactions in international corporations. He was also active in the AIA as an examiner and committee member – the Income Tax Law Committee (1923), Committee on Public Affairs (1925), Board of Examiners (1928), and Chairman of the Committee on Federal Legislation (1935). He was a CPA in Louisiana (1929) and New York (1930). *DAMA* retired from PWC in 1941 and died in 1956. He lived in New York and owned his home which was valued at $35,000 in 1930 ($391,000 in 2004 terms). His wife was born in Montana and the couple had a son.

BAIRD, John James (1879–1936)   SAE (1905)

John James Baird (*JJB*) was born in 1879 at Lesmahagow in Lanarkshire, a small market town founded in 1144 as a religious centre and situated south-east of Glasgow with a population of 10,000 in 1881. *JJB* later moved a short distance with his parents to the village of West Calder near Edinburgh. He was educated in Edinburgh at James Gillespie's School. His father was William Baird who came from the farming village of Dalry in north Ayrshire where he was a limestone quarryman before becoming a colliery agent at West Calder. He later became a commercial traveller. The paternal grandparents were John Baird, a brick manufacturer at Lesmahagow, and Marion Thomson. *JJM*'s mother, Kate Storey Anderson, was born at the fishing town of Whitehaven in Cumberland in north-west England. Her parents were John Anderson, a baker at the farming village of Straiton in south Ayrshire, and Alison Storey. *JJB*'s sister, Marion Thomson Baird, was a photographic assistant in Edinburgh but died young. His uncle, John Storey Baird, farmed 150 acres at the village of Sorn east of Ayr in Ayrshire. John Baird had seven sons, six of whom worked on his farm. The remaining son, James Baird, was described in the 1881 *Census* as a pioneer – a form of agricultural worker.

JJB was successively apprenticed to two Edinburgh CAs John Wilson (SAE 1884) and Richard Brown (SAE 1879) and became an SAE member in 1905. Wilson and Brown were both SAE Council members, and Brown was Secretary and Treasurer of the SAE at the time. *JJB* immediately immigrated to the US to be employed by the Scottish CA firm MRC in New York. In 1910, he became an accountant with the Indian Refining Company of Cincinnati in Ohio. Seven years later, when he joined the AIA, he partnered English public accountant, Richard Turner Lingley, in New York as LBD. He joined the NYSSCPA a year later and remained as a partner in LBD until 1932 when he retired to Florida. He died there in 1936. There was no record of a family.

BALDWIN, Charles Young (1884–1948)   IAAG (1911)

Charles Young Baldwin (*CYB*) was born in 1884 at the port and regimental town of Folkstone in Kent on the English Channel coast. His father, William Baldwin, was a marine engineer based in Singapore who came originally from Paisley in Renfrewshire where his parents were Charles Baldwin, a blacksmith, and Jean Young. *CYB*'s mother, Joan Hunter (formerly Donaldson), was a music teacher from the town of Kilmarnock in Ayrshire where her father, James Hunter, was a cabinetmaker and town missionary and married to Jean Gilmour. There is no information available regarding *CYB*'s education, but he was apprenticed to CAs Wallace & Tannock in Glasgow. He then became an audit clerk with CAs David Strathie & Company from 1908 to 1910 and joined the IAAG in the latter year before leaving for New York. He worked there for several months with CAs MMC before leaving for Edmonton in Alberta in Canada to work for a local firm of accountants, Webb, Read & Hagan. A year later, in 1912, he became a partner in the public accountancy firm of Nash, Soares & Baldwin in Edmonton. He also became a member of the Institute of Chartered Accountants of Alberta (ICAA) in that year.

 CYB served with the armed forces during the First World War. By 1917, he was a Captain with the Royal Munster Fusiliers and had been wounded in fighting in the Dardanelles. This was the failed British attempt to control the strategic waterway in north-west Turkey between Asia and Europe, and suggests that *CYB* fought at the unsuccessful Battle of Gallipoli in 1915 which involved 130,000 UK deaths and 262,000 wounded. In 1916, while on leave, he married Eliza Coats of Paisley, daughter of William Coats, a ham curer, and Eliza Evans. Three years later, he was a partner in the Paisley firm of CAs, Balderston, Whyte & Baldwin. In 1922, he resigned from the IAAG but was restored to membership in 1928. A year later, he became Secretary of the Vocation Gramophone Company and the Vocation (Foreign) Company in London. By 1934, he was working and residing in Lancashire as the Secretary of John Wilkinson (Manchester & Nelson) Ltd and, by 1948, he was also a director of that company (an iron and steelworks). He died in Manchester in 1948. It is unclear whether he had children.

BALLINGALL, Peter (1863–1914)   UQ

Peter Ballingall (*PB*) was born in Glasgow in 1863 and brought up by his grandmother, Margaret Arneil, who was from the farming village of Strathaven in south Lanarkshire, and his uncle, Andrew Fraser, a chemist and druggist's assistant in

Glasgow. His father, also Peter Ballingall, was a Glasgow joiner from the small farming town of Markinch in Fife, and his mother, Jessie, was from the nearby fishing village of Leven, also in Fife. *PB* worked as a commercial clerk in a millinery business in Glasgow where his brother James was born and later employed as a draper's assistant. He immigrated to Philadelphia in the US in 1888 where a relative, James Ballingall, was working as a wagon driver.

PB joined the AAPA in 1902 and established himself as a public accountant in Philadelphia, practicing on his own from 1897 until 1902. He was the thirty-sixth Pennsylvanian CPA. From 1903 to 1910, he was President of the United States Audit Company in Philadelphia. These companies were incorporated bodies funded by share investments from prominent businessmen in individual cities such as Philadelphia, New York, and Chicago. The idea behind their formation was that their shareholders could refer their businesses to the company for audit. This lack of independence created considerable criticism among CPAs and audit companies gradually disappeared by the early 1900s. In 1910, *PB* was a bank accountant living in Montgomery in Pennsylvania with his Scottish wife and a daughter. He died in 1914. A brief biography appears in N. E. Webster, *The American Association of Public Accountants: Its First Twenty Years 1886–1906* (American Institute of Accountants: New York, NY, 1954).

BANKS, Alexander Scott (1884–1948)   IAAG (1909)

Alexander M. Banks was a Dundee shipbroker and married to Marjory Hume. The couple had five children, including Alexander Scott Banks (*ASB*) who was born in Dundee in 1884. *ASB* had three brothers – George William Banks who died young, William Kenneth Banks who lived with his mother and appears to have had no occupation, and Harry Kenneth Banks, a mercantile clerk in Dundee. There was also a sister. The grandparents were George William Banks, a Dundee linen manufacturer, and Susan Kinnear, and William Hume from the village of Longforgen in Perthshire, the manager of a jute mill in the parish of Liff and Benvie in Forfarshire, and Helen Thomson. One uncle was an overseer in a jute mill in Dundee and another was a land surveyor. *ASB* was educated in Dundee before starting a CA apprenticeship with IAAG member James A. Murdoch of the Dundee firm of A. Tosh & Son. He was with this firm in 1909 when he joined the IAAG. A year later, he formed the Dundee firm of Banks & Nicol. This lasted only a few months when *ASB* joined the New York partnership of Scottish CA firm LBC and became a CPA in Minnesota.

ASB joined the AIA in 1918 and was a Vice President and director of the ASCPA by 1924. He was also a CPA in New York and became President of the ASCPA in 1925. From 1926 to 1934, he was the NYSSCPA representative in the ASCPA and was also very active with the Credit Association of Building Trades in New York. In 1927, he was a member of the Advisory Committee of the ASCPA and, in 1928, became the Chairman of its International Accountants' Congress Committee. By 1933, he was a member of the Business Advisory Council of the American Arbitration Association. His institutional activities continued into 1936 when he chaired the AIA's Committee on Cooperation with Investment Bankers. He attended the International Congress of Accountants in London in 1933 as a representative of the ASCPA and spoke on the subject of mechanical accounting. *ASB* died in New York in 1948. His home was in New York and had a value of $25,000 in 1930 ($280,000 in 2004). He had a wife and five children.

BARCLAY, Alexander Connon (1872–1948)   SAE (1908)

Alexander Connon Barclay (*ACB*) was born in the port of North Leith near Edinburgh in 1872 and became an SAE member in 1908. He was educated at George Watson's College in Edinburgh before contracting to an apprenticeship with CA George Todd Chiene Junior (SAE 1869). Chiene was the son of George Todd Chiene (SAE 1855), one of the earliest Edinburgh CAs, a SAE Council member, and one of the leading CAs of his day. He founded the firm of Chiene & Tait in the early 1880s and it exists with the same name to the present day in Edinburgh. *ACB* was the son of a Leith-based shipmaster, James Barclay, from the port town of Montrose in Forfarshire and his mother, Margaret Aitken, a former domestic servant, came from the county town of Forfar. Her parents were John Aitken, a seaman, and Helen Watson. *ACB* had a brother, James Alexander Barclay, who died at sea aged fourteen years, and a sister Helen. His grandfather, Alexander Barclay, was a seaman in Montrose and married to Jane Wylie.

A year after qualification, *ACB* went to London as an audit assistant with English CAs PWC. However, he quickly immigrated to the US and became a CPA in Missouri in 1910 where he was employed as an audit assistant with Scottish CAs MMC in St Josephs. He was there for two years before becoming a Paymaster-Lieutenant in the US Navy during the First World War until 1919. His next employment was as an audit assistant in the Chicago office of English CAs DDGC and he remained in this position until 1942 when he worked for the US Maritime Commission at the Sun Shipbuilding & Dry Dock Company at Chester in Pennsylvania and the Great Lakes Engineering Works at River Rouge in Michigan. The latter organisation was opened in 1904 with four berths and a floating dry dock, and appears to have been in continuous production producing ships for the Great Lakes until 1960. It became the largest ship builder on the Great Lakes. *ACB* retired in 1947 and died in 1948. He was never a member of the AAPA or the AIA and was not a partner in DDGC. No trace of *ACB* can be found in any US Census nor can any record of marriage.

BARCLAY, James White (1878–1924)   IAAG (1903)

James White Barclay (*JWB*) was born in 1878 in Glasgow. His father, Robert Barclay, was a merchant and muslin manufacturer from Paisley in Renfrewshire and son of Robert Barclay, a weaving manufacturer, and his mother, Susan Campbell White, was from the Glasgow suburb of Rutherglen and the daughter of James White, a Glasgow chemical manufacturer, and Francis Campbell. He had a brother, Robert Francis Barclay, who was a Glasgow Solicitor (lawyer), and five sisters – one of whom married Henry A. Roxburgh, a Glasgow Solicitor and son of a ship owner and insurance broker. The household also had seven servants, indicating that this was a wealthy family. A brother-in-law, Francis John Martin, was a lawyer who qualified as a Writer to the Signet (WS). *JWB* was educated in Glasgow and apprenticed to CAs McClelland, Mackinnon & Hay from 1890 to 1892 and its successor firm Mackinnon, Kerr & Hay from 1893 to 1895. He joined the IAAG in 1903 and remained with McClelland, Ker & Company in Glasgow until 1905 when he immigrated to the US. No information is available as to what he was doing in that country; although it is possible he was working for his Glasgow employers. However, he was resident there for four years until his relocation to Hampstead in London in 1909. He later moved to Braintree in Essex and appears to have been in the British Army during the First World War. In the IAAG records in 1923, he is stated to be a Major and retired. He died in Essex in 1924. Given the lack of occupation in the Glasgow records, it is reasonable to assume that *JWB* had been wounded in the War.

BARR, George Murray (1888–1968)   IAAG (1911)

Little background information can be found for George Murray Barr (*GMB*). He was born in Glasgow in 1888. He had a grandmother, Rachel Barr, from Glasgow and his father was named as George Murray (Barr), a machinist from Glasgow who was the stepson of John Barr, a carpet weaver. *GMB* was educated in Glasgow and apprenticed to CAs David Strathie & Company. He was admitted to the IAAG in 1911. In this year, he left Glasgow for New York to work for CAs PWC as a member of its contract staff. Such an appointment indicates he was highly regarded by the partners. He was quickly transferred to the Pittsburg, Pennsylvania office. However, by 1917, *GMB* was back with the firm in New York. He remained there as a staff member until 1934 and returned to Glasgow where he was employed outside of public practise. In 1938, he moved to London where he was, until 1953, consultant to the trustees of the late Viscount Furness. The Furness family fortune originated in ship ownership and the trust owned numerous coal and shipping companies including the Broomhill Collieries started in 1900 that, by 1940, employed nearly 1,700 men. The trust was also involved with fireclay and brick manufacturing. *GMB* was unmarried, retired in 1953, and died in 1968. His obituary appeared in *The Accountant's Magazine* of February 1968.

BAYNE, Robert (1870–1951)   SAE (1893)

Robert Bayne (*RB*) was born in Edinburgh in 1870 to Robert Bayne from Kilrenny in Fife, a small farming village south of St Andrews, and Jane Watson Inglis from the village of West Linton to the south of Edinburgh. His father was the Investment Manager of the Scottish Property Insurance Company but described as a retired accountant in 1901. His paternal grandparents were David

Clark Bayne, a tailor and clothier, and Sarah Philp, and his maternal grandparents were William Inglis, a shoemaker, and Elizabeth Hunter. *RB* was educated at Stockbridge School, Cannonmills School, and Daniel Stewart's College in Edinburgh. His sister Lizzie attended the Normal School in Edinburgh and a second sister, Sarah, became a dressmaker. There were two other infant sisters and a brother Henry H Bayne who was an SAE member (1902) in Edinburgh. *RB* had an uncle who was a farm servant at Kilrenny and several cousins also in farming occupations.

RB was apprenticed to the leading firm of Lindsay, Jamieson & Haldane, CAs, in Edinburgh and became an SAE member in 1893. He then left for Clifton in Arizona to audit the Arizona Copper Company which was a client of Lindsay, Jamieson & Haldane. By 1897, however, he was working as an audit assistant with the CA firm of JCC in Chicago. Two years later, he held a similar position in New York with the English public accountancy migrant Ernest Reckitt. Reckitt was a chemistry graduate and son of the founder of the chemical company now called Reckitt & Coleman. He immigrated to the US in 1889 to work for BWGC and became one of the leading public accountancy practitioners in Chicago. He was also a leading member of the IAPA and AIA. In 1899, *RB* joined the AAPA. From 1901 to 1922, he worked as an auditor in New York for the English CA James Yalden. Yalden was also a leading public accountancy practitioner from the UK. He came from Hampshire in England and, by 1871, had a practise in London that employed six individuals mainly involved in business liquidations. Despite an initial rejection, he was an associate member of the Institute of Accountants in London (IAL) in 1871 and a founding Council member in 1872 of the Society of Accountants in England (SAIE). However, in 1876, he was accused by the Attorney General of England of embezzling client funds from liquidations and fled with his wife and children to the US where he set up a thriving practise as a public accountant in New York. He assisted in the formation of the AAPA in 1886 and the introduction of CPA legislation in New York ten years later. Yalden was AAPA President in 1888 and 1892. Curiously, one of his specialist professional services was fraud investigation in government organisations.

RB returned to Chicago in 1922 to become the Chief Internal Auditor of the Albert Dickson Company, a firm of seed merchants. He later worked as an accountant in a bank. *RB* was married to a Scottish woman and had a son, Robert Bayne, who was an elevator operator. He owned the family home in Chicago which was valued at $10,000 in 1930 ($112,000 in 2004 terms) and died there in 1951. An obituary appeared in *The Accountant's Magazine* of May 1951 and a brief biography appears in N. E. Webster, *The American Association of Public Accountants: Its First Twenty Years 1886–1906* (American Institute of Accountants: New York, NY, 1954).

BELL, Norman James (1889–1965)   IAAG (1913)

Norman James Bell (*NJB*) was born in Dundee in 1889. His father, James Bell, was a telegraphist there and was married to Georgina Wright, a sewing machinist. His uncle, John Bell was also a telegraphist and several aunts were machinists. *NJB*'s grandparents were Robert Bell, a shipwright in Dundee, and Margaret Mackie, and Charles Wright, a Dundee shipmaster, and Mary Cassie. He was educated in Dundee and apprenticed to a local firm of CAs MIC. He joined the IAAG in 1913 and left immediately for Chicago to start work there for CAs MMC. A year later, he moved to the firm's office in Winnipeg in Canada. He appears to have then served with the armed forces in the First World War and returned to London by 1921. He practised on his own for several years in the town of Bedford as Bell & Company, CAs, and later had two partners. Vivian M. Burton was an English CA and partner from 1935 who, in 1958 became *NJB*'s wife. S. E. Clear was also an English CA and a partner from 1950. By 1960, *NJB* was chairman of Lloyds & Company and Henry Franklin & Company in Bedford and retired from public practise. These companies manufactured, respectively, farm machinery and lawnmowers. *NJB* died in Bedford in 1965.

BLACK, Ernest Charteris (1884–1915)   IAAG (1907)

The son of James Buyers Black and Jessie Charteris, Ernest Charteris Black (*ECB*), was born in the seaside village of Portobello near Edinburgh in 1884. James Buyers Black was an insurance company manager in Glasgow and came from the linoleum manufacturing town of Kirkcaldy in Fife (population 23,000) where his father, James Black, Master of Arts, was the minister of the Free Church of Scotland at the parish of Dunniker (ordained 1838). *ECB*'s grandmother was Mary Ann Sutherland from Aberdeen. Her father, John Sutherland, was an Aberdeen merchant from the farming village of Halkirk west of Wick in Sutherland. The Sutherlands were mainly farmers and masons in Halkirk. An uncle of *ECB* was John Sutherland Black, Master of Arts, a sub-editor of the *Encyclopedia Britannica*. Other uncles included Maurice Black, who trained as a lawyer, and Alexander William Black, an Edinburgh lawyer and WS (1885), who married Ellinor Wilson, daughter of Rear Admiral Thomas Wilson, Companion of the Order of the Bath, of Edinburgh. Alexander William Black was also the Member of Parliament for the County of Banff from 1900 to 1906 when he died in a railway accident at Arbroath. *ECB*'s brother-in-law was Alfred Patrick MacThomas Thoms of Aberlemno who was a WS and landowner in Fife. *ECB* also had three brothers – John Sutherland Charteris Black followed his father into the insurance industry, but no information is available about Colin Sutherland Charteris Black and Howard Charteris Black.

    ECB was educated at Nottingham High School, Halle in Germany, and the University of Edinburgh. He was apprenticed to CAs J. Wyllie Guild & Scott of Glasgow and admitted to the IAAG in 1907. A year earlier, he had moved to Edinburgh to work for CA Richard Brown and stayed with this employment until 1910 when he immigrated to the US. Brown (SAE 1879) was one of the leading CAs of his time. The son of a tenant farmer, he not only became a leading Edinburgh practitioner but also Secretary of the SAE (1892–1916), its President (1916–18), and author of a *History of Accounting and Accountants* (Jack:

Edinburgh, 1905). *ECB* worked for CAs PWC in New York for a year before becoming a partner in the firm of McDonald, Smith & Black in Montreal in Canada. This venture lasted a short time because, in 1912, he was an audit manager with DDGC in Montreal. Three years later, in 1915, *ECB* was killed in action during the First World War. He was a Second Lieutenant in the Royal Scots Fusiliers, having joined the King Edward's Horse in 1914. He is buried at Vermeilles Cemetery near Pas de Calais and appears to have died at the Battle of Loos.

ECB was never a member of an American or Canadian public accountancy body. At the time of his death, he was due to become the Chief Accountant of Consolidated Gold Fields of South Africa in London – then and now one of the largest UK mining companies. His obituary appeared in *The Accountant* in December 1915.

BLAIKIE, William Francis Garden (1849–1914)   UQ

William Francis Garden Blaikie (*WFGB*) was born in Edinburgh in 1849 and is one of the oldest migrants in this study. His father was the Reverend William Garden Blaikie, Doctor of Divinity, Doctor of Letters, the minister of Pilrig Free Parish Church in Edinburgh (1844–68), Professor of Apologetics and Pastoral Theology at the University of Edinburgh (1868–97), and Moderator of the General Assembly of the Free Church of Scotland (1892). His mother was Margaret Catherine Biggar, the daughter of Walter Biggar, a merchant, and Ann Duff from the county and market town of Banff in Banffshire (population 8,000). The Very Reverend Blaikie was a prolific author and his publications included *The Dwellings of the People* (1851), *David, King of Israel* (1856), *Outlines of Bible Geography, Physical and Political* (1861), *Better Days for Working People* (1863), *Counsel and Cheer for the Battle of Life* (1867), *The Public Ministry and Pastoral Methods of Our Lord* (1883), and *The Personal Life of David Livingstone* (1889).

WFGB's maternal grandparents were James Biggar, an Aberdeen Advocate, and Jane Garden, and his paternal grandfather was James Ogilvie Blaikie of Craigbuckler, Advocate, landowner, and Lord Provost of Aberdeen, whose father, John Blaikie, was an Aberdeen plumber. He also had three sisters and five brothers. Walter Biggar Blaikie was a Civil Engineer in India (1870–8) before becoming a distinguished printer in Edinburgh from 1879. He was also an astronomer, Fellow of the Royal Society of Edinburgh, and author of books on Prince Charles Edward Stuart (Bonnie Prince Charlie) and the military history of Perthshire. Robert Henry Blaikie was educated at Edinburgh Academy, graduated as Master of Arts in 1878, Bachelor of Medicine in 1881, and Doctor of Medicine in 1883 from the University of Edinburgh. He was admitted as a Fellow of the Royal College of Surgeons of Edinburgh in 1884 and won numerous golfing medals while at university. He became a general practitioner in Edinburgh and assistant Medical Officer at Longmore Hospital. James Andrew Blaikie, Master of Arts, Fellow of Caius College at the University of Cambridge, mathematics schoolmaster at Fettes College in Edinburgh (1870–6), was the Inspector of Schools in Scotland from 1877 to 1885. He was also a schools examiner for many years and the author of a number of texts including *Elements of Dynamics* (1887). He married the daughter of the Surgeon-General James Alexander Dunbar (a rank of Major-General). However, when James Andrew Blaikie died at Hawick in Roxburghshire, he was reported as a shepherd and the son of a shepherd. John Adrian Blaikie was the Inspector of Alkali Works at Newcastle when he died aged twenty-nine having been hit by a cricket ball. He was educated at Edinburgh Academy, graduated as Bachelor of Science and Doctor of Science (1878) from the University of Edinburgh, and lectured in chemistry at the University of Bristol. Charles Louis Blaikie was educated at Edinburgh Academy and became an Edinburgh CA (SAE 1887). He was also Honorary Lieutenant Colonel in the Royal Artillery and Secretary and Treasurer of the Scottish National Artillery Association. *WFGB*'s sister, Alice Margaret Blaikie married Murdo Campbell Mackenzie, a Free Church of Scotland minister (ordained 1870) in Inverness-shire and son of Walter Mackenzie, a farmer, and Ann Campbell. A further sister, Anne Louisa Catherine Blaikie, married James Murdoch, Professor of Surgery at the University of Edinburgh who immigrated to Australia.

WFGB was also the nephew of Robert Balfour, one of the most influential founders of the SAE in 1854. Balfour's wife, Frances Grace Blaikie, was the daughter of James Ogilvie Blaikie of Craigiebuckler, an Aberdeen Advocate and landowner and partner to the first President of the SAA, John Smith, and sister of William Garden Blaikie. Other relations of *WFGB* included James William Biggar Blaikie who was a Chartered Engineer, writer on Scottish history, senior partner in the Queen's printers, T. & A. Constable, and Chairman of the Edinburgh Chamber of Commerce in 1903. He was also a manager of the Royal Infirmary of Edinburgh and published articles on Scottish history.

WFGB was educated at Edinburgh Academy and Edinburgh Institution before studying at the University of Edinburgh in 1865. He then appears to have practised as a stockbroker and moved to London to join the London Stock Exchange from 1877 to 1882. In 1881, he married Alison Clephane, the daughter of the Reverend John Manson, Master of Arts, of the Free Church of Scotland at Fyvie in Aberdeenshire. The Mansons were landowners in Aberdeenshire and linked to the Blaikie family by marriage. His mother-in-law was Grace Edmonson Pringle, the daughter of John Pringle, Sheriff-Substitute of Banff, and Margaret Wallace. In 1884, the Blaikies immigrated to California and, in 1907, *WFGB* became a CPA in that state. From 1912 until his death in 1914, he was the Treasurer to the City of Ontario in California. He had three sons and several grandchildren whose occupations varied from ministers and army officers to a carpenter and deputy sheriff.

BOWMAN, Archibald (1878–1955)   IAAG (1900)

Archibald Bowman (*AB*) was born in Glasgow in 1878. His father, Walter Bowman, was an iron merchant's clerk who became a bookkeeper and cashier in a colliery in the village of Newton in Ayrshire. Walter Bowman was born in the seaside village of Aberdour in Fife on the north shore of the River Forth. His mother, Grace Wilson, was a former domestic servant from the market town of Dunfermline, also in Fife. Her parents were David Wilson, a general labourer, and Agnes Barrie. His grandfather, Archibald Bowman, was from Dunfermline, employed as the colliery manager at nearby Wemys, and married to Jane Beveridge. Great uncle Laurence Bowman was the coal master at Wemys and employed more than 450 men and boys in the mine. Uncle Archibald Bowman was a colliery manager and his brother, John Bowman, was a grocer.

AB was educated in Glasgow and apprenticed to CA Alexander J. Forgie of Maclean, Brodie & Forgie of Glasgow. He joined the IAAG in 1900 when he was resident in Manchester. He remained there until 1902, although it is unclear what his occupation was, and immigrated to New York and employment with Scottish CAs MMC. In 1905, he became a partner in MMC and a member of the AAPA. He also became a CPA in Ohio in 1908, Minnesota (1909), California and Louisiana (1925), Oregon (1926), and New York (1931). In 1916, he joined the AIA and was a member of its Committees on Federal Legislation (1920), Endowment (Chairman, 1931), Cooperation with the Stock Exchanges (1931–9), and Accounting Procedure (1940–3). He was also a member of the ASCPA from 1923 and the Merchants' Association of New York from 1925, and a director of the American Arbitration Association from 1926. He became deputy senior partner of MMC in 1917 and was senior partner from 1925 to 1930. He retired from the firm in 1951. *AB* died in New York in 1955 and his obituary appeared in *The Accountant's Magazine* of May 1955. He was married to an English woman whom he married prior to immigration, had a son, and owned his home in New York with a 1930 valuation of $70,000 ($783,000 in 2004 terms). His son, Archibald G Bowman, was employed in real estate in California and wrote a book on that subject.

BOYACK, Henry (1880–1952)   IAAG (1907)

Henry or Harry Boyack (*HB*) was a member of a Forfarshire family. Born in Dundee in 1880, his father, James Boyack, was a joiner and cabinet maker from Forfar, and his mother, Isabella Miller, was from the fishing town of Arbroath. The paternal grandparents were Robert Boyack, a machine fitter, and Ann Balmuir, and the maternal grandparents, James Miller, a mill overseer or supervisor, and Jane Marshall Taylor. He had five brothers. James Boyack died young. William Boyack was a chemist and druggist in Dundee. Robert Boyack was a joiner and Frank Boyack, after training with a lawyer, became an engineer. *HB*'s grandfather, James Boyack, was a waste merchant in Dundee. He had several uncles who had occupations such as factory engineer, merchant, general labourer, bellhanger and paper worker.

HB was educated in Dundee and apprenticed to CA Daniel McIntyre of McIntyre & Grant in Dundee. He joined the IAAG in 1907 and immigrated to Chicago in 1908 where he worked for Scottish CAs AYC. He remained with the firm for the remainder of his career. He joined the AIA in 1916 and was Secretary and Treasurer of the IAPA from 1919. He was a partner in AYC from 1921 to 1941 and based mainly in Chicago. He joined the ASCPA in 1923 and chaired the AIA's Credentials Committee in 1933. *HB* was boarding with a medical doctor near Chicago in 1930. On retirement from the partnership in 1941, he became a consulting associate with AYC. He died unmarried in Chicago in 1952.

BRODIE, Alexander Bertram (1876–1961)   SAE (1911)

Alexander Bertram Brodie's (*ABB*) family came from the farming and market town of Haddington in East Lothian and it appears he was distantly related to John Alison Brodie, a founder of the IAAG in 1854. If so, he was also related to Patrick Brodie, Manager of the British Linen Bank from 1860 to 1867 and William Lorrain Brodie who won the Victoria Cross for exceptional bravery in action in 1914. Born in Ceylon in 1876, *ABB* was the son of James Brodie who was a tea planter and merchant in Colombo in Ceylon before becoming an Edinburgh mortgage agent and stockbroker. He had three sisters also born in Ceylon. His paternal grandparents were Alexander Brodie, a merchant, and Elizabeth Somerville. His mother, Isabella Winifred Brodie, came from the farming village of Garvald in East Lothian. She was the daughter of Robert Taylor, an Edinburgh Advocate who, when he died in 1907, was "Father of the Bar", and Isabella Whitelaw, the daughter of Mathew Whitelaw of Berwick, a corn factor. Other Whitelaw relations of *ABB* included Charles Whitelaw, a stockbroker, and John M. Whitelaw (Doctor of Letters), a Church of Scotland minister at Athelstaneford in the county of Haddington. *ABB* was the great grandson of Robert Taylor, a farmer at Carfrae to the south of Edinburgh. His grandfather, Alexander Brodie, was a merchant in the coastal town of Dunbar and he had two uncles who were also in the business of merchanting in London and Ceylon.

ABB was educated at Merchiston School in Edinburgh before training as a CA with the Edinburgh firm of Howden & Molleson. He joined the SAE in 1911 having qualified for membership about 1900. At that time, he went to work in London for the audit firm of PWC, and two years later was recruited by English CA migrant Arthur Lowes Dickinson (ICAEW 1887) to work in the New York office of PWC. Dickinson was one of the most famous English CA migrants to the US. The son of a well-known artist and brother of a famous historian and philosopher, he graduated from the University of Cambridge, trained and practised as a Barrister, formed his own public accountancy practise in London, and entered the US in 1889 to work for the firm of JCC (later PWC). He became a partner in 1901 and was knighted for his services to the UK government in 1919. He was also an influential writer on accountancy matters and PWC partners funded academic positions at Harvard Business School in his name.

In 1906, *ABB* moved to Pittsburg in Pennsylvania to open and manage a PWC office. He remained there until 1911 when he moved to Quebec in Canada to be a PWC partner there. In 1910, he became a CPA in Missouri, and a CA in Quebec, Ontario and British Columbia. He resigned from the SAE in 1911 shortly after joining it. *ABB* was a PWC partner in the US and Canada from 1911 until 1933.

He joined the AIA in 1916 and the PWC Executive Committee in 1920. During that period, he became a leader in the development of the Canadian public accountancy profession and was Vice President of the AAM in 1920 and President of the QICA in 1924. During the First World War, he was a member of several Canadian government commissions, including the Halifax Relief Fund which dealt with the aftermath of eighteen hundred deaths when an explosives ship was rammed. He was President of the Montreal Board of Trade in 1924. *ABB* died married in Montreal in 1961. An obituary appeared in the *Canadian Chartered Accountant* in 1961 and in *The Accountant's Magazine* of February 1962.

BROWN, Robert Charles (1884–1961)   SAE (1908)

Born in Edinburgh in 1884, *RCB* was educated at the Normal School for three years and George Heriot's School for seven years. He was the son of John Law Brown, a wood engraver, and Margaret Mark. His paternal grandparents were John Brown, a journeyman engineer, and Jane Grieve. The maternal grandparents were William Mark, a shoemaker, and Margaret McKillop, both of Edinburgh. He had four elder brothers. John Brown was a printer and compositer, Alfred C. S. Brown trained as a lawyer, and William Mark Brown, as a civil servant. David Brown cannot be traced. An aunt, who was deaf and dumb, was a tobacco roller, and an uncle was a bookbinder.

Between 1901 and 1906, *RCB* was apprenticed to Edinburgh CAs Wilson & Johnston. He attended law classes at the University of Edinburgh between 1904 and 1906. He joined the SAE in 1908, two years after immigrating to the US. In fact, he joined the AAPA in 1905 and the NYSSCPA in 1907. He was also a Tennessee and Virginia CPA and appears to have worked in the relatively privi-leged position of a contracted audit assistant with PWC in St Louis in Missouri between 1906 and 1919. During that period, he also became a CPA in Ohio (1909), a member of the MSCPA (1912), and the AIA (1916).

RCB became Assistant Secretary and General Auditor of the Gilliland Oil Company in Tulsa in Oklahoma in 1920 before joining Scottish CAs TNC as a partner in Chicago in 1925. He remained in this position until his retirement to Saratoga in California in 1953. He became a CPA in Michigan in 1928 and was a member of the Fiftieth Anniversary Committee of the IAPA in 1953. He died in Saratoga in 1961 and there was an obituary in *The Accountant's Magazine* of August 1962. His wife was from Scotland and there were no children. The fam-ily home was owned and valued in 1930 at $35,000 ($391,000 in 2004 terms).

BURDEN, George Slimman (1881–1963)   IAAG (1907)

James Burden, a wine and spirit merchant in Dundee, was the father of George Slimman Burden (*GSB*) and son of John Burden, a dry dyke builder, and Catherine McEwan. His wife and cousin, Annie Slimman, was from the village of Kilfinchan in Argyllshire, and took over the family business when James

Burden died. She was originally Annie McNab and her parents were Duncan McNab, a farmer from the village of Killin in Perthshire, and Janet McEwan. *GSB* was born in Dundee in 1881 and had a brother, Duncan McNab Burden, who became a Solicitor and law agent in Dundee, and three sisters. His aunts included a Dundee housekeeper, who was born in Edinburgh, and a yarn dresser. Uncles included a lather (plasterer) and several masons in Perthshire, and Donald McNab, a farmer at Kilfinchan, also in Perthshire.

Following education in Dundee, *GSB* was apprenticed to Dundee CA Daniel McIntyre of McIntyre & Grant. He joined the IAAG in 1907 and immigrated to New York in 1908. He was employed there in the CA firm of MLC, becoming a CPA in Minnesota in 1910. He remained with this firm until 1919 when he became a Canadian CA and an employee of Creak, Cushing & Hodgson in Montreal in Canada. He became a partner in this firm in 1921 and retired as senior partner in 1954. He died in Montreal in 1963. He was a past President of the QICA. An obituary appeared in the February 1963 issue of *The Accountant's Magazine*.

BURTON, James Campbell (1886–1966)   IAAG (1909)

James Campbell Burton (*JCB*) came from a theological background. His father, the Reverend John Tudhope Burton, Master of Arts, was ordained in 1877 and the minister of the United Presbyterian Church at Newmills in Lanarkshire. His mother was Christina Boyd Campbell, daughter of James Campbell, a coal master, and Margaret Caruth. He had two sisters, a brother, John Archibald G Burton who cannot be traced, and grandparents Thomas Burton, a Lanarkshire landowner and farmer, and Janet Tudhope. An uncle, James Burton, was an unmarried farmer of 38 acres at Lesmahagow in Lanarkshire. *JCB* was born in 1886 at Newington in Edinburgh and graduated as a Master of Arts and Bachelor of Laws from the University of Glasgow. He was then apprenticed to Dundee CAs, Moody Stuart & Robertson, and joined the IAAG in 1909 having passed his final examinations with distinction. A year later, he was employed in New York with CAs MMC. He remained with this firm for five years before becoming Internal Auditor, Secretary, then General Manager of a Pittsburg, Pennsylvania furniture store, Kaufmann's.

JCB joined AYC as a national partner in 1921 and held that position until 1956. He also joined the AIA in 1921 and became an Ohio CPA in 1950. In 1923, he became senior partner in his firm. He was described as a brilliant accountant who took an early responsibility in AYC for the hiring and firing of staff. He headed the firm's management committee from 1933 that dealt with the overall administration of the firm, with Arthur Young retaining complete control over it. He was well known for taking quick decisions and separating essential from non-essential matters. He authored a private publication in 1948 entitled *Arthur Young and the Business he Founded* (Merrymount Press: Boston, MA).

JCB died at Lennox Hill in New York in 1966. He had suffered ill health for some years. He was married to a Swedish woman and had no children. An obituary appeared in *The Accountant's Magazine* of March 1966. He had been active in the administration of Mills College of Education as chairman of its board of directors, Madison Avenue Presbyterian Church as a trustee, and the Metropolitan Republican Club. His career in AYC is recounted in detail in T. G. Higgins' *Thomas G Higgins, CPA: An Autobiography* (Comet Press: New York, NY, 1965).

CAESAR, William James (1859–1917)   SAE (1881)

William James Caesar (*WJC*) was also a son of the manse. His father was the Reverend Doctor William Caesar, the Church of Scotland minister at the small farming and mining town of Tranent in East Lothian (population 4,600). Doctor Caesar was ordained in 1850 and came from Dumfriesshire. He was the son of William Caesar, a farmer, and Agnes Cowan. He had a brother, John Caesar, who was a grain merchant at Tinwald in the same county and father of seven sons between 1867 and 1880. Doctor Caesar's publications included *The Gospel of Saint John: Its Authorship and Authenticity* (1877). Eliza Ainslie Burnett from Tranent was *WJC*'s mother and a daughter of James Burnet, a land factor or manager, and Eliza Ainslie. *WJC* had three unmarried sisters and a brother, John Alfred Charles Caesar who was a bank clerk, and married to Mary Louisa Minkley, the daughter of John Wilkins Minkley, furniture warehouseman, and Eliza Brandreth. The Caesar siblings were born in a house adjacent to the manse in Tranent – which was rented out to a miner, a mason, and a schoolmaster.

WJC was born in 1859 and educated at Edinburgh Academy from 1871 to 1874. He finished his schooling at George Watson's College in Edinburgh before starting a CA apprenticeship with the leading Edinburgh firm of A. & J. Robertson. He joined the SAE in 1881. A year later, his business address was with Rutherford & Kay, an Edinburgh firm of wine merchants, although he appears to have practised on his own at that time. He remained at this address until 1885 when he worked for the property investment firm of Laurie & Ker before moving to CAs PWC in London in 1889. He also appears to have worked as an auditor in Paris in France. In 1890, *WJC* was appointed Secretary of the Florida Mortgage & Investment Company in Florida. This was a speculative company incorporated in the UK and *WJC* was sent to Florida by its shareholders to organise its management. This was a period when Scottish accountants, lawyers and merchants combined to create numerous property investment companies permitting shareholders to invest in property in the US.

A year later, in 1891, *WJC* was appointed Chicago agent for PWC and, four years later with an English CA, Lewis Davies Jones, he restructured the agency as the firm of JCC in Chicago and New York. Jones was a Welshman who joined the ICAEW in 1890 having worked for PWC in London since 1877. He had visited the US on several occasions for PWC clients and went there permanently in 1890 as PWC agent in New York. Jones found the agency difficult – it was costly, he was tightly controlled from London, and New York costs were considerable. However, he was particularly good with clients and active in professional matters, having become the first IAPA President in 1897. Because of Jones' problems, *WJC* was appointed by PWC to assist in the development of its agency in the US at a time of considerable UK investment in the US. He was perceived by the London PWC partners as more experienced than Jones in American business. However, the agency proved difficult to sustain due to a downturn in UK investment in the US in the early to mid 1890s. The result of this setback was the formation of JCC in 1895 that permitted *WJC* and Jones to acquire American clients and continue to act as the US agency of PWC. Client income gradually increased due to an active corporate merger market and audits from the late 1890s. However, Jones died of diabetes in 1899 leaving *WJC* in charge of JCC and the US PWC agency.

In 1899, following the death of Jones, *WJC* appointed PWC employees Charles James Marr (a former railroad accountant and future PWC partner) as PWC manager in Chicago, George Oliver May (ICAEW 1897 and future PWC senior partner) as New York manager, and Arthur Henry Pogson (who formed PPC in 1900) as western US manager. He retained overall control and focused on finding new clients by traveling around the US. He then started a protracted discussion with PWC in London to improve his partnership provisions due to the death of Jones. Eventually, PWC was persuaded to form an American PWC partnership in 1898 with *WJC* as one of the partners. This partnership was separate from that of JCC and included a provision for the payment to *WJC* of a sum for goodwill on his retirement or death and based on one-half of the PWC net profits in the US for the two years prior to retirement or death. *WJC* announced his intention to retire in 1901 following two years of rapidly growing revenue in the US for PWC.

WJC was a stern, enthusiastic but difficult man – particularly with staff and clients. He paid low salaries and staff turnover was always high in JCC and PWC. In 1901, he retired at the age of forty-two after prolonged negotiations with PWC over his financial settlement. He became a New York CPA in 1897 as well as a Governor of the ASCPA and a member of the AAPA. In 1900, he joined the IAPA. He did not participate greatly in the early development of these bodies and retired to Paris in 1900 where he died in 1917. *WJC* was unmarried and lived on his own in an apartment at Manhattan in New York in 1900. His contributions to JCC and PWC in the US are covered in D. G. Allen & K. McDermott, *Accounting for Success: A History of Price Waterhouse in America 1890–1990* (Harvard Business School Press: Boston, MA, 1993), C. W. DeMond, *Price, Waterhouse & Co. in America: A History of a Public Accounting Firm* (Comet Press: New York, NY, 1951), and E. Jones, *True and Fair: A History of Price Waterhouse* (Hamish Hamilton: London, 1995). A brief biography appears in N. E. Webster, *The American Association of Public Accountants: Its First Twenty Years 1886–1906* (American Institute of Accountants: New York, NY, 1954).

CAMPBELL, James Albert (1885–1946)   SAA (1910)

James Albert Campbell (*JAC*) was born in 1885 in Aberdeen. His father, James Albert Watson Campbell, was a schoolmaster there and the son of John Edward

Campbell, a clerk, and Jane Paul. His mother was Francis Neil, the daughter of John Neil, an Aberdeen bookseller, and Mary Johnston. Following schooling in Aberdeen, *JAC* was apprenticed to one of the SAA founder firms, James Meston & Company. James Meston was one of the initial organisers of the SAA in 1867 and became its first Secretary and Treasurer. *JAC* passed his examinations with distinction and joined the SAA in 1910. This was the year when he immigrated to the US and he joined CAs MMC in Chicago after a short period in its New York office.

JAC became a Minnesota CPA in 1910, joined the AAPA in 1913, and registered as a CPA in Missouri two years later. His business addresses at this time were Chicago and St Louis. Virtually his first assignment was an investigation on behalf of the bankers, J. P. Morgan & Company, of the Studebaker wagon and carriage business in South Bend. In 1919, *JAC* was admitted to the MMC partnership and remained in that position until his retirement in 1944. He became a CPA in Louisiana and Michigan in 1925 and worked in the New York office from 1930. His only institutional position was as a member of the Committee on Complaints of the IAPA. He died in 1946. The family home was in New Jersey and his wife was born in Scotland. The couple had a daughter.

CARRUTHERS, Charles Peter (1880–1960)   SAE (1902)

Charles Peter Carruthers (*CPC*) was born at Cummertrees on the Solway Firth in Dumfriesshire in 1880. He was the son of a landowner and farmer, Peter Carruthers of Portrack, who farmed more than 300 acres there and employed 14 farm labourers. His mother, Elizabeth Roddick, was also from Cummertrees, and the daughter of John Roddick, a farmer, and Nancy Skelton. Other Roddicks in the area included James Roddick, also a farmer, who had three farmer sons and three daughters, all unmarried. *CPC* had one brother, James, who qualified as a lawyer (WS 1899) and became a Lieutenant Colonel in the Royal Artillery, serving in the First World War and winning the Distinguished Service Order in 1914, and marrying the daughter of a Chesterfield engineer. *CPC*'s grandfather, Charles Hugh Carruthers, was also a landowner and farmer and married to Margaret Richardson. His other grandfather, Thomas Roddick, was born in Scotland but farmed 1,000 acres at Merionyth in Wales with his six sons and six daughters.

CPC was educated at Dumfries Academy (1889–92) and the Moreland's School for Boys (1892–6). He then entered an apprenticeship with the Edinburgh firm of CAs A. & J. Robertson, becoming an SAE member in 1902. A year later, he was recruited by English CA migrant Arthur Lowes Dickinson to the Chicago office of JCC. He joined the IAPA in 1903. In 1904, he moved to a new office in Pittsburg and then, in 1905, to New York. He stayed there for five years before leaving for the San Francisco office in California. In the same year, he was admitted to the AAPA and the CSCPA and MNSCPA. He became manager of the San Francisco office in 1911 and a PWC partner in 1914. Among his assignments was a visit to Hawaii in 1925 to consider opening an office there (which did not happen) and as an expert witness in a sugar company valuation court case in the same year. He joined the AIA in 1916, chaired its Arbitration Committee in 1927, and worked on its Committee on Cooperation with Investment Bankers in 1938. He became a member of the executive committee of PWC in 1935 and retired from the firm with the continuing status as consultant from 1945. *CPC* was married to a woman from California and they had two sons and two daughters. The family home was owned and had a value in 1930 of $10,000 ($112,000 in 2004 terms). He died in California in 1960 and an obituary appeared in *The Accountant's Magazine* of August 1960. He is mentioned several times in C. W. DeMond, *Price, Waterhouse & Co. in America: A History of a Public Accounting Firm* (Comet Press: New York, NY, 1951).

CATTANACH, Peter Lorimar (1879–1905)   SAE (1904)

Peter Lorimar Cattanach (*PLC*) was born in Edinburgh in 1879 to Peter Lorimar Cattanach and Jane Bladworth Hardie. His father was a Solicitor-at-Law (1855) and a member of the Faculty of Advocates (1863) in Edinburgh and his mother's father was James Hardie, an Edinburgh spirit merchant. He had four brothers, Joseph Hardie Cattanach (a Church of Scotland minister at Dalkeith near Edinburgh who died young), John Hardie and James E. Cattanach (both of whom cannot be traced), and David Lorimar Cattanach (Master of Arts, ordained 1913, and minister at Golspie in Sutherland). He also had a sister. *PLC*'s paternal grandparents were William Cattanach, an Edinburgh distiller and wine merchant, and Ann Gardiner Marwick. His uncle, James Gibson Cattanach, was a medical practitioner in Edinburgh.

PLC was educated at George Watson's College in Edinburgh and graduated Master of Arts from the University of Edinburgh in 1900. He was apprenticed to CAs Lindsay Jamieson & Haldane and admitted to the Faculty of Actuaries in 1903 and the SAE in 1904. He immigrated to the US in 1905 for employment with CAs PWC in New York. Transferred to the St Louis office, he died there of typhoid fever in 1905. He was unmarried. Obituaries appeared in *The Accountant's Magazine* in October 1905 and *The Accountant* of November 1905.

CHAMBERS, Norman Gilbert (1882–1948)   IAAG (1908)

Norman Gilbert Chambers (*NGC*) was born in Hammersmith in London in 1882. His parents were William Chambers, a commercial traveller in wool, from Failand in Somerset, and Catherine Chambers from Dalzeil in Lanarkshire. He had three sisters and one brother and was boarding in Kelvin in Glasgow by 1901 where he had an apprenticeship with Glasgow CAs Moores, Carson & Watson. He was presumably educated in London. *NGC* joined the IAAG in 1908. In that year, he left for New York and employment with CAs MMC. In 1910, he became a CPA in Minnesota and moved to the firm's Toronto office in Canada. In 1919, he joined the AIA and became a partner in MMC in New York in 1920. Three years later, *NGC* was recorded as a CPA in California. In 1931, he was a member of the NYSSCPA. *NGC* was a speaker on taxation at the annual convention of the

American Institute of Banking in 1928 and was a member of the AIA's Committee on Double Taxation in 1931. He retired in 1940 and died in New York in 1948. His wife was a Canadian and there were no children. The family home in New York was owned in 1930 and valued at $42,000 ($470,000 in 2004 terms).

CHERRY, Gladstone (1881–1980)   IAAG (1906)

Born in Hutchesontown in Glasgow in 1881, Gladstone Cherry (*GC*) was the son of John Cherry from Paisley in Renfrewshire and Margaret Sproul from Linwood in the same county. John Cherry was a grocer's assistant who became a restaurant owner in Renton in Dumbartonshire. Renton is a small town to the north-west of Dumbarton. Margaret Sproul had money from property and lived in Sproul's Land in Glasgow prior to her marriage. She was 12 years older than her husband and was born in Ireland. *GC*'s uncle, John Sproul, was a master joiner who employed 16 men, and his brothers, Matthew and William Sproul, were commercial travellers. *GC*'s brother, John Sproul Cherry, was an engineering fitter and there were three sisters.

GC was apprenticed to CA William McMillan of Glasgow and admitted to the IAAG in 1906. From 1905 to 1906, he was employed as an audit clerk by CAs MacLean, Brodie & Forgie. In 1907, he moved to Milwaukee in Wisconsin to work for CAs AYC. He remained with this firm in Milwaukee until 1920 when he became a partner. He was also a member of the AAPA and a Wisconsin CPA from 1910, becoming President of the WSCPA from 1917 until 1922. He joined the AIA in 1916 and served in the US army during the First World War. Then, in 1923, he founded his own firm in Milwaukee, Gladstone Cherry, Cheyne & Company. This remained his occupation until at least 1936 when he appears to have retired. He died in 1980 in San Diego in California at the age of ninety-nine. There is no record of a family.

CONNER, Andrew King (1877–1912)   IAAG (1900)

Andrew King Conner (*AKC*) was born in 1877 at Lochwinnoch in Renfrewshire, a small textile manufacturing town eight miles west of Paisley and with a population in 1871 of 3,300. His father was Robert Buchanan Conner, Clerk and Treasurer to the School Board at Catrine in southern Ayrshire, and Inspector of the Poor and Collector of Rates at the farming village of Sorn. Robert Conner was born at Campsie in Stirlingshire, a farming town of 6,700 inhabitants in 1871. Sorn was linked to the larger marketing town community of Catrine which had an 1881 population of 2,900. *AKC* appears to have had one brother, John King Conner, who died young. His mother, Jane Thomson King from Glasgow, also died when he was young and she was Robert Conner's second wife. The Conners in Campsie were mainly general labourers who originated from Ireland. Bernard Conner was a grandfather and a carting contractor who married Jane Buchanan. Jane King's father was Andrew King, a spirit merchant and husband of Agnes Young.

It is not known with which firm of CAs *AKC* trained as there is no record of his apprenticeship surviving. When he joined the IAAG in 1900, he was employed by CAs Ivory & Sime in Edinburgh and remained with them until 1902. He then appears to have been unemployed and residing with his father at Catrine in Ayrshire until 1904 when he spent two years in London. This was followed by a further three years to 1908 at Catrine. In 1909, he left for New York and employment with CAs TNC. However, a year later, he was deported from the US because he was suffering from tuberculosis. As he had no money or living relations, he received the sum of £50 from the Council of the IAAG to pay for three months of treatment at a sanatorium in Crieff in Perthshire. He then moved to London in 1910 to work for PWC but a year later, received a further £25 from the IAAG to pay for medical treatment in London. The IAAG also waived three years of arrears of membership dues. A last payment of £35 from the IAAG was made in 1912, the year of *AKC*'s death.

COOK, James Thompson (1887–1927) IAAG (1911)

Born in the district of Kelvin in Glasgow in 1887, James Thomson Cook (*JTC*) was the son of a railway plant superintendent for the Caledonian Railway Company, William Cook from the farming village of Penpont in Dumfriesshire, to the north-west of Dumfries. The Caledonian Railway Company was a major Scottish rail transportation company formed in 1847 with a line from London to the Borders region. It connected to Edinburgh and Glasgow a year later and, by 1895, had the fastest locomotives to link to Aberdeen. It became part of the London, Midland & Scottish Railway Company in 1923. William Cook's father was William Cook, a general merchant in Penpont, and his mother was Elizabeth Taylor. *JTC*'s mother was Ellen Beattie from the iron and steel manufacturing town of Coatbridge in Lanarkshire, the daughter of John Beattie, a draper, and Maria Money, also a draper. *JTC* had an uncle, James Beattie, who was a railway clerk, a brother, John William Cook, a shipping clerk, and a sister. Other Pen Point relatives included uncles who were masons.

JTC was educated at the Glasgow High School and then apprenticed to CAs John Mann & Son. When he died in 1910, John Mann was the last surviving founder of the IAAG in 1854. The son of an east of Scotland landscape artist, his son, also John Mann, joined the IAAG in 1885 and was knighted in 1919 for his cost accounting advice to the government during the First World War. *JTC* was admitted to the IAAG in 1911 when he formed his own practise in Glasgow. This cannot have lasted more than a few months because in the same year he immigrated to the US and joined CAs MMC in Minneapolis in Minnesota. A year later, he became a Minnesota CPA and transferred to Kansas City in 1913. He became a member of the AIA in 1916. Two years later, he transferred to the MMC office in Dallas in Texas. He served there in the US military between 1917 and 1918. In 1920, *JTC* had moved to New York to become a partner in the CA immigrant firm of Harris, Kerr & Company. He remained in this position until his death in New York in 1927. There is no record of a marriage or children.

CRAIG, Andrew (1880–1918)   IAAG (1909)

There is very little information available concerning Andrew Craig (*AC*). He was born in 1880 to John Craig, a cab proprietor from Hamilton in Lanarkshire, and Isabella Craig from Kilsyth in Stirlingshire. Approximately 100 miles south of Glasgow, Hamilton was a coal and iron ore mining town and a military depot in the late nineteenth century, and had a population of 14,000 in 1881. At the same time, Kilsyth had a population of 6,800 – predominantly working in the coal and iron industry and in paper manufacturing. *AC* had three brothers and four sisters and was apprenticed to Glasgow CAs John Mann & Son. He joined the IAAG in 1909 and immigrated a year later to the US where he joined CAs MMC in Minneapolis and became a Minnesota CPA. He then became a partner in a firm he founded in London in 1911, Craig, Gardner & Harris, but a year later was working in New York for CAs Harris, Allan & Company. He remained with this firm until 1918 when, during an audit of the Atlantic Fruit Company, he was recruited by Arthur Young and admitted to a partnership with AYC in New York. He died there in the same year as a result of influenza. He was a New York CPA. As with several other immigrants, there is no sign of marriage or children.

CRAIG, William (1885–1955)   SAA (1911)

William Craig (*WC*) was born in Kintore on the River Don in Aberdeenshire in 1885, the son of James Craig, a quarry master, and Ann Jackson. His grandparents were David Craig, a farm labourer, and Mary McAllan, and Alexander Jackson, a farmer, and Ann Boak. Quarrying was the major industry in Kintore from the 1830s and employed up to 400 individuals. The village of approximately 600 inhabitants in 1881 is located 13 miles west of Aberdeen. Educated in Aberdeen, *WC* was apprenticed to CA A. S. Mitchell of Aberdeen and admitted to the SAA in 1911. He immediately immigrated to Brooklyn in New York and started work with CAs MMC in 1912. A year later, *WC* was employed by CAs, Harris, Allan & Company, and three years later had moved to St Louis in Missouri to work for CAs PWC as a non-contract staff member. He then moved to Houston in Texas to work for the Humble Oil & Refining Company (now part of the Chevron Oil Corporation) between 1923 and 1927 when he moved back to St Louis to become the Comptroller of the Roxana Petroleum Corporation (a Dutch company based in East Chicago and now part of the Royal Dutch Shell Corporation). He remained with this company until 1935 when his address was Aurora in Illinois. In 1948, *WC* was retired in Eugene in Oregon and, in 1952, in Reno in Nevada. He died in 1955 at Menlo Park in California. An obituary appeared in *The Accountant's Magazine* of November 1955. *WC* was married to a woman from Texas who was 13 years his junior. They had one daughter.

CRAWFORD, John (1881–1936)   IAAG (1907)

John Crawford (*JC*) was born in Glasgow in 1881. His father, William Crawford, was a tinsmith in the shipbuilding town of Govan in Renfrewshire and it is assumed his mother died in childbirth as the family home had a servant in the year of his birth without the presence of his mother. He was apprenticed to Glasgow CAs Dunlop & Murray and admitted to the IAAG in 1907 having migrated to New York in 1904. His first employer was a Scottish firm of CAs MLC and he remained with them for a year until he moved to work for a small firm of accountants at Butte in Montana. In 1910, *JC* started to practise on his own and became a CPA in Minnesota. Six years later, he became a Montana CPA and a member of the AIA. In 1923, *JC* moved his practise to Portland in Oregon and remained there until his death in 1936. In the 1930 US Census, he was living in a home in Portland valued at $7,500 ($84,000 in 2004 terms) with his Scottish wife and two sons who were born in Montana.

CUNNINGHAM, Robert Thomson (1881–1963)   IAAG (1911)

Born in the small shipping port of Girvan in south Ayrshire in 1881 (population 5,500), Robert Thomson Cunningham (*RTC*) was the son of Francis Thomson Cunningham, a tailor's cutter from Dumfries in Dumfriesshire, and Margaret Hunter, a milliner from Girvan. His paternal grandfather was James Cunningham, a sailor, and his maternal grandfather William Hunter, a hotel manager. He had three brothers including James Thomson, a tailor. *RTC* was educated in Girvan before serving an apprenticeship with a firm of Glasgow CAs Moores, Carson & Watson. He qualified as a member of the IAAG in 1911 and, one year later, was in New York working for Scottish CAs MMC.

   RTC remained with MMC in New York until 1923 when he moved to the Dallas, Texas office. During the First World War, he served in Europe in the British Army and won the Military Cross for bravery in action. By 1930, he was living in Dallas and the family home was valued at $17,500 ($196,000 in 2004 terms). His wife was from Texas and they had a daughter. In 1931, *RTC* became a Canadian CA and, two years later, a partner in the Winnipeg office of MMC. He retired in 1948 and was removed from the membership roll of the IAAG in 1949. He was reinstated in 1959 and served on the Council of the CICA. *RTC* died in Winnipeg in 1963.

CUTHBERT, Hugh Thornton (1878–1966)   SAE (1901)

Hugh Thornton Cuthbert (*HTC*) was a member of a remarkable family from the West of Scotland. He was the grandson of Robert Cuthbert from the village of Alloway to the immediate south of Ayr in south Ayrshire. Robert Cuthbert was a ship owner. *HTC*'s father, Hugh Cuthbert, was also a ship owner and his mother,

Anne Wilkinson, was the daughter of Lieutenant-Colonel Sir Thomas Wilkinson of the Honorable East India Company, a Westmoreland landowner. *HTC* was born in 1878 at the shipping and shipbuilding town of Greenock on the River Clyde in Renfrewshire and married Lucy Bishop Smith of New London in Connecticut. He had several brothers, including the oldest and next biographee in this book, Robert Lancelot Cuthbert. Most of these siblings were involved in the British Army prior to and during the First World War.

The second eldest brother, Thomas Wilkinson Cuthbert, was born in 1873 and educated at Edinburgh Academy where he was a member of its rugby team. He was a land agent in Devon and a factor in Aberdeenshire where he was also a Justice of the Peace and County Councillor. Other offices held by Thomas Cuthbert included a governorship of Aberdeen & North of Scotland College of Agriculture. He served as a Lieutenant-Colonel in the Seaforth Highlanders in France between 1914 and 1916, was wounded twice, and awarded the Distinguished Service Order, George Star and Victory Medal. Brother James Mackie Cuthbert was born in 1875 and educated at Edinburgh Academy where he was a member of the school's rugby and gymnastics teams. He graduated as a medical doctor from the University of Edinburgh in 1898 and became a Major in the Royal Army Medical Corps and pathologist for Scottish Command in 1910. He was President of the Medical Board of Scottish Command (1916–17), medical officer at general hospitals in France, Mesopotamia, and Persia (1914–20), and holder of the 1914 Star, George Star and Victory medals.

Brother Reginald Vaux Cuthbert was born in 1880 and also educated at Edinburgh Academy where he was a member of the gymnastics team. He became a broker in Singapore and a Lieutenant in the Singapore Artillery before joining the Seaforth Highlanders in France in 1916. He was awarded the George Star and Victory medals before dying of his wounds in 1917. Brother William Arthur Cuthbert was born in 1893, educated at Edinburgh Academy, before serving during the Boer War with the Scottish Horse Regiment. He was awarded the Queen's Medal with four clasps and became a farmer in Canada. Brother Ronald Wingrave Cuthbert was a Captain in the Royal Army Medical Corps and the Black Watch in France and Mesopotamia during the First World War. He was awarded the George Star and Victory medals and was killed in action in 1916.

HTC was educated at Edinburgh Academy between 1889 and 1896 where he was a member of the school's rugby and cricket teams. He appears to have served in the British Army during the Boer War between 1901 and 1904 where he was awarded the South Africa Medal with three clasps. He had been admitted to the SAE in 1901 following an apprenticeship with Frederick Walter Carter (SAE 1868) of CAs Carter, Greig & Company in Edinburgh. Carter was the son of Frederick Hayne Carter, a founder member of the SAE in 1854, SAE President in 1904, and a Lieutenant-Colonel in the Royal Artillery Militia. *HTC* worked for Carter during 1905 and 1906 and then immigrated to Chicago in 1906 to work for English CA Ernest Reckitt. He remained with Reckitt until 1909 when he set up his own public accountancy firm, H. T. Cuthbert & Company, at Douglas in Arizona. The firm transferred to Phoenix in 1924. In 1911, he became a CPA in

Ohio and a member of the AAPA in 1912. The latter membership was transferred to the AIA in 1916.

HTC was one of the founders of institutionalised public accountancy in Arizona and was described as the "dean of Arizona public accountants". He became the second Arizona CPA in 1919, President of the first Arizona State Board of Accountancy (1919–21), Secretary of the Board (1932–3), and President of the AASCPA in 1939. He was on the first Arizona Examinations Board in 1932 and also a member of various committees of the AIA during the 1930s. His firm became Cuthbert, Johnson & Tisor in 1948 and Cuthbert, Johnson & Company in 1953. He specialised in livestock accounting, was active in promoting the use of local accountants by the State of Arizona government in 1933, and challenged the State to enforce the public accountancy law in 1940. *HTC* was married and had one son. The family home in 1930 was in Phoenix and valued at $16,000 ($179,000 in 2004 terms). *HTC* was the first Treasurer of the Southwest Tennis Association in 1912 and became its sixth President in 1917. He died in Phoenix in 1966 and was the sixth most senior member of ICAS. His career is covered in N. J. Stowe and B. Luey, *Accountancy in Arizona: A History of the Profession* (Arizona State Society of Certified Public Accountants: Phoenix, AR, 1990). He also appeared in *Who's Who in Arizona* (1913) and *History of Arizona* (Record Publishing Company, 1930)

CUTHBERT, Robert Lancelot (1868–1915)   SAE (1891)

Robert Lancelot Cuthbert (*RLC*) was born in 1868 at Greenock in Renfrewshire as the eldest son of Hugh Cuthbert and Anne Wilkinson. He was educated at the Collegiate School in Edinburgh and Wimbledon School in London, and then apprenticed to CA Patrick Turnbull (SAE 1858) of A. & J. Robertson in Edinburgh. Patrick was a farmer's son who had also worked as an estate factor. *RLC* was a prize-winner in the examinations of the SAE to which he was admitted in 1891. Immediately on qualification, he left Edinburgh for London to work for CAs DDGC. He was unmarried and boarded in East Dulwich. He worked in London for three years until immigrating to New York and practised there on his own. *RLC* became a New York CPA in 1896 and, two years later, partnered migrant Frederick William Menzies as Cuthbert & Menzies. Menzies was a member of the Society of Incorporated Accountants & Auditors (SIAA).

The partnership lasted until 1906 when *RLC* became a partner in the New York office of DDGC. Menzies formed a new firm with James Hussey Robertson, an SAE member, and C. H. Patrick who was not a CA. The DDGC partnership lasted until 1910 when *RLC* became a partner in AYC and a member of the AIA. Four years later, while on vocation in London, he enlisted in the British Army. He was 47 years of age and had lied about his age. His decision was presumably influenced by the service of his younger brothers in the Boer and First World Wars. He was a private in the King Edward's Horse Regiment attached to the 1st Canadian Division, and died in Flanders while on hazardous scouting duty in 1915. *RLC* was buried in the Plus Douve Farm Cemetery at Hainaut in Belgium.

He was unmarried and had been a keen racing yachtsman and golfer in New York. Obituaries appeared in *The Accountant's Magazine*, the *Journal of Accountancy*, *The Pace Student*, and *The Accountant*. A biography was published in the November 1952 issue of *The New York Certified Public Accountant* and is reproduced in J. Grant, *The New York State Society of Certified Public Accountants: Foundation for a Profession* (Garland Publishing: New York, NY, 1995).

DAVIDSON, James Ramsay (1891–1951)   IAAG (1914)

Mary Ramsay, a domestic servant from the farming village of Glenshee in Perthshire, and William Davidson, a house joiner from the village of Arngask in Fife, had a son, James Ramsay Davidson (*JRD*), in 1891 at Hamilton in Lanarkshire. *JRD* had three brothers and three sisters. Grandfather William Davidson was a labourer from the village of Monzievaird in Perthshire and grandfather John Ramsay was a crofter with 11 acres to farm. Uncle James Davidson was a joiner, and uncle Thomas Ramsay was a shepherd. *JRD* was educated in Motherwell, a Lanarkshire coal mining and ironworks town of 13,000 inhabitants in 1891, and started an apprenticeship in 1910 with Glasgow CA George McKean. This lasted three years and the remaining two years were served with CAs McLean, Brodie, & Forgie. He was a clerk with this firm in 1913 and 1914 when he was admitted to the IAAG and joined CAs MMC at Boston in Massachusetts. *JRD* appears to have remained there until 1920 when he returned to Glasgow. However, it is possible he had served during the First World War. In 1923, he became a partner in the firm of CAs Russ & Cree in Glasgow and remained there until his death in 1951.

DAWSON, John Peterkin (1880–?)   UQ

John Peterkin Dawson (*JPD*) was born in 1880 at Aberdeen. His father was Henry Dawson of Woodside in Aberdeen, a house carpenter who became a laboratory assistant then janitor at the University of Aberdeen. His mother Euphemia Peterkin, was the daughter of John Peterkin a mason, and Ann Watt. His paternal grandfather was Charles Dawson, a town's officer, and Jessie Gibb. Of his siblings, Henry Dawson was a university laboratory assistant, and James Perterkin Dawson was an electrical engineer in Aberdeen.

JPD was educated at Robert Gordon's College and apprenticed to CA John Craigen in Aberdeen. He failed to complete his contract of service and, in 1905, immigrated to New York. In 1916, he became a New York CPA and, a year later, joined CAs PWC. In 1920, he was moved to the firm's Seattle office to supervise the audit staff there. He opened the Oregon office in 1921 as its manager and initiated meetings to facilitate joint activities for the public accountancy societies of British Columbia in Canada, Washington, and Oregon. In 1928, *JPD* moved to Chicago to help in various merger investigations and became a partner in 1933. He was a Vice-President and then President of the IAPA. He retired in 1941 at the same time as fellow UQ immigrant Donald Arthur and went to Florida where he was living in the mid-1960s. His wife was from Scotland and there is no record of children or of his death.

DEWAR, Douglas (1883–1965)   IAAG (1905)

Douglas Dewar (*DD*) was born in the Glasgow suburb of Rutherglen in Lanarkshire in 1883. His father was Duncan Dewar, a bank accountant from Coylton in Ayrshire (a farming village three miles east of Ayr) and son of John Dewar, a gamekeeper, and Jane Brodie. His mother was Janet Gray, a daughter of farmer John Gray and Mary McLarty. He had three brothers, two of whom were commercial clerks, and a sister. *DD* was educated at the Glasgow High School and apprenticed to Glasgow CAs Moores, Carson & Watson. He was admitted to the IAAG in 1905 and migrated to New York in 1906, having been recruited by James Marwick of CAs MMC. He had initially responded to an advertisement in *The Glasgow Herald*, and left for the US against the advice of his father.

In 1908, *DD* transferred to the MMC office in Chicago and became a CPA in Ohio and Illinois. A year later, he was admitted to a partnership in the firm and remained in that position until 1939. He became a Canadian CA in 1912 and a member of the AAPA in 1913. *DD* served with the Canadian armed forces in Europe from 1914 until 1919 and returned to the MMC partnership in New York in 1920. He became an active member of the New York Chamber of Commerce from 1925 and was his firm's deputy senior partner from 1930 to 1939 when, despite a fifteen per cent share in the firm's profits, he left as a result of illness due to bronchitis and a continuing row with the firm's senior partner James William Hall, a fellow migrant and Glasgow CA. *DD* had refused Hall's request to become a US citizen.

DD left New York for Canada in 1940 to work for the Canadian government, first as foreign exchange controller for British Columbia and then as Deputy Chairman of the Price & Control Board of the federal government. He became a Commander of the Order of the British Empire for these services and also had non-executive directorships including the Celanese Corporation, a former audit client at MMC. During his time at MMC and later, *DD* was known for a very harsh management style. In 1941, he published a lecture to the Vancouver Institute entitled "Certain Aspects of Foreign Exchange Control". He retired in Vancouver and died there in 1965. His obituary appeared in the December issue of *The Accountant's Magazine* in 1965 and his role in MMC is explained in T. A. Wise, *Peat, Marwick, Mitchell & Company: 85 Years* (Peat, Marwick, Mitchell & Company: New York, NY, 1982). *DD* was married and had a son and daughter. The son, also Douglas Dewar, appears to have been a scientist and received a Doctorate in Chemistry for identification of toxins in mussels.

DICKIE, Charles Swappe (1882–1944)   SAA (1906)

A member of the SAA from 1906, Charles Swappe Dickie (*CSD*) was born in Aberdeen in 1882. He was the son of Aberdeen CA George Dickie and grandson of George Dickie, an Advocate's bookkeeper in Aberdeen. His mother was Annie Grant, a lady's maid in Aberdeen. He had four sisters and three brothers, two of whom can be traced – George Robertson Dickie was an Aberdeen Solicitor who died of asthma aged 29, and Forbes M. M. Dickie was an arts student at the University of Aberdeen in 1901 who later became a member of the SAA. Great grandfathers included Andrew Dickie, a house painter, and John Grant, a clothes merchant in Aberdeen. A cousin, Ann Swappe, was a draper's cashier in Aberdeen, and the daughter of Alexander Swappe, an Aberdeen cabinet maker. *CSD* was educated in Aberdeen and apprenticed there to CAs Milne & Milroy. After qualifying, he left Aberdeen for London in 1907 to become the managing assistant to Sir (later Lord) William Plender of CAs DDGC. Plender (ICAEW 1884) was the son of a north of England grocer in Newcastle who was ICAEW President on three occasions (1910–12 and 1929–30). He was knighted in 1931 and made a Baron in 1931 for his work on various Royal Commissions and other public service work. In 1908, *CSD* transferred to the DDGC office in New York. He returned to the managing assistantship in London in 1909. He stayed with the firm until 1923 when he became the financial director of a large steelworks in Sheffield, Thomas Firth & John Brown Ltd. He was there in 1944 when he died. *CSD* was married and did not join any American public accountancy body during his short stay in the US.

DOUGHERTY, Richard (1882–1926) IAAG (1905)

Richard Dougherty (*RD*) was born in Glasgow in 1882. His father, James Dougherty, was a fruit merchant and his mother was Mary McGowan. Grandfather William Dougherty was also a fruit merchant and married to Susan Grant. His maternal grandparents were Thomas McGowan, an iron merchant in Glasgow, and Agnes McKechnie. His brothers, William and Thomas Dougherty, were fruit salesmen, brother John Dougherty a manufacturer's apprentice, uncles Peter and John Dougherty, clerks in his father's business, and aunt Sarah Dougherty, a fruit saleswoman.

Following education in Glasgow, *RD* left the family fruit business and served an apprenticeship with CAs Wight & Wight in Glasgow. He joined the IAAG in 1905 and almost immediately immigrated to the US where he joined MMC in New York in 1906. However, by 1907, he had set up his own practise in Minneapolis with fellow Glasgow CA William Alexander Frame as Frame, Dougherty & Company. Two years later, he became a Minnesota CPA and, in 1911, was working for immigrant CA firm J. Gordon Steele & Company in Minneapolis. A year later, *RD* was practicing as Richard Dougherty & Company and had joined the AAPA. He died in Minneapolis in 1926 and an obituary appeared in *The Accountant's Magazine* of June 1927. There is no record of a marriage.

DREVER, Thomas (1882–1965) SAE (1905)

Thomas Drever (*TD*) was born in Edinburgh in 1882. His father, John Barry Stewart Drever, was a master draper from the island of Shapinsay north of Kirkwall in the Orkney Islands off the north coast of Scotland. The Orkneys were initially inhabited by Norsemen and comprise 67 islands mainly devoted to fishing and agriculture in the nineteenth century. The overall population in 1881 was 32,000, with 4,000 in the capital of Kirkwall. *TD*'s mother Jane Ross was also from the Orkneys, John Drever's second wife, and a daughter of William Ross, a butler, and Christina Menzies. *TD*'s paternal grandfather, also Thomas Drever, was a land steward in Shapinsay and married to Margaret Maxwell. An uncle, David Drever, was an Edinburgh tailor and a further uncle from Kirkwall, William Peace Drever, was a Writer (lawyer) in Paisley in Renfrewshire. An aunt worked as a tobacconist in Edinburgh. *TD* had a brother, John Barry Stewart Drever, who was an apprentice to a CA George Lisle (SAE 1887). George Lisle was admitted to the SAE in 1887, a Fellow of the Faculty of Actuaries, and a well-known Edinburgh practitioner, lecturer, and writer on accounting matters. His principal texts were *Accounting in Theory and Practise* (1900, William Green & Son, Edinburgh) and the six-volume *Encyclopedia of Accounting* (1903–4, William Green & Son, Edinburgh). John Barry Stewart Drever was a medalist in the principles of accounting class at Heriot Watt College in 1911 and admitted to the SAE in 1920. He served as a non-commissioned officer in the British Army between 1915 and 1919. On return from France, he left for the US and held audit appointments there with PWC and James Angus Steven, an immigrant member of the IAAG. A CPA of Illinois and Wisconsin, John Drever became County Auditor of Cook County in Illinois, a jurisdiction that included Chicago. He was married with two sons and died in 1944. His biography is not included in this study in full as he left Scotland for the US in 1919.

TD was educated at the Royal High School and apprenticed to W. J. Arthur Drummond, CA (SAE 1885), in Edinburgh. He joined the SAE in 1905 and remained with Drummond for two years until immigrating to New York in 1907. His initial employment was with PWC in New York as a seasonal member of staff. Despite the lack of regular employment, however, *TD* was appointed in 1908 as Comptroller of the US Coal & Oil Company in Boston, Massachusetts. In the same year, when he also became a CPA in Ohio (almost uniquely for an industrial accountant), he moved to the American Steel Foundries in Chicago, becoming its Treasurer and a Vice-President in 1910. A year later, *TD* was appointed as Comptroller and President of the company. In 1912, he became the chairman of the board of directors and a member of the AAPA and the IAPA. American Steel Foundries was incorporated in New Jersey in 1902 and remains the largest producer of steel castings in the US with plants in East St Louis, Chicago, Pittsburg and Chester. It initially supplied castings for rails in the railway industry but expanded into other industries such as oil, shopping, and munitions. The company supplied castings in 1943 for the construction of the two atomic bombs dropped on Japan. Its profits in its first year of trading were $1.5m. By the time of his retirement in 1959 to Pompano Beach in Florida, *TD* had an honorary degree of Doctor of Laws from the Illinois Institute of Technology in Chicago (1954). The Institute was founded in 1893 as the Armour Institute and offered courses in engineering, chemistry, architecture, and library science. It continues today as a private university with 6,000 students and specialises in engineering, science, architecture, law and business on several campuses throughout the US. *TD* died at Pompano Beach in 1965 and left a widow, Edith E. Drever.

DUNCAN, Ernest Bailey (1882–1923)   SAE (1908)

Ernest Bailey Duncan (*EBD*) was born in Edinburgh in 1882. His father, Thomas Duncan, was a boot manufacturer there and employed 31 individuals. Grandfather James Sandilands Duncan was an Edinburgh boot maker, merchant, and husband of Ann Elizabeth Wingrave. *EBD*'s mother was Eliza Mary Bailey, a governess. Maternal grandparents were William Bailey, a manure manufacturer in Edinburgh, and Elizabeth Black. Thomas Duncan was educated at Edinburgh Academy and the University of Edinburgh before starting his business career as a merchant in Liverpool. *EBD* was also educated at Edinburgh Academy between 1892 and 1893 where he was a member of the cricket and gymnastics teams. His brother, Ronald Wingrave Duncan, was educated at Edinburgh Academy and the Universities of Edinburgh and Glasgow where he graduated as a dental surgeon in 1907. An elder brother, William Arthur Duncan, followed a similar educational path – Edinburgh Academy and the University of Edinburgh where he graduated as a medical practitioner in 1901. Other known relatives of *EBD* followed non-professional careers as, respectively, a seaman, a plumber and a commercial traveller.

EBD served an apprenticeship with Edinburgh CAs Whitson & Methuen from 1893 to 1898 and was admitted to the SAE in 1908. Thomas B. Whitson, son of Perthshire CA Thomas Whitson (SAE 1872), entered the SAE in 1893 and became Lord Provost of Edinburgh. His partner, Harry T. Methuen, became a member a year later. In 1908, *EBD* left Edinburgh for San Francisco to become an assistant audit manager with CAs PWC. However, approximately a year later, he returned to the family home in Craigmillar Park in Edinburgh. He became a grain merchant and, in 1915, married Anna Gwendolen Thomson, daughter of William Thomson, a carpet designer, and Jean Montgomery. He died in the Chalmer's Hospital in Edinburgh in 1923 from bronchitis at the age of 41.

ELDER, David (1882–1967)   IAAG (1905)

Born in Dundee in 1882, David Elder (*DE*) was the son of Peter Elder, a public school teacher in Edinburgh who was originally from the market town of Cupar in Fife, and Catherine S. Fleming of Dundee, also a teacher and from the fishing town of Arbroath in Forfarshire. His paternal grandfather, also David Elder, was a mason in Cupar and married to Ann Collier. Grandfather David Fleming was a grocer in Arbroath and married to Elizabeth Spink. A great uncle was a house painter in the Fife fishing village of Anstruther, and uncles included a baker and confectioner and a potato merchant in Cupar, and a grocer and bank clerk in Arbroath. Cupar was and remains the county town of Fife. It is a market town and, in 1881, had a population of 5,000.

DE was educated in Dundee and apprenticed to a local firm of CAs Mackay & Ness (later MIC). The firm had an office in New York. *DE* was admitted to the

IAAG in 1905 and continued to work with MIC in Dundee until 1907 when he left to join CAs MLC in New York. He became a CPA of Ohio in 1908 and a partner in MLC in 1909. He joined the AAPA in 1912 and the AIA in 1916. *DE* left MLC in 1919 to form his own practise in New York as David Elder & Company. Two years later, he admitted fellow Dundonian, Carestin Dakers Fairweather, to a partnership. *DE* lived at Richmond in New York by 1920 with his parents, Scottish wife (who had migrated in 1911), three daughters, and son. He died at his home on Staten Island in 1967 when he was senior partner in his firm and the ninth most senior member of ICAS. An obituary appeared in the January 1968 issue of *The Accountant's Magazine*.

FAIRNIE, Alexander Adamson (1875–1961)   IAAG (1911)

Alexander Adamson Fairnie (*AAF*) was admitted to the IAAG in 1911 following an apprenticeship with the firm of CAs Macfarlane, Hutton, & Partick. He had been born in the small farming village of Hoddom in Dumfriesshire in 1875 where his father, Alexander Adamson Fairnie, was a teacher in the parish school. Alexander senior was born in 1842 in the fishing village of Earlsferry on the south coast of Fife and was married to Jane Ann Rodger from Ecclefechan in Dumfriesshire. Grandfather Robert Fairnie was a coal and iron mine overseer, and grandfather William Rodger a hotel keeper. *AAF* had two brothers and a sister.

By 1910, *AAF* was working for a local firm of accountants, Helliwell, Moore & Maclachlan, in Vancouver on the west coast of Canada. A year later, he had moved to Minneapolis, Minnesota, and employment with CAs MMC. He remained there until 1919 when he returned to Vancouver and Helliwell, Moore & Maclachlan. In the same year, he joined the BCICA, becoming its Vice-President in 1926 and President in 1933. He was a partner in Helliwell by 1936 and retired in 1952. *AAF* died in 1961 at Vancouver and had served on the Council of the CICA. He was not a member of an American public accountancy body. An obituary appeared in the April 1961 issue of the *Canadian Chartered Accountant*.

FAIRWEATHER, Carestin Dakers (1881–1923)   IAAG (1912)

Born at some time after 1881, Carestin Dakers Fairweather (*CDF*) was the son of Daedelus Fairweather, a grocer in Dundee, and Margaret Reid, a power loom weaver who was born in France. He had two brothers. His paternal grandfather, William Fairweather, was a Dundee grocer, and his maternal grandfather a ship's smith in the same city. *CDF* was educated in Dundee and apprenticed to CAs MIC. He qualified as a member of the IAAG in 1912 by which time he was working for MIC in New York and was a Minnesota CPA (1910). He remained with MIC until 1920 when he started employment with CAs MMC in New York, was admitted to the AIA, and became a Missouri CPA. A year later, in 1921, he was admitted as a partner to David Elder & Company in New York. He joined the ASCPA in 1923, the year in which he died. There is no record that *CDF* was married.

FIELD, Richard Sydney (1884–1944)   IAAG (1907)

James Field was a paint manufacturer from England with a business in Glasgow and an Irish wife. The couple had three children including Richard Sydney Field (*RSF*) born in the market town of Pontefract in west Yorkshire in 1884. He was educated at Ackworth Friends School in Pontefract prior to a CA apprenticeship with Dunn & Todd in Glasgow. *RSF* was admitted to the IAAG in 1907 and immigrated in that year to work for CAs MMC in New York. Two years later, he returned to the UK to work in London for Cooper Brothers & Company (CBC), CAs. CBC was founded in 1854 in London by William Cooper who assumed his three brothers as partners between 1854 and 1864. The firm did not open a US office (in New York) until 1926. In 1911, and until 1926, *RSF* was an accountant with the British international trading company of Harrison & Crossfield. The latter traded predominantly in the Far East and Australasia. During his time with Harrison & Crossfield, *RSF* appears to have served during the First World War. By 1927 and until 1940, he was a partner in the firm of CAs Ford, Rhodes & Ford in London. He died in 1944 leaving a widow and son serving in the armed forces. An obituary appeared in *The Accountant's Magazine* of November 1944.

FLEMING, Henry Hamilton (1880–1941)   IAAG (1905)

Henry Hamilton Fleming (*HHF*) was born in the Glasgow suburb of Rutherglen in 1880. His father, John Fleming, was a Writer (lawyer) from Glasgow and his mother was Isabella Wark Pinkerton. His paternal grandfather was John Fleming, a landowner and husband of Ann Pinkerton. John Pinkerton was the maternal grandfather, a farmer and landowner of 100 acres near Rutherglen (employing five individuals), and married to Jane Brown. Uncle Henry Pinkerton was a cashier in a shipping company in Glasgow. Nothing more is known of *HHF*'s family other than he married Jessie Keith in 1910. She was a daughter of John Keith, a Glasgow iron merchant, and Elizabeth Kincaid.

HHF was apprenticed to Mackay & Ness (later MIC), CAs in Dundee and he was admitted to the IAAG in 1905. In that year, he was employed by CAs Moores, Carson & Watson of Glasgow. In 1906, he became a partner in the Glasgow firm of CAs Wight, Wight, Myles & Fleming and this lasted until 1912 when he immigrated to the US. He worked for the Scottish CA firm of J. Gordon Steele & Company in Minneapolis, Minnesota and became a Minnesota CPA in 1912. He was also an associate member of the AAPA. This employment lasted one year and he went to work for immigrant CAs Frame, Dougherty & Company in 1913 in Minneapolis. A year later, he was employed by PWC in Winnipeg in Canada. In 1920, *HHF* was the general auditor of an industrial company in Winnipeg, Stobarts Ltd. Three years later, in 1923, he founded his own practise in Winnipeg, H. Hamilton Fleming & Company, and remained in that position until his death in 1941. No record can be found of any marriage.

FLEMING, Thomas Reid (1860–1924)   SAE (1882)

Thomas Reid Fleming (*TRF*) was born in the farming and weaving town of Campsie in Stirlingshire in 1860 (population 6,500). He was a member of a well-known Scottish family. His father was Alexander Fleming, a linen merchant and brother of James Simpson Fleming, the Cashier and Manager of the Royal Bank of Scotland between 1871 and 1891. His grandfather was Sir James Young Simpson, Professor of Midwifery at the University of Edinburgh, the Queen's Physician in Scotland (1847–70), and the first user of ether and chloroform in surgery. *TRF* was also the brother-in-law of lawyer Thomas Skene Esson, a WS (1882) and son of George Auldjo Esson, one of the founders of the SAE in 1853–4 and Accountant of Court (1856–78). Other brother-in-laws included Philip Robert Dalrymple Maclagan, the Manager of the North British & Mercantile Insurance Company (1882–1906) and son of David Maclagan, another SAE founder, and Sir Robert Russell Simpson, WS (1869) and son-in-law of SAE founder Samuel Raleigh. *TRF*'s mother was Elizabeth Reid, daughter of Thomas Reid, land owner, and Helen Duncan, both of Campsie. His brother, James Alexander Fleming, was an Advocate who was appointed as Advocate Depute (1898), Sheriff of Dumfries (1900), Vice-Dean of the Faculty of Advocates (1905–20), and Sheriff of Fife (1913). He also had three sisters.

TRF was educated at Glasgow Academy, Abbey Park in St Andrews, and Uppingham School in Rutland. He then entered a CA apprenticeship with the leading firm of Lindsay, Jamieson & Haldane in Edinburgh. He was admitted to the SAE in 1882. Two years later, he was working in Threadneedle Street in London and, in 1885, in Colorado in the US. It is probable that he was working for or with mining clients of Lindsay, Jamieson & Haldane. Thirteen years later, he was located in South Africa, strengthening the argument that he was involved in mining. However, he died in California in 1924. In the 1920 US Census, he is recorded with his Scottish wife as living on his "own income" at Redwood in California. There were no children. No information is available to specifically determine *TRF*'s employment details and he was never a member of an American public accountancy body. An obituary appeared in *The Scotsman* of March 1924.

FORSYTH, Stephen (1863–1924)   SAA (1889)

Stephen Forsyth (*SF*) had an unusual career path. His father, Alexander Forsyth, was an English Presbyterian minister at Bowington in Northumberland in England and husband of Amelia Harvey Stephen from Aberdeen. The paternal grandfather was Morris Forsyth, an official with the Inland Revenue in Aberdeen, who was married to Jane Brand from Forfarshire. The maternal grandfather was Alexander Stephen, a ship master in the merchant marine service and husband of Janet McDonald, a daughter of James McDonald, an annuitant from the Isle of Skye and brother of Archibald McDonald, an accountant with a steam shipping company.

SF was born in Bowington in 1863 but, from 1876 to 1880, lived with his unmarried uncle Alexander Stephen, an Aberdeen stockbroker, and widowed great aunt, Jessie Stephen (McDonald). He was educated at Aberdeen Grammar School and the University of Aberdeen where he graduated as Master of Arts in 1884. His CA apprenticeship was with the leading Aberdeen firm of Marquis, Hall & Milne and he joined the SAA in 1889. He then appears to have immigrated to the US and, by 1896, was working in the town of Zillah, in Yakima County in the State of Washington. This was a mining area in the north-west. *SF*'s residency in the US lasted until 1905 when he returned to Glasgow to study divinity at the University of Glasgow. He graduated as a Batchelor of Divinity in 1908 and was ordained in Glasgow in the same year. In 1909, *SF* resigned from the SAA and two years later had a ministry in Dundee. He died there in 1924 from a lung disease. His widow was Isabella Templeton, daughter of William Pettigrew Templeton (stated on the birth certificate as a Glasgow veterinary surgeon) and Isabella Fleming. William Templeton, however, was described on his death certificate as a foreman blacksmith from Barony in Lanarkshire and his father, John Templeton, was also a blacksmith from Ireland.

FRAME, William Alexander (1880–1949)   IAAG (1906)

William Alexander Frame (*WAF*) was born in 1880 in the farming town of Bridge of Weir in Renfrewshire to the west of Paisley and Glasgow. His father, Thomas Frame, was the schoolmaster there and came from Hamilton in Renfrewshire. His mother, Nelly Arthur Alexander, came from Bridge of Weir and was a shopkeeper. Paternal grandfather, John Frame, was a weaver and maternal grandfather, William Alexander, was a cattle dealer and married to Margaret Spens. It is presumed that *WAF* was educated at Bridge of Weir before starting an apprenticeship with CA Edward Hutchison of Walker & Marwick, the Glasgow firm founded by MMC founder James Marwick. *WAF* qualified as a member of the IAAG in 1906 and set up his practise Frame Dougherty & Company in Minneapolis in the US in 1907. His partner was fellow Glasgow immigrant, Richard Dougherty.

In 1909, *WAF* became a CPA in Minnesota but, two years later, was working for the immigrant CA firm of J. Gordon Steele & Company, also of Minneapolis. However, Frame Dougherty appears to have survived and, by 1912, *WAF* was back as a partner. The firm remained until 1927 when *WAF* relocated to Fruitland Park in Florida. However, by 1936, he was back practicing on his own in Minneapolis and died there in 1949. He was a member of the AAPA (1913) and the AIA in 1916. *WAF*'s wife was born in Pennsylvania and there were no children. The family home in Florida in 1930 was valued at $5,000 ($56,000 in 2004 terms).

FRASER, Edward (1877–1968)   SAE (1901)

Edward Fraser (*EF*) was a prominent member of the early public accountancy profession in Missouri in the US. He was born in Edinburgh in 1877, the son of a printer, Alexander Fraser, who was the senior partner in the family printing firm at Canonmills in Edinburgh. Alexander Fraser was also the son of a print master, William Fraser, and his mother was Agnes Moulluie. *EF*'s mother was Mary Sang, the daughter of John Sang, a Solicitor in the Supreme Courts (SSC), and Mary Sang (a cousin). The Sangs were a well-known Edinburgh legal family. Uncle George Sang was an SSC, and his son, also George, was a WS (1899). Cousin John Henry Sang was also a WS (1884) as was David Sang (1871). *EF* was the great nephew of one of the outstanding actuaries of the nineteenth century. Edward Sang was a mathematician, lecturer and writer of more than one hundred scientific works including many on actuarial mathematics. He was a founder member of the Faculty of Actuaries in 1856 and its lecturer for many years. The Fraser family printing firm employed more than 180 individuals who were predominantly female. The family home at Canonmills was a large estate and included a lodge for the resident gardener and his family.

EF had three brothers. The eldest was William Fraser who died young. George Fraser was educated at Edinburgh Academy and immigrated to farm in New Zealand. He was a private in the New Zealand Medical Corps in 1915 and ended the First World War as a sergeant having won the George Star and Victory Medal. Brother John Fraser was also educated at Edinburgh Academy and became a printer in his father's firm. Alexander Fraser was the Dux at Edinburgh Academy in 1890, a Fellow of the Faculty of Actuaries (1897), Institute of Actuaries (1901), and Royal Society of Edinburgh (1910), and the Actuary for the Scottish Life Assurance Company.

EF followed his brothers to Edinburgh Academy (1888–91) and served an apprenticeship with CA and Actuary Hugh Blair (SAE 1869) of MacAndrew & Blair in Edinburgh. Blair was the son of Hugh Blair, WS (1827), partner of SAE founder James McLean MacAndrew from 1874, and member of the Councils of the SAE and Faculty of Actuaries. *EF* was admitted to the SAE in 1901. Following two years of post-qualification employment with MacAndrew & Blair, he immigrated to Chicago and worked as a non-contract staff member for PWC. In the same year, he became a CPA in Illinois. He worked for PWC for two years in Chicago before moving in 1905 to work for the Audit Company of New York. In 1907, *EF* moved back to Chicago to work for CAs AYC and transferred with this firm in 1909 to Kansas City in Missouri. He became a Missouri CPA in 1910 and a member of the AIA in 1916. He devoted considerable time to the administration of both bodies. He was Treasurer (1919–37) and President (1920–2) of the MSCPA, and served on several AIA committees including those of Procedure (1925), Bylaws (1930 and 1935), and State Legislation (1932–6). At some time in the early 1920s, he formed Edward Fraser & Company, CPAs, in Kansas City, and this firm became Fraser, Dell & Company in 1926, reverting in 1941 back to Edward Fraser & Company.

EF died in 1968 in Kansas City. His widow was Lydia Rachel Binkerhoff, daughter of Indiana farmer Jacob Oscar Binkerhoff and Lydia Elizabeth Hunt, also the daughter of an Indiana farmer. He had a son, daughter and five grandchildren.

FRASER, James Crichton (1890–1914)   SAE (1914)

Born in 1890, James Crichton Fraser (*JCF*) was the son of a Leith schoolmaster, James Fraser, from the farming village of Abernethy in Inverness-shire. His mother, Elizabeth Robertson Turner, was a telegraph clerk and the daughter of Peter Turner, a carter, and Catherine Thomson. Grandfather James Fraser was a road contractor married to Elizabeth Kennedy. His grandfather and uncle were woodcutters in Abernethy and a great uncle was a farmer there of more than 700 pastoral acres employing five individuals. *JCF* was educated at Daniel Stewart's College in Edinburgh and apprenticed to CA George Todd Chiene. He qualified as a member of the SAE in 1914 and immediately left for the US where he was employed in the New Orleans office of CAs MMC. Unfortunately, soon after his arrival, he was drowned in a bathing accident. He was not a member of any American professional body and obituaries appeared in *The Accountant's Magazine* of August 1914 and *The Accountant* of July 1914.

GIBSON, Archibald Parker (1878–?)   UQ

Born at Kilmarnock in Ayrshire in 1878, Archibald Parker Gibson (*APG*) was the son of Robert Gibson, a tweed manufacturer from Stevenson in Ayrshire, and Agnes Wallace Parker. Kilmarnock in east Ayrshire was a market and textile manufacturing town of 25,000 in 1881. *APG*'s brother William Gibson was a blanket manufacture, at the village of Closeburn in Dumfriesshire. Grandparents were William Gibson, a ditch digger, and Mary Reid, and John Parker (no occupation recorded) and Margaret Lyon. He was apprenticed to Glasgow CAs Mitchell & Smith and became an associate member of the IAAG in 1897. He did not complete his training and, two years later, he immigrated to Colorado in the US and resigned from the IAAG. No other information is available regarding his career thereafter and it not known where and when he died.

GILLIES, John (1879–1962)   IAAG (1903)

John Gillies was a slate master at Rothesay, the county town and shipping port of the Island of Bute to the west of the north Ayrshire coast. In 1881, Rothesay had a population of 8,000 and the quarry employed sixteen men. John Gillies was married to Agnes Marshall and had four daughters and a son, also John Gillies (*JG*), born in Rothesay in 1879. *JG*'s grandparents were Andrew Gillies, a soldier, and Elizabeth Leslie, and Samuel Marshall, a shoemaker, and Agnes Wilson. There is no information concerning *JG*'s education but he was apprenticed to Glasgow CAs Carswell & Murray joining the IAAG in 1903. He then practised in Glasgow on his own for seven years before immigrating to New York in 1911. He was employed for three years with CAs MMC, and moved to CAs DDGC in 1914. It is presumed he served with the military during the First World War because there is no further information on his career until 1920 when he is a partner in a Glasgow firm of CAs J. & J. Gillies (presumably with a son). He remained in this position until his death in 1962. *JG* was not a member of any public accountancy body in the US.

GRANT, Robert Monteath (1885–1941)   IAAG (1911)

Born in the small fishing village of Lochgoilhead in Argyllshire in 1885, Robert Monteath Grant (*RMG*) was the son of Francis Wallace Grant, a teacher of English in Govan who was born in England and a Fellow of the Educational Institute of Scotland (EIS), and Williamina Lawrie from Glasgow. The EIS was founded in 1847 and remains the principal professional body for schoolteachers in Scotland. *RMG* had three brothers, including James Wallace Grant, a hotel waiter, and John Grant, a law clerk, and two sisters. His paternal grandfather, John Grant, was a spirit merchant, and his maternal grandfather, William Lawrie, a ship's carpenter in Glasgow. Little is known of *RMG*'s education other than, unusually for the times, he graduated as a Master of Arts and Bachelor of Laws from the University of Glasgow. He was then apprenticed to Glasgow CAs Wilson & Nelson and worked as an audit clerk with them until 1909. He was admitted to the IAAG in 1911 and immigrated in 1912 to Chicago to work for CAs MMC. However, in 1914, he moved to Vancouver in Canada and worked there as a lawyer.

RMG presumably served in the armed forces during the First World War as he had a postal address with a firm of Glasgow lawyers during that period. He then returned to Vancouver and practised as a Barrister and Solicitor until 1929 when he was appointed as the managing director of the Anglo-Eastern Finance Corporation in Bishopsgate in London. Three years later, he became a partner in the legal firm of Herbert Hill & Company in London and remained in that position until his death in 1941. His obituary appeared in the August 1941 issue of *The Accountant's Magazine*.

GRAY, John Bird (1868–1944)   SAE (1889)

John Bird Gray (*JBG*) was born in 1868 in the burgh of Lewisham in London to a Scottish dairy farm accountant, James Adams Gray from the market town of Dalkeith in East Lothian, and Ann Arrenton Johnston. He had one brother, William Croft Gray, who was a Bachelor of Laws, SSC (1899), and law examiner, and three sisters. His paternal grandparents were David Gray, a Dalkeith merchant, and Barbara Scott. *JBG* was educated by and boarded with Thomas S. Henderson, an English teacher, and George Heriot's School in Edinburgh. His CA apprenticeship was served with the leading Edinburgh firm of A. & J. Robertson and he joined the SAE in 1889. He was then employed by A. & J. Robertson until 1893 when he worked for Edinburgh CA Adam Davidson Smith (SAE 1872). This employment lasted four years and his next job was with an Edinburgh firm of lawyers. Two years later, his employer became CAs A. & A. Paterson for whom he worked for seven years. Then, in 1906, he formed his own firm in Queen Street in Edinburgh. This lasted no more than three years when he immigrated to the US in 1909. He was therefore 41 years of age when he immigrated.

By 1910, *JBG* was a Minnesota CPA and an audit staff member of MMC in New York. A year later, he was working as a non-contract staff member of PWC in New York. In 1915, he formed his own firm in Brookline in Massachusetts. This venture lasted no more than two years and, in 1917, he was back in New York working for BWGC, CPAs. *JBG* appears to have remained with this firm until 1931 when he was employed by D. W. Harris & Company, a firm of migrant British CAs in New York. This was his last employment and he died in New York in 1944. He was unmarried and residing at the Waldorf Astoria Hotel in New York. He does not appear to have been a partner in any of his employers and was not a member of the AAPA or AIA.

GRAY, William (1878–1972)   IAAG (1910)

William Gray (*WG*) was born south of Glasgow in the farming village of Bothwell in south Lanarkshire in 1878. His father, William Gray, was an agricultural implement maker from Glasgow who was married to Janet Inglis also from Glasgow. William Gray had one other son, Robert, and a daughter. *WG* was a clerk with Glasgow CAs Rattray Brothers & Company between 1903 and 1904 before serving an apprenticeship with the firm at the age of 26. He was admitted to the IAAG in 1910 and soon left to work for CAs MMC in Chicago. He transferred within this firm in 1912 to Winnipeg in Canada and, in 1913, started to work for a local firm of accountants, F. C. S. Turner & Company. This employment lasted until 1923 when, at the age of 45, he started to practise on his own in Winnipeg as William Gray & Company. He remained in practise until 1962 when he retired aged 84. *WG* died in Winnipeg in 1972. He was never a member of an American professional accountancy body and his obituary appeared in the January 1973 issue of *The Accountant's Magazine*. There is no record of a marriage.

GREY, David Langton (1875–1942)   SAE (1899)

David Langton Grey (*DLG*) was the son of an Edinburgh Writer (lawyer) John Edward Ogilvie Grey and the grandson of Alexander Grey, Member of the Royal College of Veterinary Surgeons, a veterinary surgeon practicing in Edinburgh, and Margaret Simpson. He had an uncle, William Grey, who was an architect in Edinburgh, and another uncle John Edward Grey, Member of the Royal College of Veterinary Surgeons who practised with his father. *DLG* also had a great uncle, Henry Grey, who was a Doctor of Divinity and the minister of the Free St Mary's Church in Edinburgh. Henry Grey (ordained 1801) wrote several publications under the name Anglicanus between 1811 and 1843. Some were related to sermons as a visiting preacher in support of Edinburgh bodies such as the Edinburgh Lunatic Asylum and the Edinburgh Bible Society. A further great uncle, Edward Grey was an unmarried and retired army officer.

DLG was born in the Newington district of Edinburgh in 1875 and educated at George Watson's College. His mother was Lydia Margaret Gavin, a daughter of Hector Gavin, an Edinburgh engraver, and Marion Walker, and a sister of William

Gavin, a corn factor. He had six brothers and a sister. Edward Simpson Grey was an Edinburgh CA (1886) who practised in London until his death in 1902. Hector Gavin Grey was a law apprentice who failed to become a SSC. John Ogilvie Grey, however, did become a SSC in 1898 and practised in Edinburgh for many years. Alexander Grey was an Edinburgh insurance manager. Gavin Grey was an army Captain. Uncle Edward Simpson Grey followed his father's career in veterinary medicine in the army and died single in 1887. *DLG* was always described as the Honorable David Grey which suggests that he held a judicial appointment in the US. A nephew, Henry Gavin Grey became a member of the SAE in 1935, qualifying with distinction. He worked as Comptroller of a Chilean nitrates company from 1952 to 1970 and as an Edinburgh electronics factory accountant from 1971 to 1982.

DLG was apprenticed to CAs A. & J. Robertson and became a member of the SAE in 1899. He immigrated to the US a year later. From 1901 to 1903, he was employed as an auditor with the English migrant firm of PTD in New York and had become a CPA of New York. He was also a member of the AAPA (1903). In 1904, he moved to Pittsburg in Pennsylvania to work for PWC. He transferred to the firm's St Louis office in 1905 where he was a partner from 1912 to 1937. He married in 1906 to a Glaswegian and they had two daughters. In 1910, he became a CPA in Missouri and was President of the MSCPA from 1911 to 1913 and a member of the State's Board of Accountancy from 1914. During his presidency, he challenged the extensive use by US firms of British CAs. *DLG* was also a CPA in Louisiana (1929), Arkansas (1930), Mississippi and Texas. He joined the AIA in 1916 and was a Council member from 1923 to 1928 and a member of its Endowment Committee from 1932 to 1937 when he retired. He chaired the Missouri State Board of Exchange in 1917 and, in 1933, attended the fourth International Congress of Accountants as representative of the Missouri State Society. *DLG* died in St Louis in 1942. He was an Episcopalian and a member of the Noonday, Racquet, and University clubs, and of the Businessman's League and the Civic League of St Louis. His career is mentioned in D. E. Breimeier, *A History of the CPA Profession in Missouri* (Missouri State Society of Certified Public Accountants: St Louis, MO), and an obituary was published in *The Scotsman* in November 1942. He also appeared in W. B. Steven's *Centennial History of Missouri (The Center State): One Hundred Years in the Union 1820–1921* (S. J. Clarke Publishing, 1921).

GUTHRIE, William (1882–1945)   IAAG (1908)

Born in Dennistown to the east of Glasgow in 1882, William Guthrie (*WG*) was the son of William Muir Guthrie, a stationer, and Martha Thompson. His grandparents were William Guthrie, a Glasgow muslin manufacturer, and Janet Pollock, and Richard Thompson, a gun powder agent, and Martha Carnie. *WG* was apprenticed to CA James M. Davies of Davies, Tait & Company in Glasgow and admitted to the IAAG in 1908. He then immigrated to the Gold Coast in West Africa and worked as a mining accountant there for two years. In 1911, he immigrated to the US and worked for CAs J. Gordon Steele & Company in Minneapolis. Two years later, he moved within the city to work for another immigrant CA firm, Frame, Dougherty & Company.

In 1914, *WG* opened his own practise in Minneapolis as William Guthrie & Company and quickly moved to Sioux City in Iowa. He joined the AAPA in 1915 and was a charter member of the IASCPA in the same year. In 1916, he became a member of the AIA and, in 1920, a member of the Iowa State Board of Accountancy. He chaired the Board in 1926. By 1932, he appears to have retired to California and died there in 1945 having been removed from membership of the IAAG in 1940. His wife was from Iowa and he had a daughter. An obituary appeared in *The Accountant's Magazine* of November 1945.

HALL, James William (1876–1953)   IAAG (1901)

James William Hall (*JWH*) was born in Ireland in 1876. His father was William Hall, a machine printer from Edinburgh, and his mother was Christina Wood from Aberdeen. He had two brothers, William and John, and five sisters. Most of his siblings were born in Aberdeen, suggesting that William Hall had worked there for some time. By 1881, the family was living in Dundee and had a domestic servant. *JWH*'s paternal grandfather, also James Hall, was a drayman in Edinburgh and married to Helen Brunton. The maternal grandparents were John Wood, an iron moulder in Aberdeen, and Hannah Leslie. *JWH* was educated in Dundee and his CA apprenticeship was with Mackay & Ness (later MIC) in Dundee. He was then employed as an audit clerk from 1898 to 1904 with Glasgow CAs Dunlop & Murray. He was admitted to the IAAG in 1901.

JWH moved to London in 1905 to work for CAs W. B. Peat & Company and, one year later, moved to New York and MMC. William Barclay Peat was a Scot from a farming family near Montrose in Forfarshire who, in 1870, after training as a lawyer, moved to London to work for SAA founder Robert Fletcher. Peat's mother was a daughter of the founder of Barclays Bank. After the death of Fletcher and his partner, Peat formed his firm in 1891, was a founding Council member of the ICAEW in 1880 (President 1906–8), and received a knighthood in 1918. In 1911, he merged his US operations with MMC to become MMPC and, in 1925, his firm and the latter merged to become PMMC. At some time during 1905 and 1906 *JWH* worked in Portuguese East Africa investigating fraudulent trading reports for William Barclay Peat. In 1908, he transferred to *MMC*'s Chicago office and took charge in 1914. He has been reported as a ruthless administrator and, having introduced a time clock, induced a strike by his 13 employees (12 of whom were British CAs). He eventually had to back down. He also built a reputation as an investigator of frauds (including gas companies in Chicago and New York).

JWH quickly became an American public accountant. He was a CPA in Ohio (1908), Minnesota (1909), Missouri and Massachusetts (1910), Illinois (1912), Louisiana (1920), California (1925), Oregon (1926), Washington (1928), and New York and Michigan (1931). He is recorded as being a CPA in a further nine (unnamed) states. His other memberships included the AAPA in 1911, the AIA (1916), and the ASCPA (1923). He chaired the Illinois State Board of Accountancy in 1914, and served on several AIA committees over several years – Executive (1927 and 1932), Professional Ethics (Chair, 1928), Council (1930–5), Nominations (1931), Bank Examinations (Chair, 1935), and Discipline (1940).

JWH became a partner in MMC in 1905 with a 15 per cent share in profits and retired from the partnership in 1947. He was a favourite of James Marwick and in charge of the Chicago office from 1914 to 1925 when he moved to New York to become the deputy senior partner from 1925 to 1930 and senior partner from 1930 to 1947. He attended the Fourth International Congress of Accountants in London in 1933. *JWH*'s retirement was abrupt and full of political intrigue relating to his successor. He had alienated younger partners with his apparent desire for "yes" men in the partnership and also transferred the pension fund into the firm's funds, thus increasing the size of his 15 per cent of profits. He retired to California with approximately $500,000 ($5,600,000 in 2004 terms) from the firm, never returned to the latter, and died in 1953. His obituary appeared in *The Accountant's Magazine* of March 1953. His career is covered in T. A. Wise, *Peat, Marwick, Mitchell & Company: 85 Years* (New York: Peat, Marwick, Mitchell & Company, 1982). His wife was Scottish and they had a daughter.

HARDIE, Steven James Lindsay (1885–1969)   IAAG (1908)

Steven James Lindsay Hardie (*SJLH*) was born in 1885 as the son of John Hardie, a mathematics teacher in Paisley in Renfrewshire who came from the small fishing village of Kinghorn in the east of Fife. John Hardie was married to Ann Eliza Lindsay from the farming village of Dollar in Clackmannanshire. She was the daughter of James Lindsay from Dunfermline in Fife, a mathematics, physics, and civil engineering teacher at Dollar Academy, and sister of James P. S. Lindsay, a law clerk. The couple had three children in addition to *SJLH*. Of these, John Alexander Hardie was born in Calcutta in India and became a Civil Engineer. *SJLH*'s uncles included James Hardie, a colliery manager at Shotts in Lanarkshire, and a CA, William Hardie. Their parents were James Hardie, a United Presbyterian Church of Scotland clergyman at Kinghorn (ordained 1824), and Elizabeth Birrell. William Hardie was born in 1857 and had the distinction of joining the SAE in 1878 and the IAAG in 1890. He had been apprentice to the Edinburgh firm of CAs Lindsay, Jamieson & Haldane and was an SAE prizewinner in 1875 and 1877. He moved to Glasgow and founded the firm Hardie, Caldwell, Ker & Hardie and later founded a practise in Greenock in Renfrewshire with SAA member Robert Houston Rowan, son of a Greenock merchant. William Hardie was the Secretary and Treasurer of the Greenock Chamber of Commerce for 40 years and wrote two accounting texts – *Manual of Bookkeeping for Law Agents* (1893) and, with CA Alexander Allan, *Manual of Bookkkeeping by Double Entry* (1893).

SJLH served his CA apprenticeship with his uncle in Glasgow and joined the IAAG in 1908 and soon left for the US. It is not clear what his employment was there, but he resided for two years in Brooklyn in New York. In 1910, he returned to the UK and was employed by CAs DDGC in London. A year later, he was a partner in his uncle's firm, Hardie, Caldwell, Ker & Hardie in Glasgow. He then served as an officer with the armed forces in the First World War until 1918, during which time he was awarded the Distinguished Service Order. He then returned to the family firm in Glasgow until his retirement to Perthshire in 1951. *SJLH* married Mary McGlashan Nicholson in 1919. She was the daughter of David Nicholson, a Greenock linen manufacturer, and Florence Edith McGlashan. He received an honorary degree of Doctor of Laws from the University of Glasgow and was heavily involved in industry as a non-executive director. For example, he was chairman of the Iron & Steel Corporation (1950–2), British Oxygen Ltd, and George Dobie & Company. He was also on the boards of the Scottish Council for Development & Industry, the British Transport Commission, and the Cinematographic Council. He died in Perthshire in 1969 and his obituary appeared in the July 1969 issue of *The Accountant's Magazine* and the August 1969 issue of *The Accountant*.

HARRIS, Robert James (1887–1965)   IAAG (1912)

Robert James Harris (*RJH*) was born at Campsie in Stirlingshire in 1887. His father, Henry Harris, was born in England and owned an underclothing factory in Stirlingshire that employed 300 individuals. His mother, Fanny Gertrude Hawkins, was Henry Harris' second wife. The paternal grandparents were Robert Harris, a farmer, and Mary Johnson, and the maternal grandparents were James Hawkins, an army Major, and Mary Curtin. *RJH* was educated at Campsie and apprenticed to CAs Thomson McLintock & Company in Glasgow. He was admitted to the IAAG in 1912 when he immigrated to the US. Thomson McLintock was the son of a Dumfriesshire house factor, trained with a Glasgow CA, became an associate member of the ICAEW in 1880, and an IAAG member in 1891. He formed his firm in Glasgow in 1877 and it became one of the pre-eminent British firms for several decades, with the largest office in London. The firm became part of PMMC in 1968 and KPMG in 1991.

   RJH was employed by the American accountancy firm of PPC in Butte, Montana from 1912. His next employment was in Madison in Wisconsin with the Gisholt Machine Company. This lasted from 1914 to 1923 when he moved to Cleveland in Ohio where he was an accountant with an electrical power company. He remained there until his retirement in 1943 when he relocated to Gainesville in Florida. His wife was from Wisconsin and they had no children. He later moved to Santa Barbara in California where he died in 1965. He was a Wisconsin CPA. His obituary appeared in *The Accountant's Magazine* of February 1965.

HARRIS, David William (1874–1956)   IAAG (1909)

David William Harris (*DWH*) was born in 1874 at the Glasgow suburb of Anderston to James Harris, a merchant, and Alexandrina Johanna Ross, a milliner. His paternal grandparents were David Harris, also a Glasgow merchant, and Jane Ferrier, and his maternal grandparents were Hugh Ross, a commercial agent, of St Quinox in Ayrshire, and Margaret McDonald. He had two brothers. In 1907, he married Effie Sadler Campbell, a daughter of William Campbell, house factor, insurance agent, and wine and spirit merchant employing eight individuals in Glasgow.

Following education in Glasgow, *DWH* was apprenticed to CA David Strathie (IAAG 1878) of Finlay, Kidson & Goff in Glasgow from 1894 to 1899. A decade later, he was admitted to the IAAG. He immigrated to New York in 1900 and employment with the public accountancy firm of Wichert & Gardiner in Brooklyn. In 1912, he entered a partnership with Gardiner as Gardiner & Harris in Brooklyn. Five years later, the firm was located in Chicago. *DWH* was living at Brooklyn in New York by 1920 with his Scottish wife (who had migrated 1907), and two sons. He founded his own firm of D. W. Harris & Company in New York in 1923. He had no memberships with American public accountancy bodies and appears to have resigned from the IAAG in 1926. Despite this, he is described in the 1930 US Census of Queens in New York as a self-employed CA. This official description of an immigrant accountant is almost unique at this date. *DWH*'s residence was valued at $11,000 ($123,000 in 2004 terms). *DWH* died in Randolph County in Missouri in 1956.

HENDERSON, Thomas Best Gibson (1886–1945)   SAA (1911)

Born in Aberdeen in 1886, Thomas Best Gibson Henderson (*TBGH*) was the son of Joseph Henderson, a ship's master in the mercantile marine, and Helen Grant Gibson. His paternal grandfather was James Henderson; also a ship's master, who was married to Mary Allan. Thomas Best Gibson, an Aberdeen grocer, and Helen Grant were his maternal grandparents. He had four sisters and a brother, Francis Joseph Henderson. The latter was educated at Aberdeen Grammar School and apprenticed to CA James Milne. In 1906, he became an estate manager in the West Indies without qualifying as a CA. James Milne (SAA 1877) trained as a lawyer and developed an extensive audit practise. He was SAA President from 1903 to 1907.

From 1894 to 1900, *TBGH* was educated at Aberdeen Grammar School. A gap of three years exists before he started a CA apprenticeship in 1903 with James Milne & Company in Aberdeen. He joined the SAA in 1911, five years after immigrating to the US. It is unclear what his initial employment was but, by 1912, he was General Auditor with the General Motor Company at Detroit in Michigan. A year later, he was working for CPAs Lybrand, Ross Brothers & Montgomery (LRBM) in Chicago and became a manager there in 1915. He was admitted to the partnership in 1919. He was one of a very few British CAs who joined this US firm. LRBM was formed in Philadelphia in 1898 by William M. Lybrand, T. Edward Ross and Adam A. Ross and Colonel Robert H. Montgomery. It became one of the largest US public accountancy firms. *TBGH* also became a member of the AIA and the IAPA in 1919 and a Michigan CPA in 1920 (he was a director of the Michigan Society of Certified Public Accountants, MISCPA). Similar memberships were obtained in Louisiana in 1930 and Ohio in 1939. *TBGH* moved to his firm's New York office in 1931 and died in that city in 1945. He was author of "Yield on Plant Investment" in *Administration* of March 1922 and "Obsolescence – What is It?" in the *American Appraisal News* of September 1927. *TBGH* was a director of the Greenwich, Connecticut YMCA. A brief biography appeared in *Fiftieth Anniversary 1898–1948* published by LRBM in 1948 and he was described as "a Scotsman with all the finest attributes of that race". *TBGH* was married to a Canadian and had a daughter. His home in 1930 was owned and valued at $30,000 ($336,000 in 2004 terms) in Chicago.

HILTON, Ernest Denison (1878–1930)   IAAG (1908)

Ernest Denison Hilton (*EDH*) was born in 1878 at Walkden, a small village to the south of the textile manufacturing town of Bolton in Lancashire and west of the industrial city of Manchester, to John Hilton, a mill mechanic from Patricroft in Lancashire, and Isabella Ann Hilton. He had five sisters and step sisters who were all cotton weavers. His brothers, James Harrop and William Thomas Hilton, were railway workers. Grandfather Simon Hilton was a shoemaker from Tyldsley in Lancashire (a cotton town to the west of Walkden) and an uncle, William Hilton, was a colliery labourer at Tyldsley. By 1901, *EDH* was working as an accountant's clerk with Leman & Sons in Nottingham, married to Annabella Hilton who was from Northern Ireland, and had a daughter. Thomas Leman was an 1878 member of the SAIE who became a founding Fellow of the ICAEW in 1880. *EDH* was then apprenticed to CAs Fraser & Ferguson in Glasgow and admitted to the IAAG in 1908. There is no record as to why he switched from English to Scottish CA training. He immigrated to the US in 1909 with his wife and daughter, becoming a Minnesota CPA and audit clerk with CAs BWGC in New York. In 1913, he transferred to the firm's office in Philadelphia. Then, in 1917, he was working for the Molme Plow Company at Molme in Illinois. However, two years later, he was a partner in BWGC although he appears to have served in the armed forces during the First World War. The partnership with BWGC was based in Chicago by 1923. *EDH* was a member of the AIA in 1921 and the ASCPA in 1923. He was a CPA in Michigan and Indiana. He wrote a paper "Determining Selling Price" published in the *Journal of Accountancy* in 1918. He died in Chicago in 1930. He was then living in Evanston with his wife in rented property with a monthly rental of $340.

HOURSTON, Charles Marshall (1883–1941)   IAAG (1909)

Charles Marshall Hourston (*CMH*) was born in 1883 in the port of Greenock in Renfrewshire. His father, George Peter Hourston, was a bookkeeper for a sugar manufacturer there, and his mother, Griselda Mair Davies, a daughter of John Davies, an ironmonger, and Eliza Donald, was also from that town. He had four brothers, none of whom can be traced, and a sister. Shortly after his immigration to the US, *CMH* married Jessie Patience in 1911. She was a daughter of James Patience, a river pilot at West Greenock who came from Bonar in Sutherland. *CMH*'s brother-in-law, Alexander Patience, was a general clerk.

CMH was educated in Greenock and apprenticed to CAs Nairn, Bowes & Craig, in Glasgow. He was admitted to the IAAG in 1909 and immigrated to New York in 1910 where he was employed by CAs MMC. He remained with this firm for three years before working for a firm of bankers Hayden, Stone & Company in New York. It is unclear when he returned to the UK, and whether he served during the First World War, but by 1920 he was the Chief Accountant at the Royal Ordnance Factory at Woolwich in London. He was appointed an Officer of the Order of the British Empire for his work there and, by 1925, was employed in the London firm of J. & R. Morley Ltd. He became its Secretary in 1927. By 1939, *CMH* was retired and residing in a hotel in Helensburgh in Ayrshire. He died of tuberculosis in 1941 at West Peterculter a few miles outside of Aberdeen in Aberdeenshire. His usual address was stated as Blackheath in London.

HOUSTON, Alexander Muir (1871–1972)   IAAG (1905)

Colin Houston was a steamship engineer, master mariner, and partner in the Govan firm of mechanical engineers and boilermakers, Muir & Houston. The firm employed 15 men and his partner was Robert Muir from Kilmarnock in Ayrshire, a master boilermaker. Colin Houston was married to Robert Muir's sister, Marion Anderson Muir. The couple had four children, including Alexander Muir Houston (*AMH*) who was born in 1871 in Govan. *AMH*'s grandparents were Campbell Houston, a steamship engineer, and Martha Whitehill; and Alexander Muir, a boilermaker, and Marion Jamieson. He was educated in Govan and apprenticed to Glasgow CAs Mitchell & Smith, joining the IAAG in 1905 at the age of 34.

AMH immigrated to St Louis in Missouri in 1905 and started work there with CAs MMC. He joined the AAPA in 1906. His next employment was with CAs JCC in St. Louis in 1908. However, he moved to an industrial position as an internal auditor in 1910. The company was the Chicago Lumber & Coal Company in St. Louis. He became a Missouri CPA in 1910. Ten years later, he was appointed Comptroller of the Fulton Iron Works Company in St Louis and, in 1923, the Treasurer of the Asiatic Petroleum Company in New York. This company was formed as a joint venture in London in 1903 by the Shell Transport & Trading Company and The Royal Dutch Petroleum Company. Its operations were based in Shanghai in China. *AMH* remained with this company until his retirement in 1948 to San Antonio in Texas. He later moved to Bowling Green in Ohio where he died in 1972. An obituary appeared in the January 1973 issue of *The Accountant's Magazine*. He was 101 years of age. In N. E. Webster, *The American Association of Public Accountants: Its First Twenty Years 1886–1906* (American Institute of Accountants: New York, NY, 1954), there is a report of Andrew M. Houston, a New York accountant and Glasgow CA who was invited to join the organisation of the AAPA in 1897. He declined and is stated to have become a

Missouri CPA. This appears to be *AMH*. His wife was from Texas and they had a son and daughter. The family home in New York in 1930 was valued at $32,500 ($364,000 in 2004 terms).

HOUSTON, David Arthur (1881–1924)   IAAG (1907)

David Arthur Houston (*DAH*) was born at sea in 1881. His father, John Houston, was a ship's master, and his mother was Annie Hill Quinn. Parental grandparents were David Houston, a blacksmith, and Agnes Galt. Maternal grandfather, John Quinn, was an umbrella manufacturer and married to Ann Hill. The family appears to have originated from Glasgow. Five years after immigrating to the US, *DAH* married Lena Margaret Burden of Stirling, a daughter of Peter Burden, a brewery owner from Stirling with nine employees, and Janet Thomson Dalgleish also from Stirling.

DAH was educated and trained in Glasgow. His apprenticeship from 1899 to 1903 was with CAs John E. Watson & Son and then, from 1903 to 1904, with Macfarlane, Hutton & Patrick. John E. Watson was one of the earliest Glasgow CAs (IAAG 1855) and IAAG President from 1887 to 1890. *DAH* joined the IAAG in 1907. This was the year he immigrated to New York to work for CAs MMC. He worked as an audit clerk for three years before accepting an internal audit appointment with the American Asphalt & Rubber Company in Chicago. He boarded as a single man in that city in 1910 and became a CPA in Minnesota in 1911. *DAH* had an address for communications with MMC in Chicago in 1914 and 1915 and it is presumed he was serving with the armed forces during the First World War. He was not recorded in the US Census of 1920. By 1923, he was a partner with public accountants Smart, Gore & Company in Chicago. Allen Richard Smart was a UQ public accountant who immigrated to the US in 1890 to work on assignments for his English-based CA brother. He remained in New York and became a BWGC manager in Chicago in 1895 and a partner in 1911. Eleven years later, Smart formed the firm of Smart, Gore & Company with another BWGC partner Edward Everitt Gore, an American-born CPA. *DAH* died in this city in 1924. He was an Illinois CPA and a member of the AIA.

HOUSTON, Edward McDowall Scott (1889–1933)   IAAG (1911)

Edward McDowall Scott Houston (*EMSH*) was born at the district of Maryhill in Glasgow in 1889. He was the son of William Henry Houston (born in England), the cashier of George McClellan & Company, rubber manufacturers, and Grace Dick Alexander, from Glasgow and the daughter of David Alexander, a joiner, and Mary Paterson of Glasgow. He had three brothers and two sisters. His paternal grandparents were Robert Houston, a shipping agent, and Amelia McDowall. Nothing is known of *EMSH*'s education in Maryhill. However, he was apprenticed from 1906 to 1911 to Glasgow CA Robert Paterson (IAAG 1877) of Paterson, Pewlands & Company (later Paterson & Steel) and admitted to the IAAG in 1911. A year later, he was working as an audit clerk for CAs MMC in

New York. In 1913, he moved to the firm's office at Winnipeg in Canada and returned to Glasgow in 1914. He appears to have served in the armed forces and been wounded in the First World War. When he returned from Europe, he worked for CAs Thomson McLintock & Company in Glasgow between 1920 and 1923 and then in London until 1927. He worked as an advisory accountant to the Inland Revenue in London and returned to Glasgow in 1929 where he died in 1933 from acute alcoholism. He was never a member of an American public accountancy body and does not appear to have married.

HURST, John William (1864–1943)   SAE (1911)

John William Hurst (*JWH*) was born in South Leith near Edinburgh in 1864, the son of John Hurst, a baker and confectioner employing four individuals in his bakery in Roseneath Terrace in Edinburgh. His paternal grandparents were John Hurst, a baker, and Margaret Torrance. His mother was Jane Smail Lambert, the daughter of Andrew Lambert, a contractor, and Robina Walker. *JWH* had one brother, Andrew Hurst, a bookseller, and five sisters. He was educated at James Gillespie's and George Heriot's Schools. In 1911, he married Camilla Cooper Oliver of Edinburgh, the daughter of John Oliver, minister at the Free Church of Scotland at Crossford near Carluke in Lanarkshire from 1904.

JWH was working as a bookseller by 1904 but soon after began a CA apprenticeship with CA William S. Brown of Edinburgh (SAE 1899). He joined the SAE in 1911 and immediately left for the US where he was one of 17 accountants who formed the TSCPA in Dallas in 1911. He was employed in the Dallas accountancy firm of Peter & Company. However, in 1913, he became a partner in the firm of Schoolar, Bird & Hurst, Corporation Audit Company in Dallas. Charles H. Schoolar was an American-born (1868) public accountant who formed his firm in 1906 with George H. Bird. Schoolar attended the foundation meeting, was one of the founding directors of the TSCPA, and became a Texas CPA by waiver in 1915. George H. Bird was also American born, attended the third meeting of the TSCPA, and became a Texas CPA in 1916. In 1914, *JWH* was Secretary of the Southland Life Insurance Company, an organisation that exists today as part of the North America Insurance Corporation. By 1920, he was residing in Dallas with his Scottish wife and daughter (also born in Scotland). In 1921, however, his residence was in East Trinity Road in Edinburgh followed, a year later, by an address in Middlesex. Seven years later, in 1929, he was back in the US as the Assistant Secretary of the North American Reassurance Company in New York. In 1931, his address reverted to Harrow in Middlesex. He died in Stow in Midlothian in 1943 of heart failure and was described as a life insurance clerk. He had a son, John William Hurst, who lived in Harrow in Middlesex.

It has to be assumed that *JWH*'s employment in insurance involved work in the UK and the US. Although he helped to create organised public accountancy in Texas when attending the planning meetings in 1911, he was never a Texas CPA. A nephew, however, became a leader of the Texan public accountancy community. John Kenneth Stuart Arthur was the son of one of *JWH*'s sisters and

Scottish CA John F. Stuart Arthur who immigrated to Dallas in Texas in the 1920s. Kenneth Arthur was a graduate of Harvard Business School, a partner in public accountants Coopers & Lybrand (previously CBC and LRBM), and President of the TSCPA in 1966.

HYSLOP, George Kennedy (1889–1954)   SAE (1913)

William B. Hyslop was a master draper from the remote farming village of Durisdeer in the county of Dumfries who was living in the late 1880s as a travelling draper in London in the county of Middlesex. His wife, Mary A. Hyslop, was from Dumfries. She provided for several boarders from Scotland who were also travelling drapers. The couple had a son, George Kennedy Hyslop (*GKH*), born in London in 1889. His grandfather, William Hyslop, was also from Dumfries and worked as a commercial traveller in drapery in Middlesex. He was married and had several unmarried children working as travelling drapery salesmen. Drapery therefore appears to have been the family business as several relatives in the county of Dumfries also worked in the industry. A great-uncle of *GKH*, however, was an exception. Hugh Hyslop was the manager of an insurance company in London.

GKH was educated at Dumfries Academy before serving a CA apprenticeship with the leading firm of Romanes & Munro in Edinburgh from 1902 to 1907 and working with them as a clerk from 1908 to 1913. He was admitted to the SAE in 1913 and immigrated to the US in 1914 where his initial employment was as a non-contract audit staff member with PWC in New York. He became a New York CPA and member of the AIA in 1917. Two years later, he left PWC to work for a firm of migrant CAs LBC in New York. He remained with this firm for three years before setting up his own firm there as Hyslop & McCallum. This partnership appears to have been with fellow immigrant and IAAG member Dougall McCallum. It lasted two years until 1924 when *GKH* was appointed a partner in the Chicago-based public accountancy firm of Smart, Gore & Company. The association lasted until 1937 when *GKH* formed Hyslop & Boehm in New York. A series of brief associations with other firms took place between 1942 and 1954 when he died in Clinton, Connecticut – i.e. Smart, Gore & Company, E. C. Martin, Thomas Nelson & Company, publishers, and Civil Air Transport in Hong Kong. *GKH* does not appear to have been involved in the administration of any American public accountancy body. He had a review published in 1926 in the *Atlantic Monthly*. His wife was a French Canadian and the couple had a daughter.

INGRAM, Robert Scott (1871–1959)   IAAG (1904)

Robert Scott Ingram (*RSI*) was born in 1871 in the farming and fishing community of Tongue in Sutherland on the Atlantic Ocean coast – although US Census records state the date as 1879. He was the eldest son of William Ingram, a domestic gardener working at Kincardine in Aberdeenshire (who came from Gamrie in

Banffshire), and Jane Scott from the fishing town of Fraserburgh in Aberdeenshire. *RSI* had three brothers (Thomas, William and John) and two sisters. None of the siblings can be traced. He appears to have been sent to Glasgow at an early age and educated there although his family continued to live in rural Aberdeenshire. He was apprenticed to Glasgow CAs Nairn, Bowes & Craig. He also worked as an audit clerk with this firm and joined the IAAG in 1904. Two years later, he was employed by MMC in New York and remained with them until 1914. He was transferred to the firm's Boston office in 1908. By 1910, *RSI* was working as an accountant in local government and resident at Brookline in Massachusetts with his two sisters. Both of the latter were employed – respectively as a saleswoman in a department store and as a bookkeeper with an industrial company. In 1914, *RSI* was appointed Secretary of the American Pneumatic Service Company in Boston. Nine years later, he held a similar position with the Ames Shovel & Tool Company in Boston. The Ames company was founded in the 1850s by Oakes Ames and Oliver Ames. Oakes Ames later founded the Union Pacific Railroad Company in the 1860s and channeled considerable federal funding for the project to his own company, Credit Mobilier. He was a member of Congress (1863–73) and survived a Congressional inquiry into the fraud. In 1936, *RSI* retired and, 23 years later in 1959, he died unmarried. An obituary was published in the January 1960 issue of *The Accountant's Magazine*.

KELLY, William Patrick (1884–1936)   SAE (1909)

William Patrick Kelly (*WPK*) was the son of a customs officer, Patrick Kelly, from Hamilton in Lanarkshire, and was born in Leith in 1884. His mother, Mary Ellen Alsop, was from Dublin in Ireland. He was educated at the cotton manufacturing town of Rochdale in Lancashire and then the Leith Convent School, Albany Street School (also in Leith), and George Heriot's School in Edinburgh. These locations presumably reflect the nature of his father's occupation. In 1913, he married Christina Reid Crawford, a daughter of George Crawford, a spirit merchant in Edinburgh, and Mary Ann Reilly.

WPK was apprenticed to an Edinburgh CA William D. Stewart (SAE 1896) and, following admission to the SAE in 1909, immigrated to the US. He worked as a non-contract audit staff member from 1909 to 1916 in Chicago with CAs PWC. He became a Minnesota CPA in 1910 and a member of the AIA in 1916. He also remained with PWC until 1921 and worked for the firm in the US, Russia and France. In 1921, he moved to the International Harvester Company in Chicago as its Comptroller and was with this company in this capacity when he died in 1936. The company was formed in 1901 from the merger of three agricultural machinery companies and sold to the Tenneco Corporation in 1984. The earliest company was that of Robert McCormick and founded in Virginia in the 1830s. *WPK* did not get involved with any public accountancy body other than as a member. He was married to a Scot and had two sons and three daughters. The family home in 1930 at Highland Park in Illinois was worth $30,000 ($336,000 in 2004 terms) and had two servants.

KERR, David Smith (1878–1937)   IAAG (1901)

James Kerr from Antrim in Northern Ireland was a minister of the Reformed Presbyterian Church in the port of Greenock in Renfrewshire and then in Glasgow. He was ordained in 1869. His wife was Jeanie Smith from the iron and steel town of Airdrie in Lanarkshire. They had six children including David Smith Kerr (*DSK*) who was born in Greenock in 1878. His grandparents were Robert Kerr, a Northern Ireland farmer, and Mary Ann Carson, and David Smith, a Glasgow iron founder, and Jean Barry. *DSK* was educated in Greenock and Glasgow, and then apprenticed to CA Alexander J. Forgie of Maclean, Brodie & Forgie of Glasgow. He was admitted to the IAAG in 1901.

Once qualified, *DSK* spent two years working for a firm of accountants in Nottingham in England before immigrating in 1903 to work for Scottish CAs TNC in New York. He remained with them until 1905 when he transferred to become a partner in CAs MMC in New York. In 1908, he became an Ohio CPA and, in 1910, transferred to MMC's office in Montreal in Canada. He also became a CPA in Minnesota in that year and a member of the AAPA in 1912. He joined the Council of the AAM in 1920 – the year in which he founded his own firm of public accountants styled as Kerr, Payne & Company. He wrote a number of papers that were published between 1912 and 1919. Ten appeared in the *Canadian Chartered Accountant* and included topics such as cost accounting and tariffs (1912), how to read a balance sheet (1913), over-capitalisation (1914), sinking funds (1914), goodwill and watered stock (1914, 1915, and 1916; also in *The Public Accountant*), consolidated balance sheets (1915; also published in *The Accountant*), deferred charges (1915), and watered stock and the cost of living (1919). In 1935, he retired to Cliftonville in Kent and died there in 1937. His wife was from Basford in Nottinghamshire.

KERR, Errol (1878–1951)   SAE (1905)

Errol Kerr (*EK*) was born in Edinburgh in 1878. His family came from Inverness-shire. Angus Kerr was his father – a stockbroker and member of the Edinburgh Stock Exchange who was born in the village of Kirkhill west of Inverness and married to Elizabeth Wilson Cumming from Edinburgh. Grandparents were Angus Kerr, a blacksmith, and Janet Douglas, and James Cumming, an Edinburgh linen merchant, and Margaret Wilson. He had two brothers, John N. and Douglas Kerr, and an uncle who was a bank teller in Inverness.

EK was educated at George Watson's College in Edinburgh and apprenticed to CAs Brewis & Rainie. Edward Brewis joined the SAE in 1893 and George T. Rainie in 1894. *EK* joined the SAE in 1905 and almost immediately immigrated to Egypt where he formed the accountancy firm in Cairo of Russell & Kerr. In 1908, the firm expanded to Russell, Kerr & Wyatt and moved to Alexandria. Five years later, in 1913, it had migrated to New York. It did not last long there and, by 1915, *EK* was a partner in the public accountancy firm of Harris, Allan & Company in New York. In 1917, he was a member of the AIA and the NYSSCPA.

In 1926, the firm became Harris, Kerr & Cook on Madison Avenue in New York and, in 1934, Harris, Kerr & Forster & Company, CPAs. This remained *EK*'s occupational address until his death in New York in 1951. He was admitted as an Officer of the Order of the British Empire in 1930 and presumably served the UK government in some advisory capacity during or after the First World War. He did not participate in the administration of the American professional bodies to which he belonged. His wife was English and they had a daughter and a son. The family home in New York in 1930 was valued at $18,000 ($201,000 in 2004 terms).

KERR, James Craig (1843–1917)   UQ

James Craig Kerr (*JCK*) was born at the mining community of Crawford and Leadhills in Lanarkshire in 1843. He was the son of William Kerr, a lead smelter, and Mary Craig from Dalry in Ayrshire. He was an accountant in Glasgow then a railway inspector at Stranraer in Wigtonshire prior to his immigration to New York in 1893. He became a New York CPA in 1896 and practised in the city until 1916. He was also a Fellow of the AAPA from 1896 and a member of the ASCPA in 1897. *JCK* died at West Stockbridge in Massachusetts in 1917. He immigrated to the US with a wife, Elizabeth T. Kerr from Glasgow and four daughters.

KINNAIRD, Peter William (1884–1916)   IAAG (1907)

Peter William Kinnaird (*PWK*) was born at the Glasgow suburb of Pollockshaws in Renfrewshire in 1884. His father, Thomas Kinnaird, was a bank agent or manager for the Glasgow Bridgeton Cross branch of the British Linen Bank. Thomas Kinnaird came from the farming village of Kinloss in Morayshire and his wife, Margaret Armour, from Ayrshire. She was a daughter of Allan Armour from Kilmarnock in Ayrshire, a house factor, and Jane Wilson from Govan near Glasgow. Margaret Armour's siblings included three clerks with East Indies merchants and a dry-salter. *PWK* had three brothers including John Armour Kinnaird who was a shipping clerk. Grandfather William Kinnaird was a shop owner and fisherman from Findhorn in Morayshire and married to Margaret Smith. *PWK* was apprenticed to Glasgow CAs Grahams & Company and admitted to the IAAG in 1907. He immigrated to New York in that year and was employed by CAs MMC. However, he returned to the UK and was residing in Brighton in 1910. He died in a Glasgow hospital in 1916 from tuberculosis from which he had been suffering for several years. He was single and had no family present when he died.

KIRKCALDIE, William John (1874–1933)   SAE (1897)

Born in the village of Norwood in Surrey in 1874, William John Kirkcaldie (*WJK*) was the son of William John Kirkcaldie, a colonial broker of Enfield in Middlesex. His mother was Rosa M. A. Cullen from Kerroway in Fife. Her sister, Hannah D. Cullen from the farming village of Markinch in Fife, was *WJK*'s guardian in 1891. His brothers were Robert Cullen (who trained to be banker) and

James Cullen Kirkcaldie, and he had three sisters, including one born in Sydney in Australia – suggesting the family had immigrated there in the early 1870s. The paternal grandparents were Robert Kirkcaldie, a shoemaker, and Margaret Meldrum, a domestic servant. *WJK*'s maternal grandfather was James Cullen, a mill manager at Kerroway. His great-aunt, Catherine Cullen, was a lodging house keeper at the farming village of Kettle in Fife.

WJK was educated at Mill Hill Grammar School and Merchiston Castle School in Edinburgh, suggesting the family was well off. He was then apprenticed to CA Thomas Goldie Dickson of T. G. & L. W. Dickson in Edinburgh. Dickson was one of the most influential SAE founding members in 1854 and became SAE President in 1889. His son, Leonard Walter Dickson (SAE 1892) was a considerable figure in the life assurance industry. *WJK* joined the SAE in 1897 and remained with T. G. & L. W. Dickson until 1899 when he was employed by another Edinburgh CA firm, Barstow & Miller. Charles Murray Barstow was also an SAE founder and SAE President (1869–76). His partner, Robert Cockburn Miller (SAE 1877) was a well-known lecturer and writer as well as practitioner who became SAE President (1910–13). *WJK* was therefore gaining experience with very reputable firms.

In 1901, *WJK* left Edinburgh for training as a Barrister at Lincoln's Inn Fields in London. This venture lasted a year before he resided for two years in Cork in Ireland. His next occupation was as a public accountant from 1904 to 1913 with Sydney Merritt & Company in Valparaiso in Chile. His experiences there are contained in articles written in *The Accountant's Magazine* ("Accountants in Chile", 1904) and *The Businessman's Magazine and Bookkeeper* ("Auditing in the Desert of Tarapaca", 1906; reprinted in *The Accountant*). In the latter, he describes his audits of nitrate mines in Chile. The nitrate was used for fertilisers and explosives. The Chilean desert had no wind, rain or cold and travel from the coast was by train. He spent months on the pampas when on audit and much of the travelling was by mule. He was responsible for putting the mining transactions into a journal which was sent monthly to Europe. He audited the mining expenses and costs of departments and reported on this back to the client in Europe.

WJK's next assignment lasted for 14 years in New York as a public accountant practicing on his own account as Kirkcaldie & Company. Then, from 1927 to 1933, his address was the Mexican Pacific Company in New York. He died in that city in 1933. He did not belong to any American public accountancy body and does not appear to have married.

KIRKLAND, Robert Smith (1887–1960)   IAAG (1910)

Robert Smith Kirkland (*RSK*) was born in Glasgow in 1887 to William Davidson Kirkland, a house factor or real estate agent, and Annie Waddell Borland Dickie. His paternal grandparents were Robert Kirkland of R. Kirkland & Son, house factors and insurance agents, and Janet Davidson. He had a brother, William Kirkland, who was a shipping clerk, and two sisters. The Kirkland family seems to have been descended from weavers. Grandfather Robert Dickie was a marine engineer and married to Jane Robertson. *RSK* was educated in Glasgow and apprenticed to CA Mackie Clark in Glasgow. He joined the IAAG in 1910 when he immigrated to New York and employment with CAs MMC. He transferred to their Pittsburg office in 1912 and remained there until 1923 when he worked for Leon Israel & Brothers on Wall Street in New York. He appears to have returned to MMC in Minneapolis in 1923 and transferred to the San Francisco office in 1930. He joined the AIA in 1929 and became a California CPA in 1936. *RSK* was married to an English woman and had a son, William Robert Kirkland, who was born in Canada and appears to have been unemployed in 1930. The family home in San Francisco was valued at $13,000 ($145,000 in 2004 terms) and had a servant. *RSK* retired to Redwood City in California in 1951 and appears to have died circa 1960. He was never a partner in MMC.

LAMB, James Alexander (1890–1961)   IAAG (1913)

Born in 1890 in the village of Lasswade in Midlothian and south of Edinburgh to Thomas Lamb, a master grocer and manager of the cooperative store, and Isabella Cairns, James Alexander Lamb (*JAL*) was the grandson of James Lamb, a mason, and Marion Affleck, and John Cairns, a paper factory worker, and Isabella Walker, all from Lasswade. He was educated locally and apprenticed to CAs Brown, Fleming & Company in Glasgow. Although *JAL* was admitted to the IAAG in 1913, he had immigrated to Pittsburg in Pennsylvania to work for CAs MMC in 1910. He became a CPA in Pennsylvania in 1920, a member of the AIA in 1922, and transferred to MMC's Los Angeles office in 1919. In 1920, *JAL* was living in Los Angeles with his Scottish wife whom he married prior to immigration. There were no children. He was described in the US Census of that year as an "expert accountant". In 1923, he became a Vice President of the Broadway Department Store in Los Angeles and remained there until 1952 when he returned to Ayr in Scotland. He died there in 1961 and an obituary appeared in the January 1962 issue of *The Accountant's Magazine*.

LAMB, James Stewart (1868–1949)   IAAG (1893)

James Stewart Lamb (*JSL*) was born in 1868 at the village of Old Kirkpatrick in Dumbartonshire between Dumbarton and Glasgow. His father was James Lamb from Perth, the minister of the United Presbyterian Church at Old Kilpatrick (ordained 1867), and his mother was Mary Fleming, a daughter of David Fleming, a surgeon and general practitioner of Kinnoull in Perthshire who was born in Glasgow, and Mary Allan. David Fleming was a Licentiate of the Faculty of Physicians and Surgeons of Glasgow and a Parochial Medical Officer of Health in Perthshire. *JSL*'s paternal grandfather was James Lamb, a naturalist, and husband of Christina Stewart. He had two brothers, David Fleming Lamb and George Lamb, and a sister. David Lamb became an IAAG member.

There is no information regarding *JSL*'s education but he was apprenticed from 1888–1893 with Glasgow CAs Reid & Mair. He was admitted to the IAAG in 1893 and employed by Reid & Mair until 1898 when he entered a partnership with his brother, David Fleming Lamb, as J. & D. Lamb, CAs, in Glasgow. This lasted until 1911 when he immigrated to Toronto in Canada and relocated in 1914 to New York and employment with CAs MMC. A year later, he was working for CAs TNC and, in 1917, with BWGC. *JSL* appears to have left the US at some time after this and been re-admitted to the country in 1919 with his Scottish wife. The couple had no children and boarded at Manhattan in New York in 1920 where he worked as an accountant. In 1921, *JSL* joined the AIA and, in 1923, was practicing on his own. He was re-admitted to the IAAG in 1935 and removed from the roll in 1950 following his death in New York in 1949.

LAUGHLAND, David Stanley (1889–1949)   IAAG (1912)

David Stanley Laughland (*DSL*) was born in Glasgow in 1889. His father was David Laughland, a bank clerk with the Bank of Scotland, and his mother was Margaret Fulton, daughter of Thomas Fulton, Sheriff Clerk Depute for Kilmarnock in Ayrshire (population 25,000 in 1881). Fulton was from Kilmarnock and a member of its Faculty of Procurators (1841). Grandfather David Laughland from the coastal village of Stevenston in the north of Ayrshire was the minister of the United Presbyterian Church at Bothwell in Lanarkshire (from 1844) and married to Mary Black, also from Stevenston. Three uncles were warehousemen in Glasgow. *DSL* was apprenticed to Glasgow CAs McAdam & Shaw and admitted to the IAAG in 1912. He immigrated in that year to Milwaukee in Wisconsin to work for Scottish CAs AYC. No further information is available about his employment and career. By 1917, he was residing in Glasgow and he moved to London in 1937. He was awarded the Military Cross for gallantry during the First World War and it appears the lack of work-related information in the IAAG's records may indicate ill health as a result of his military service. *DSL* died in London in 1949.

LAURIE, John (1876–1957)   IAAG (1899)

John Laurie (*JL*) was the second son of Joseph Laurie from the village of Carnwarth in Lanarkshire, the chief claims clerk of the North British Railway Company, and Agnes McKechnie from Glasgow. He had one brother, Archibald M. Laurie, and was born in Glasgow in 1876. The Laurie family appears to have been farmers of small holdings in the Carnwath area. Although educated in Glasgow, *JL* was first apprenticed to George Lisle, an Edinburgh CA and then to Glasgow CAs Rattray Brothers & Cairnie before joining the IAAG in 1899. He worked for a non-accounting firm between 1899 and 1900, and then founded his own practise in Glasgow in 1901. He immigrated a year later to Pittsburg in Pennsylvania to work for CAs PWC. He soon moved to the New York office. Unusually for PWC, he was a contracted member of staff between 1902 and 1905. In 1903, he became a CPA in Illinois. Four years later, he was working in PWC's Boston office as a casual staff member. Then, in 1908, *JL* was appointed as the Comptroller of the US Smelting, Refining & Mining Company in Boston and New York. He remained in that position until his retirement in 1951. The company was formed in Utah in 1918 and had expanded with the 1965 merger with Mueller Brass Corporation. In 1972, it was renamed UV Industries and, in 1978, liquidated its assets to prevent an aggressive takeover by asset strippers Victor Posner and Saul Steinberg. In 1988, it entered Chapter 11 bankruptcy and was reformed as Mueller Industries in 1990. *JL* was married to a Scottish woman from Colorado Springs and had no children. He died in Boston in 1957 and his obituary appeared in *The Accountant's Magazine* of November 1957. He was the 22nd oldest member of ICAS and the ninth senior member of the IAAG.

LEITH, John (1869–1934) UQ

John Leith (*JL*) was a Fellow of the AAPA from 1899. He was born at Aberdeen in 1869, the eldest child of John Leith, a customs officer from the farming village of Oyne in Aberdeenshire (west of Aberdeen) and Mary Leith from the coastal village of St Fergus in Aberdeenshire (north of Peterhead). The couple had a second son, James M. Leith, and four daughters. In 1881, they also had a domestic servant and two boarders who were students at the University of Aberdeen. This suggests a relatively humble background, although *JL* came from a landed family at Oyne. His paternal grandfather was Lieutenant-General Sir Alexander Leith. Sir Alexander was Colonel of the 90th Regiment of Foot (the Perthshire Regiment) and a Deputy Lieutenant of Aberdeenshire for many years. A great grandfather, Sir James Leith (1763–1816) was also a Lieutenant-General, present at the Battle of Corunna (1809), with the Peninsula Army (1810–12), and Commander of the Forces in the West Indies and Governor of the Leeward Islands (1814).

JL was educated at the local parish school and immigrated to Chicago in 1892. His employment details between 1880 and 1892 are unknown. However, he obviously had accounting skills (probably bookkeeping learnt at school in Aberdeenshire) and was employed by Scottish migrants and public accountants Stuart & Young (later AYC) in Chicago from 1897 to 1899 before partnering fellow immigrant, Robert Nelson, as Nelson & Leith in Chicago from 1899 to 1901. In the latter year, he became the Vice-President of the International Audit Company and remained there for a year before entering practise on his own for the next 16 years in Chicago. He was single and boarding in Chicago in 1900, and recorded as an "expert accountant". From 1918 to 1934, *JL* was practicing in the mining town of Eureka in Colorado. He was an Illinois CPA. He died in Eureka in 1934. There is no record of a family.

LESLIE, William (1872–1939) SAE (1895)

William Leslie (*WL*) was born in the coastal village of Culross on the River Forth in Fife in 1872. He was the son of James Leslie, a carpenter, and Helen Drysdale, a domestic servant. His grandparents were William Leslie, a labourer, and Janet

Brewster from Edinburgh, and James Drysdale, also a labourer, and Jane Morgan. He had one brother James. By 1881, *WL*'s father had died and he was residing in Culross with his uncle, John Drysdale, a railway surfaceman, mother and brother. *WL* was educated at Culross Parish School and Dunfermline High School in Fife and apprenticed to CA George Lisle in Edinburgh. His cautioner was his uncle John Drysdale. He was Lisle's first apprentice and admitted to the SAE in Edinburgh in 1895.

Two years later, in 1897, *WL* was in New York working for the immigrant CA firm of Cuthbert & Menzies. He remained there for five years before starting to work in 1902 for the American Bank Note Company in New York. However, in the same year, he founded his own public accountancy firm in New York as Leslie & Company. This lasted four years and, in 1906, he worked briefly for CAs DDGC before setting up the public accountancy firm of LBC with Glasgow CA immigrant Alexander Scott Banks. In 1908, he became the first instructor in accounting at the Teacher's College of New York City. At about this time, he employed a student at the New York University's School of Commerce, John Thomas Madden. The latter was to become one of the US' leading educational-ists in accounting and was Dean of the School from 1925 to 1948. *WL* also became a CPA in Ohio (1908), Michigan (1912), and New York (1932), a mem-ber of the AIA (1934) (having been a member of the AAPA prior to 1916). LBC lasted until 1939 when *WL* died. The firm directed various relief agencies for the US government during the First World War.

WL was married to a woman from Virginia whose family came from Ireland. He had one son, William Leslie, junior. When he died in New Jersey, he was a member of the Mountain Lakes Borough Council in New Jersey. He wrote a paper on "Loose Leaf and Card Ledgers" in *The Accountant* in 1908. His obitu-ary appeared in *The Accountant's Magazine* of May 1939. He did not become involved in any of the public accountancy bodies to which he belonged and was one of a small number of the Scots accounting migrants to be involved in accountancy education.

LITTLEJOHN, Charles (1879–1917)   SAA (1906)

Born in Banchory in Kincardineshire in 1879, Charles Littlejohn (*CL*) was the son of a farmer, John Littlejohn from Coul in Aberdeenshire. Banchory was a farming and salmon fishing town on the River Dee to the west of Aberdeen and had a population in 1881 of more than 6,000 individuals. The farm was 14 acres in size and John Littlejohn's main occupation was as quarry manager at Craigton Quarry in Banchory. *CL*'s mother was Catherine Hoey from Banchory. The Hoeys appear to have been weavers from Fife. *CL* had two brothers, including James a quarry worker, and five sisters, including Mary, a domestic servant. Uncle James Littlejohn was a mason in Banchory.

CL was educated in Banchory before serving an apprenticeship with CAs James Meston & Company in Aberdeen. This was one of the founding firms of the SAA in 1867. James Meston was the primary influence in the formation. He practised as a lawyer and a public accountant and developed auditing as part of public accountancy practise. *CL* was admitted to the SAA in 1906 and immigrated a year later to New York. He appears to have practised on his own and became a CPA of Minnesota in 1910. In 1910, he was boarding as a single man at Brooklyn in New York and in 1912 was residing in New Jersey. He returned to Aberdeen in 1914. Three years later, he died in hospital in Aberdeen of congestion of the lungs.

LOGAN, Cornelius (1876–1953)   IAAG (1898)

Cornelius Logan (*CL*) was the son of James Logan, a commission iron merchant, and Margaret Brand, a dressmaker, from the small village of Holytown in Lanarkshire to the east of Glasgow and north of Motherwell. He was born in Glasgow in 1876. His paternal grandfather was John Logan, a quarrymaster in Perthshire, and husband of Isabella Parland. The maternal grandparents were James Croft Brand, a Glasgow cab proprietor, and Margaret Fairley Duncan. He had four siblings including John Logan, the next migrant. An uncle, also Cornelius Logan, was a boilermaker in Greenock in Renfrewshire.

Following school, *CL* was apprenticed to Thomas Guthrie of Glasgow CAs Thomson McLintock & Company. According to the official history of this firm, Guthrie was never a partner. He was the son of a grocer at Erskine in Renfrewshire and admitted to the IAAG in 1886. *CL* was admitted to the IAAG in 1898 and worked for a non-CA firm in Glasgow between 1899 and 1903. Then, in 1904, he and his brother John Logan formed a practise titled J. & C. Logan & Steven. It lasted until about 1911 when *CL* immigrated to Chicago and work with CAs BWGC. How long this employment lasted is unknown, but *CL* was mainly involved in mining operations in the western states of America. In 1917, he returned to Glasgow and resided with his brother John Logan. It is not known whether he was employed before he immigrated again – this time in 1921 to Madras in India. Two years later, he was resident at Rangoon in Burmah. Again, it must be presumed that he was involved in non-accountancy activities in these locations. By 1927 and at the age of 51, *CL* was living with his brother and a sister in retirement in London. He died there in 1953. His obituary appeared in the January 1954 issue of *The Accountant's Magazine*. He was never a member of an American public accountancy body.

LOGAN, John (1873–1938)   IAAG (1902)

Cornelius Logan's brother John Logan (*JL*) was born in 1873 in Glasgow. He was also apprenticed to CA Thomas Guthrie of Thomson McLintock & Company in Glasgow. He joined the IAAG in 1902 and practised on his own until 1903 when he worked for a non-accountancy firm in Glasgow. Then he became a partner with his brother Cornelius in Glasgow from 1904 to 1910 as J. & C. Logan & Steven. He immigrated to New York in 1912 and worked there for CAs PWC, until 1914 when he returned to Glasgow. It is not known what he did between

1914 and 1917 when his brother returned to Glasgow. It may be he was serving in the armed forces during the First World War. However, he remained in Glasgow until 1925 when he joined his brother and sister in London. He died there in 1938 unmarried.

LOWSON, Frank (1873–1961)   SAE (1903)

Frank Lowson (*FL*) came from a family heavily involved in the linen manufacturing industry of Forfarshire. He was born in Forfar (population approximately 12,000) in 1873 as the son of linen manufacturer James Lowson. His great grandfather, James Lowson, was a linen manufacturer in Forfar and his grandfather, also James Lowson, was the senior partner of John Lowson & Son, bleachers and manufacturers. Uncles Andrew and William Lowson were linen manufacturers and uncles John and Francis Lowson were clerks in the family business. Francis Lowson was educated at Edinburgh Academy and the University of Edinburgh where he received a Master of Arts degree in 1874. *FL*'s mother was Catherine Fyfe Craik. Her father was Andrew Craik from Forfar, a private lodging housekeeper in that town. Her mother came from Stirling. *FL* had five brothers and three sisters. He also had an uncle, William Lowson, who was a Writer (lawyer), Notary Public, and bank agent in Forfar. The banks were the Union Bank of Scotland and the National Securities Savings Bank (cashier and actuary). William Lowson was also an agent for the Scottish Union Fire and Life Insurance Company. *FL* had cousins who were dressmakers and a law clerk in the same town.

   FL was educated at Forfar Academy and Dundee High School before a CA apprenticeship with A. & J. Robertson in Edinburgh. He was admitted to the SAE in 1903 and worked in the family business in Forfar for two years before immigrating to New York in 1905. He worked with the American public accountancy firm of PTD. This firm was formed in 1901 from the merger of two firms founded by American-born accountants – Patterson, Corwin & Patterson and Teele & Dennis. Rodney Strong Dennis, Andrew Stuart Patterson, Arthur Wellington Teele, and Hamilton S. Corwin were, respectively, New York CPAs numbers 5, 13, 14, and 56 in 1896 and charter members of the NYSSCPA in 1897. Teele was the first Secretary of the NYSSCPA (1897–9), and Vice-President (1919–21) and Treasurer (1922–8 and 1933–40) of the AIA. Corwin was the first President of the NYSSCPA.

   FL worked for PTD until 1909 when he joined the Hodgman Rubber Company in New York. A year later, he was back with PTD and, in 1913, returned to the Hodgman Rubber Company. Employment with PTD resumed in 1914. It must be presumed that the rubber company was a client of the accountancy firm and that *FL* was seconded to the former from the latter. By 1922, *FL* was a partner in PTD, and a member of the AIA and the NYSSCPA. The partnership was relatively unique – an immigrant CA becoming a partner in a US public accountancy firm. *FL* was seconded to the US Treasury in Washington in 1921 and 1924. He was active in the AIA, chairing its Committee on Meetings in 1922, being a Vice-

President, member of the Committee on the Form and Administration of Income Tax Law, and chairing the Committee on Federal Legislation in 1923. He joined the ASCPA in 1924. By 1926, he had his own public accountancy firm in Washington and in 1930 he was living there in a gentleman's club although he was married. He retired in 1940 to Oakey Bend Farm at Hubber in Georgia and died there in 1961. *FL* does not appear to have had children.

McARTHUR, Robert (1887–1962)   SAA (1911)

Robert McArthur (*RM*) was born in Aberdeen in 1887. His father, Robert McArthur, was a house painter in the city and married to Margaret Steele, a paper mill worker. His grandparents were William McArthur, a general labourer, and Margaret Dempsey, and Thomas Steele, a blacksmith, and Margaret Wilson. *RM* was educated in Aberdeen and apprenticed from 1905 to 1910 with CA Alexander S. Mitchell of Aberdeen. He was admitted to the SAA in 1911 and immediately immigrated to Chicago to work for CAs MMC. Three years later, he was in Washington, DC but his employment there is unknown. In 1917, he was working for the American Zinc, Lead & Smelting Company in Boston in Massachusetts. From 1923 to 1948, he worked for CPAs Scovell Wellington & Company in Brookline in Massachusetts and was a member of the AIA. Then, from 1948 to 1961, he was the Comptroller of the Copper Range Company in Boston. He was widowed by 1930 and living with a sister-in-law. He retired in 1961 and died in Waban in Massachusetts in 1962. An obituary appeared in the March 1962 issue of *The Accountant's Magazine*.

MacBAIN, Robert Cowan (1878–1946)   IAAG (1901)

Born in Dumbarton in 1878, Robert Cowan MacBain (*RCM*) was the son of James MacBain, a Church of Scotland minister (ordained 1871) at the village of Dalreoch in Dumbartonshire (population 3,600), and Margaret Cowan. His paternal grandfather was James MacBain, a wood surveyor and husband of Jane Davidson. His maternal grandfather was Robert Cowan from Bothwell in Lanarkshire, a Doctor of Medicine from the University of St Andrews, Licentiate of the Faculty of Physicians and Surgeons of Glasgow (1857), and Parochial Medical Officer for the district of Barony in Lanarkshire. His maternal grandmother was Isabella Patrick from Glasgow. *RCM* had a brother and two sisters, a great uncle Charles MacBain who was a grocer in Govan, and uncles who were, respectively, a cashier in Whitburn in Linlithgowshire, a spirit dealer, and an engineman in a coalmine. Another uncle was the Reverend David Hogg (ordained 1844), the Church of Scotland minister at Killearn in Perthshire.

    RCM was apprenticed to CA Alexander Sloan of Glasgow. Sloan was the son of a Glasgow shipping agent, became a member of the IAAG in 1866, and held the Secretaryship of the IAAG from 1873 to 1909 when he became IAAG President. *RCM* was admitted to the IAAG in 1901 and was an audit clerk with the Glasgow firm of CAs Kerr, Anderson & McLeod from 1900 to 1902. He then moved to London to work for CAs PWC from 1903 to 1905. He transferred to that firm's New York office. In 1907, he made a further internal transfer to the office in San Francisco in California. A year later, he was back with PWC in New York. He remained in this employment until 1923 when he went to work for CAs CBC in New York. In 1924, he was admitted to the AIA. Then, in 1932, he became Treasurer of a steamship company at Pier 13 of East River in New York. He remained in this position until his death in 1946. He had been a widower since at least 1930. There do not appear to have been children of the marriage.

MacBEAN, Donald Campbell (1864–1939)   SAE (1891)

Donald Campbell MacBean (*DCM*) was born in Inverness in 1864 and educated at the town's Inverness Royal Academy. His father was a farmer, Duncan MacBean from Dingwall, the son of John MacBean, a messenger at arms (legal court officer), and Henrietta Urquhart Mackenzie. His mother was Margaret Campbell from Dingwall in Ross & Cromarty, the daughter of Donald Campbell, an innkeeper, and Barbara Macdonald. He had a brother, also Duncan MacBean. His father was a patient in the Royal Lunatic Asylum in Aberdeen by 1881 and his cautioner for his CA apprenticeship was William Ross Grant from Inverness who was a SSC.

The apprenticeship was with Moncrieff & Horsburgh in Edinburgh and resulted in admission to the SAE in 1891. *DCM* continued to reside in Edinburgh until 1896 when he immigrated to Seattle in Washington. However, by 1902, he appears to have returned to Edinburgh and was working with the CA firm of Wilson & Johnson with whom he remained until 1931 when he retired. He died in Edinburgh in 1939 of pneumonia. He was single and his brother Duncan registered his death. He was never a partner in Wilson & Johnson, and there is no record of his membership of American public accountancy bodies.

McCALLUM, Dougall (1883–1952)   IAAG (1907)

Dougall McCallum (*DM*) was born in Glasgow in 1883. His father, also Dougall McCallum, was a master joiner (carpenter) employing four individuals, and his mother, Jeannie Dunn Graham, was a dressmaker. He had two brothers, Peter McCallum who was a journeyman joiner, and Daniel Park McCallum, who died in infancy. There were also three sisters. His grandparents were Peter McCallum, a house joiner, and Christian McDougall, and John Graham, a pattern maker, and Janet Boyle. Educated in Glasgow, *DM* was apprenticed to Rattray Brothers & Company, CAs in that city. His service finished in 1905 and he worked as a clerk for CAs, Alexander & France until 1907 when he joined the IAAG. *DM* immigrated in 1908 to work for CAs BWGC in New York. A year later, he was employed in a similar capacity by CAs MMC. Little is known about his employment from 1910 to 1920 and it is possible he served in the First World War.

However, in 1920, *DM* was the Director of the British Ministry of Food in the US. He was also a member of the AIA. A two-year partnership with immigrant SAE member George Kennedy Hyslop lasted from 1922 to 1924. From 1924 to 1929, *DM* worked for CPAs LRBM in New York and became Treasurer of the National Radiator Corporation for the next three years. This company manufactured sanitary products. Then he was back to LRBM until 1948 when he was employed by the Brookside Distilling Products Corporation in Scranton in Pennsylvania. He retired to New York in 1951, died there in 1952, and his obituary appeared in *The Accountant's Magazine* of December 1952. He was never a partner in LRBM.

McCAW, Alexander St George (1887–1972)   IAAG (1913)

Daniel McCaw was a lithographer in Glasgow and married to Margaret Georgina Robertson. They had two sons, one of whom was Alexander St George McCaw (*ASM*) who was born in 1887. No other information is available about the family. Indeed, there were almost no Scottish residents called McCaw in successive censuses of the period. *ASM* was apprenticed to William Waddell, a Glasgow CA and partner in Hourston & Macfarlane. He was admitted to the IAAG in 1913. A year later, he immigrated to New York and employment with CAs MMC. He remained there until 1917 when he became an auditor with a firm of Pittsburg brokers, Moore, Leonard & Lynch. He worked in this capacity for six years and was admitted to the AIA in 1922. A year later, he started a four-year stint with a New York firm of public accountants founded by immigrant accountants LBD. By 1927, he was practicing on his own and remained in that capacity until retirement in 1967. He died in New York in 1972 and an obituary appeared in *The Accountant's Magazine* of that year.

McCONNELL, John (1890–1960)   IAAG (1914)

John McConnell (*JM*) was born in Glasgow in 1890 to Thomas Barr McConnell, a bleacher and dyer, and Margaret Lang McDonald. The paternal grandparents were William McConnell, also a bleacher and dyer, and Isabella Aitkenhead. Alexander McDonald, master plumber, and Margaret Lang were the maternal grandparents. *JM* had an unmarried sister and, following education in Glasgow, was apprenticed to CAs McAuslin & Tait in Glasgow before admission to the IAAG in 1914. This was the year he immigrated to Mexico then the US where he worked as an audit clerk with CAs BWGC in New York. This was followed by service in France during the First World War with the Royal Garrison Artillery. By 1917, he had returned to Glasgow and was working for CAs McOmish & Arthur and, by 1929, he was the senior partner in the Glasgow firm of W. Smith Tait & McConnell, CAs. *JM* was general secretary of the Glasgow Grocers & Provision Merchants Association, and a member of the Glasgow Incorporation of Wrights, Bridgeton Business Club, Rutherglen Incorporation of Tailors, and Glasgow Eastern Merchants Association. He retired in 1959 and died in 1960 at Rutherglen. His obituary appeared in the February 1960 issue of *The Accountant's Magazine* and in the *Glasgow Herald* at that time.

McEWAN, Matthew Clark (1865–1899)   SAE (1888)

The son of the Hope Park United Presbyterian Synod minister Thomas McEwan (ordained 1858) from the village of Strathaven in Lanarkshire (who was the son of James MacEwan, also a United Presbyterian clergyman, and Helen Smart), Matthew Clark McEwan (*MCM*) was born in Edinburgh in 1865. His mother was Agnes Clark from Glasgow. She was the daughter of Matthew Clark, a thread manufacturer in Paisley in Renfrewshire, and Jane McLaren. He had several brothers. James McEwan was educated at Edinburgh Academy and a well-known rugby player who was a trialist for the Scottish national team. He became an architect. Thomas McEwan was also educated at Edinburgh Academy and a member of its rugby fifteen. He became an electrical engineer. William McLean Clark McEwan was at the Edinburgh Academy and played rugby for Scotland on 16 occasions between 1894, when he was still at school, to 1900. He was an Edinburgh stockbroker who served with the South African Sharpshooters during the Boer War and as a private with the Argyll & Sutherland Highlanders during the First World War. *MCM* also had three sisters. His uncle, James McEwan, was a merchant in Govan in Lanarkshire whose sons were, respectively, a salesman, clerk, and engine fitter.

Like his brothers, *MCM* was educated at the Edinburgh Academy (1877–82). He played rugby for the school and then proceeded to a distinguished playing career with the Scotland team. He won 15 caps between 1886 and 1892 playing against England, Ireland and Wales. He captained the winning Scottish team against England in 1891. A year later, he became a Vice-President of the Scottish Rugby Union. He was apprenticed to Edinburgh CAs F. H. & F. W. Carter from 1883 to 1888 and was placed first in 1885 in the intermediate examination of the SAE. He joined the SAE in 1888 and became a partner in F. H. & F. W. Carter in 1889. The firm was renamed Carter, Greig & McEwan. The other partners were Frederick Walter Carter (SAE 1868), son of Frederick Haynes Carter, a founder member of the SAE, and President in 1907, his brother Walter Henry Carter (SAE 1884), and James Greig (SAE 1883). In 1890, *MCM* left for the US when seconded to work as Comptroller for the New York thread manufacturers of Clark & Company. This was a company owned by uncle John C. Clark and cousins John, James and Ann Clark. He resigned from Carter, Greig & McEwan in 1895 to assume the permanent position of Comptroller with Clark & Company (which was subsequently taken over by the Scottish thread manufacturers, J. A. & P. Coats of Paisley).

MCM remained with Clark & Company until 1899 when he left to work for wholesalers Carson, Pirie, Scott & Company in Chicago. He died there of pneumonia in the same year. He was never a member of an American public accountancy body and obituaries were published in *The Accountant's Magazine* of May

1899 and *The Accountant* of April 1899. He wrote two articles on income tax in *The Accountant* in 1893.

MacGREGOR, James Peter (1878–1939) SAA (1899)

James Peter MacGregor (*JPM*) was born in 1878 in the farming village of Ellon 16 miles north of Aberdeen in Aberdeenshire. His father was George MacGregor from nearby Old Deer in Aberdeenshire who was a druggist and chemist in Ellon. His mother, Mary Keith, came from a farming background and he had three brothers. William John MacGregor was a druggist in Ellon after schooling at Aberdeen Grammar School. George Alexander MacGregor became a school teacher in the West of Scotland. Robert Leys MacGregor was a bank secretary in Aberdeenshire. There were also three sisters and an uncle in Aberdeen who was a master grocer. *JPM* was educated at Ellon and apprenticed to Aberdeen CAs G. & J. McBain. He was admitted to the SAA in 1899. He continued to work for McBain until 1900 when he moved to Hull in Yorkshire for two years. He boarded with an English CA and an audit clerk from Scotland and it must be presumed he was working in public accountancy in Hull. The only firm there at that time was Carlill & Burkinshaw, CAs.

In 1903, *JPM* immigrated to the US. His first employer was the immigrant CA firm of MRC in New York. He moved to the firm's Chicago office in 1904 and became an Illinois CPA. In 1907, he started work for CAs DDGC in Chicago and became a partner in 1912. He held this position until 1918 when he was admitted to a partnership with Scottish CAs AYC. He was Secretary and Treasurer of the IAPA in 1914 and a member of the AIA from 1916. He became a national partner in AYC in 1921 and remained in that position until 1939. His professional appointments included membership of the Illinois State Board of Accountancy (1922), the ASCPA (1923), President of the State Board (1923–5), and Council member of the AIA (1932–6). *JPM* died in Chicago in 1939. A brief biography appears in T. G. Higgins, *Thomas G Higgins, CPA: An Autobiography* (Comet Press: New York, NY, 1965) in which he is described as small, quiet, and dignified. He does not appear to have married.

MacGREGOR, Malcolm (1878–1911) SAE (1902)

Malcolm Macgregor (*MM*) was born in Edinburgh in 1878. He was the son of Malcolm Macgregor, a SSC, a son of John Macgregor, an Advocate's first clerk, and Margaret McCowan from the village of Monzievaird in Perthshire. His mother was Mary Ann Russell from the village of Cadder, a mile or so to the north of Glasgow. She was a daughter of John Russell, a provision merchant originally from Cumberland. In addition to six sisters, *MM* had one brother, John Macgregor, who qualified in 1888 as a WS after school at the Edinburgh Institution. He was Procurator-Fiscal of the Lyon Court in 1918 and the Clerk to the Admission of Notaries in 1931. His son, and *MM*'s nephew, Malcolm Robertson MacGregor, was also a WS (1928) and joint Procurator Fiscal of the

Lyon Court in 1933. *MM*'s cousins included several merchants' clerks and an accounting clerk.

MM was educated at Edinburgh Academy from 1891 to 1895. He served a CA apprenticeship with T. G. & L. W. Dickson in Edinburgh and joined the SAE in 1902. Remarkably, he lost an arm six months prior to his final examinations yet still passed. In 1903, he immigrated to the US. There is no information to say how he earned his living for the next three years. However, by 1906, he was in Chicago working for English public accountant Ernest Reckitt of Wilkinson, Reckitt, Williams & Company. A year later, he was working for this firm in New York and, in 1908, had founded his own firm in Chicago. He found practise in Chicago difficult because of the level of competition from other public accountants and died there in 1911. He was married to Mary Ducat and had one daughter. His wife was the daughter of General Arthur Charles Ducat of the US Army who was born in Illinois. Her grandfather was Arthur Charles Ducat, a fire insurance agent at Evanston in Illinois. *MM* bred Scottish terriers and won prizes when showing them. Obituaries appeared in *The Accountant's Magazine* of November 1911 and *The Accountant* of September 1911. *MM* was not a member of any American public accountancy body.

MacGREGOR, William David (1887–1969) IAAG (1912)

William David MacGregor (*WDM*) was known as Mac. He was a likable and boisterous character and an extraordinarily able public accountant. He also had a violent temper and everybody in AYC was apparently scared to death of him. This was the assessment of *WDM* by his partner Thomas G. Higgins in *Thomas G Higgins, CPA: An Autobiography* (Comet Press: New York, NY, 1965). *WDM* was born in Govan in 1887. His father, Daniel MacGregor, was a mechanical draughtsman in Govan and had been born in Canada. His mother, Elizabeth Nicholson, was from the village of Glenlyon in Perthshire. The couple had three sons and five daughters. John Duncan MacGregor trained as an accountant but became a ship builder's clerk, and Alexander K. MacGregor was a worker in a pottery. Following education in Govan, *WDM* was apprenticed to Glasgow CAs Moores, Carson & Watson between 1904 and 1909. He joined the IAAG in 1912 when he moved to New York and employment with CAs MMC. In 1917, he joined AYC and remained with this firm throughout his career. He joined the AIA in 1917 and became an AYC partner in 1918. He was a national partner from 1921 to 1948 and an AIA Council member from 1924 to 1929 and 1932 to 1937. He joined the NYSSCPA in 1931. *WDM* retired in 1948 to Montclair in New Jersey and died there in 1969. An obituary appeared in the September 1969 issue of *The Accountant's Magazine*. As with many other accounting immigrants, he does not appear to have married.

MacINNES, Duncan (1865–1935) UQ

Duncan MacInnes (*DM*) spent much of his childhood in very humble circumstances in the fishing village of Musselburgh near Edinburgh. He was born on the

Island of Barra in the Outer Hebrides in 1865, the son of Angus McInness, a crofter, and Margaret Campbell. His grandparents were Donald McInnes, also a crofter, and Rachel McDonald, and Archibald Campbell, a crofter, and Marion McNeil. His sister, Rebecca MacInnes, was a mill worker who married Donald Smith Morrison, a coal miner and the son of John Morrison, also a coal miner, and Agnes Gordon. An uncle from Barra, Donald MacInnes, was a riveter in the shipyards at Govan near Glasgow.

It is not known where he was educated but *DM* was a ticket seller for the North British Railway Company in Edinburgh from 1874 to 1880 before immigrating to New York at the age of 15. From 1880 to 1897, he worked in New York as a time-keeper and accountant and became a New York CPA in 1901. He joined the AAPA in 1901. His main employment between 1897 and 1935 was as the Deputy Comptroller for the City of New York. He also was active in public accountancy administration during this period – the New York Board of Certified Public Accountant Examiners (1907–9) and as a trustee for Koehler's New York School of Accounts (1905). He died at Brooklyn in 1935 in accommodation with a monthly rental of $100 ($1,100 in 2004 terms). His wife was born in New York of Scottish parents. The couple had no children. A brief biography appears in N. E. Webster, *The American Association of Public Accountants: Its First Twenty Years 1886–1906* (American Institute of Accountants: New York, NY, 1954). *DI* presented several papers on governmental accounting at conferences of the National Association of Comptrollers and Accounting Officers and these were published as part of the proceedings. The subjects included municipal balance sheets (1904; also published in *The Businessman's Magazine*, 1904), uniformity in municipal accounts (1910), financial statements of cities (1910), and the purpose and principles of municipal balance sheets (1911).

MACKAY, Charles Gordon (1882–1958)   SAE (1904)

Donald Mackay from the fishing village of Farr in Sutherland on the north coast of Scotland was a spirit merchant and hotelkeeper in the farming community of Duns in Berwickshire. He had four daughters and one son, all born in Edinburgh. His wife, Henrietta Gordon, was a general servant and his father, William Mackay, a master mason and husband of Christina Mackay. Henrietta's father, Donald Gordon, was a carter and married to Janet Mackay. Donald Mackay's son, Charles Gordon Mackay (*CGM*), was born in 1882 and educated at the Chalmer's Private School and George Watson's College in Edinburgh before proceeding to an apprenticeship with CA and SAE Council member Adam Davidson Smith (SAE 1872) in Edinburgh. He joined the SAE in 1904.

CGM worked for Adam Davidson Smith for two years after qualification before setting up in sole practise in Edinburgh. However, in 1909, he immigrated to the US and worked on a part-time basis with PWC in New York. A year later, he transferred to the firm's Toronto office in Canada and remained there until 1917 when he was employed in the manufacturing concern of Scrippo-Booth Company in Detroit, Michigan. By 1921, *CGM* was Comptroller of the Hayes

Motor Truck Wheel Company in Jackson, Michigan and the Albion Bottle Company at Albion in Michigan. This industrial experience lasted until 1929 when *CGM*'s next employer was Pack Shops Incorporated in New York. He was living in accommodation with a very high monthly rental of £459 ($5,100 in 2004 terms) in Manhattan by 1930 with his wife and mother-in-law from Michigan. The Pack appointment appears to have been his last position as, by 1941, he was resident in New York. He died in West Cornwall in Connecticut in 1958. An obituary appeared in *The Accountant's Magazine* of March 1958. There is no record of *MGM*'s membership of an American public accountancy body.

MacKENZIE, Thomas Alexander (1878–1962)   SAE (1907)

Thomas Alexander Mackenzie (*TAM*) was born in Edinburgh in 1878. His father, Donald Mackenzie, was an Edinburgh bank clerk from the crofting village of Cromdale in the county of Elgin and married to Ann McIver, daughter of Donald McIver, a gardener from near Haddington in East Lothian. He had one brother, Allan Mackenzie, a bank clerk who was married to a woman 29 years older, and three sisters. Education was received at the Royal High School in Edinburgh prior to a CA apprenticeship with Lindsay, Jamieson & Haldane that resulted in membership of the SAE in 1907. *TAM* remained with Lindsay, Jamieson & Haldane until he immigrated to the US in 1909 to work for CAs BWGC in New York. A year later, he was residing in Los Angeles in California and then returned in 1911 to work for R. B. Davis Company at Hobokin in New Jersey. This employment was presumably in industry and remained until 1916 when *TAM* was employed by the Frem Splitdorf Electrical Company in New Jersey.

Two years later, *TAM* returned to public accountancy and worked for the next 12 years for the firm of CPAs Harris, Allan & Company in New York. In 1929, he joined several public accountancy bodies including the AIA, and the NYSSCPA and MISCPA. In 1930, he became a partner in BWGC in New York. He remained in this position until 1952 and his retirement to Stonybrook in New York. He died in 1962 and an obituary notice was published in *The Accountant's Magazine* of September 1962. It cannot be determined whether *TAM* was married.

MacKINNON, Barclay (1884–1954)   IAAG (1911)

Barclay MacKinnon (*BM*) was born in the Old Machar district of Aberdeen in 1884. His father, James McKinnon, was a commercial traveller for a lime company and his mother, Beatrice Mary Peat, was from the fishing and farming town of Montrose in Forfarshire. His grandparents were James McKinnon, a coach builder, and Christina Scott, and James Peat, a farmer, and Margaret Barclay. This means that *BM* was the nephew of Sir William Barclay Peat, founder in 1891 of W. B. Peat & Company, CAs in London, the firm that eventually merged with MMC to become MMPC and then PMMC. There is no information regarding his education, but his CA apprenticeship was with James Alexander Murdoch of

A. Tosh & Son in Dundee. He was admitted to the IAAG in 1911. He also immigrated to New York in 1911 and worked for CAs BWGC. Six years later, he became a partner in this firm. By 1923, he was working for John H. Koch & Company in New York and had ceased to be a member of the IAAG for several years. By 1930, he was living in New Jersey in a property valued at $14,000 ($157,000 in 2004 terms), with his wife (who was 16 years his junior), two daughters, and a son. In 1948, he moved to Los Angeles in California to practise on his own. He died there in 1954. He was not a member of an American public accountancy body and an obituary appeared in *The Accountant's Magazine* in March 1954.

MacLACHLAN, Murdoch Wright (1881–1941)   IAAG (1904)

Born at Ayr in 1881 (population 21,000), Murdoch Wright MacLachlan (*MWM*) was one of seven children, four boys and three girls. His father was James MacLachlan from Irvine in Ayrshire (population 9,000), a master builder employing 42 males, and husband of Elizabeth Johnston. The grandparents were Walter MacLachlan, a builder, and Ann Wright, and James Johnston, the Town Clerk of Irvine, and Jane Crichton. Great uncle Alexander MacLachlan from Irvine was an Ayr magistrate and builder. *MWM* was educated at Irvine Royal Academy and the University of Glasgow – although he does not appear to have graduated. He then entered an apprenticeship contract with Glasgow CAs Brown, Fleming & Murray and was admitted to the IAAG in 1904. Between 1904 and 1912, he appears to have worked in South Africa in its mining industry. He published a paper in 1913 in the *Journal of the Chemical, Metallurgical and Mining Society of South Africa* on a "System of Keeping Mine and Mill Accounts and Metallurgical Records". He immigrated to the US to work for the US Smelting, Refining & Mining Company in Boston in Massachusetts. By 1915, he was employed by CAs DDGC in Cuba, followed by his own practise in Vancouver in Canada from 1917 to 1920 when he transferred it back to Cuba. Then, in 1925, he became a partner in CAs MMC in Cuba – an arrangement that lasted until 1929 when he became a New York partner of the firm. He was a member of the AIA from 1925 and a member of its Committee on Stockbroking from 1938. *MWM* died in New York in 1941. He was never a member of his firm's senior board of management and does not appear to have married.

McLAREN, Thomas (1886–1956)   IAAG (1910)

Thomas McLaren (*TM*) was born in 1886 in the farming and market town of Blairgowrie in Perthshire to the north of Perth. His father was Thomas McLaren, a local joiner and cabinetmaker, and his mother was Jane Dick, a dressmaker. Grandparents were James McLaren, a farmer in the farming village of Dalrymple in south Ayrshire, and Janet Robertson, and William Dick, a woodman and toll keeper at nearby Kirkmichael, and Elizabeth Logan. An uncle was a factory worker and an aunt a domestic servant. There is no information available regarding *TM*'s education but he was apprenticed to CAs MacFarlane, Hutton & Patrick in Glasgow. He joined the IAAG in 1910 and immigrated in that year to work for CAs MMC in New York. He remained with this firm until 1914 when he was appointed as the Internal Auditor of the Minnesota & Ontario Power Company at International Falls in Minnesota. By 1920, he was the assistant Treasurer of Peabody, Houghteling & Company in Chicago, and he was promoted to a Vice-Presidency in 1923. In 1932, *TM* became a Vice-President and Treasurer of the Crown Zellerbach Corporation at San Francisco in California. This company was acquired and asset stripped by British financier, James Goldsmith, in 1985. It had started as the Columbia River Paper Company at Camas in Oregon to produce newsprint. Through a series of mergers from 1905 to 1928, it became the second largest paper company in the US. The Camas mill continues to operate to the present day. *TM* retired in 1952 but remained a consultant and director of the company until his death in 1956 in California. He was married. An obituary appeared in the November 1956 issue of *The Accountant's Magazine*. He was never a member of an American public accountancy body and was not recorded in the US Censuses of 1910, 1920, and 1930.

McMURTRIE, William (1871–1962)   IAAG (1904)

William McMurtrie (*WM*) was born in 1871 in the port town of Irvine (population 8,500) in Ayrshire to William McMurtrie, a clerk, and Martha Stewart. His paternal grandfather was James McMurtrie, a factory overseer, and husband of Jane Black. The maternal grandfather was Neil Stewart, a grocer, and husband of Martha Durie. *WM* was educated at Irvine Royal Academy before an apprenticeship in Glasgow with CAs J. Wyllie Guild & Scott. He qualified as a member of the IAAG in 1904 and worked for CAs John Wilson & Stirling until 1905 when he immigrated to New York. He was employed there by CAs MMC until 1916 when he appears to have served during the First World War. His next employment was with PWC in London from 1923 until 1925 when he transferred to the firm's Rotterdam office in Holland. He remained there until 1940 when he retired to the mill town of Nelson near Burnley in Lancashire. He later moved to the town of Higham Ferrers to the east of Northampton in Northamptonshire where he died in 1962. He was not a partner in PWC and never a member of an American public accountancy body. His obituary appeared in *The Accountant's Magazine* of April 1962. There is no record of a marriage or family.

McONIE, Ronald John (1887–1915)   IAAG (1911)

Ronald John McOnie (*RJM*) was born in 1887 in the town of Kingston-on-Thames south of London in Surrey where his father, John McOnie, was a draper. His mother was Agnes Jessie Strange, also a draper and a daughter of Edward Hilden Strange, a draper at the village of Speldhurst near Tunbridge Wells in Kent, and Mary Agnes Montier. The Stranges had seven daughters and four sons.

Edward Strange was a draper at Colchester in Essex and employed nine individuals in his business. Neville Strange was also a draper in Eastbourne in Sussex. Charles Strange was a builder's manager in Tunbridge Wells and Felton Strange was a builder in Speldhurst. Each of these families appears to have been reasonably well off and employed several servants. John McOnie was working on his own in Frant in Sussex prior to his marriage. He was born at the small village of Balonock in Dumbartonshire in 1851 (a mile or so north of Glasgow), the son of James McOnie, a farmer at Strathblane and from Gartmore (both in Stirlingshire), and Agnes Cameron. He had eight siblings, including three unmarried farming brothers at Strathblane. *RJM* had two sisters and one brother.

Following education at Tunbridge Wells, *RJM* was apprenticed to Glasgow CAs John Mann & Son and joined the IAAG in 1911. The apprenticeship was with John Mann (IAAG 1885), son of John Mann, one of the IAAG founders in 1854, and later to be knighted for wartime services to government. *RJM* was a part-time sergeant in the Fife & Forfarshire Yeomanry before immigrating to New York in 1911 and working for CAs MMC. Two years later, he was employed as a financial and real estate agent in Winnipeg in Canada. He was a member of the Manitoba Institute of Chartered Accountants (MICA), Secretary of the Winnipeg branch of the Overseas Club, and worked with the Young Men's Christian Association and the St. John's Ambulance Association. *RJM* joined the army in 1914 and refused a commission. He was killed in action in 1915 at the Battle of St Julien as a private in the Manitoba Regiment of the Canadian Infantry. He was last seen charging the retreating enemy and his name appears on the Menon Gate at Ypres. An obituary appeared in the June 1916 issue of *The Accountant*. He was unmarried.

MacTAGGART, James McNab (1887–1941)   IAAG (1912)

Born in the fishing village of Bowmore on the Island of Islay in Argyllshire in 1887, James McNab MacTaggart (*JMM*) was the son of a Solicitor and bank agent, Murdoch MacTaggart, who had been an Assistant Registrar of Births at Bowmore and a police constable in Glasgow. His grandfather was Archibald McTaggart, a farmer in Islay, and husband of Betsy McNab. The McNabs were farm labourers at Bowmore. A great uncle, Murdoch MacTaggart, was a quarry owner at Rothesay in Argyleshire. *JMM*'s mother, Flora Ann McGilchrist, was a daughter of John McGilchrist (ordained 1859), the Church of Scotland minister at Bowmore and Clerk to the Presbytery of Islay and Jura, and Betsy Currie. Educated at Bowmore, he was apprenticed to CAs John Parker & Son in Glasgow. His membership of the IAAG started in 1912 when he immigrated to Chicago to work for MMC. Two years later, he transferred to the Kansas City, Missouri office and, in 1915, set up J. M. Mactaggart & Company in Kansas City. In 1923, he became a Michigan CPA when his practise moved to Detroit in Michigan. He moved to Port Huron in 1927 and died there in 1941. No trace can be found of any family there.

MAIN, Ralph Drummond (1887–1941)   IAAG (1910)

Ralph Drummond Main (*RDM*) was born in the suburb of Maryhill in Glasgow
in 1887. His parents were William Davidson Main from the village of Doune in
the parish of Kilmadock in Perthshire, Agent (manager) for the National Bank of
Scotland at Maryhill, and Christian Dawson Drummond from Edinburgh. The
grandparents were Robert Main, a bank agent for the Royal Bank of Scotland at
Doune employing six individuals, and agent for the Stamp Office, and Margaret
Somerville, and Ralph Drummond, from Glasgow, a carver and guilder, and
Christian Dawson. Doune was a farming and market village and country seat for
the Earl of Moray. Other relations of *RDM* included uncles David Main, an
author, John Main, a partner in tailors R. Main & Son, and John Weir, a baker in
Doune. Cousin Ralph Drummond was a carver and guilder.

RDM was apprenticed to CAs Brown, Fleming & Murray in Glasgow. He
joined the IAAG in 1910 and left Scotland for the US in that year. Initially, he
worked for immigrant CAs Mellis, Pirie & Company in Minneapolis in
Minnesota. He then moved in 1912 to MMC where he remained for two years. In
1914, *RDM* was appointed as the Treasurer of the Hood Agency in Minneapolis
and worked in this position until 1925 when he became the Comptroller of the
Minnesota & Ontario Paper Company. He later became the company's Secretary
and Treasurer. By 1930, *RDM* was described in the US Census as a "manufacturer
in paper mills". He was married to a Minnesota music teacher with a Scottish
father, had no children, and was living in a home in Minneapolis valued at
$25,000. He was still employed with the paper company in 1941, the year of his
death. The company was formed in 1912, entered receivership in 1931, but
remained in production until at least 1986.

MARWICK, James (1862–1936)   IAAG (1886)

One of the best known immigrants from Scotland to the US was James Marwick
(*JM*). He was born in Edinburgh in 1862. His father was Sir James David
Marwick (1826–1908), the son of William Marwick, a grocer and merchant in
Kirkwall, the main town of the Orkney Islands. Sir James trained as a law agent,
was admitted a SSC in 1858, and became a member of Edinburgh Town Council.
He was uniquely the Town Clerk of Edinburgh from 1861 to 1873 and of
Glasgow from 1873 to 1903. *JM*'s mother was Jane Watt, a daughter of Solicitor
James B. Watt. Sir James edited *Records of the Convention of the Royal Burghs
of Scotland* and other books, and supervised many of Glasgow's utility projects,
including its tramways, water supplies, and electricity provision. He received an
honorary doctorate from the University of Glasgow in 1878 and was knighted in
1888. *JM*'s brother David William Marwick was educated at Fettes College in
Edinburgh, the University of Glasgow where he graduated as a Master of Arts and
Bachelor of Laws. He became a WS in 1885, a partner in Simpson and Marwick
in Edinburgh, and Food Officer for the City of Edinburgh during the First World
War. Brother William Marwick was a manufacturing confectioner in Edinburgh

employing five individuals and following his uncle Joseph Marwick as a confectioner. Brother Magnus Marwick was also a confectioner and brother John S. Marwick became a commercial traveller. An uncle, Thomas P. Marwick, was an Edinburgh architect.

JM was educated between 1872 and 1873 at the Edinburgh Academy, and then moved to King's College at Canterbury for two years, before returning to Fettes until 1880. He was a rugby player at the school. Between 1880 and 1887 he was employed as an audit clerk with Glasgow CA James Wyllie Guild. Guild, the son of a SSC from Arbroath in Forfarshire, was a founder member of the IAAG in 1853. He became one of Glasgow's leading CAs, was Secretary of the IAAG (1867–73), President (1873 & 1878), and Secretary (1881–94). *JM* studied law at the University of Glasgow between 1881 and 1886 but did not graduate. He was admitted to the IAAG in 1886 before becoming a partner in the Glasgow firm of CAs Walker & Marwick. He was a member of the Chartered Institute of Secretaries. In 1890, *JM* travelled to Australia for a bank audit. He moved on to Vancouver in Canada in 1892 where he first realised the potential of public accountancy practise in North America. Two years later, he arrived in the US with a letter of introduction from Australian, Canadian and Scottish contacts. By 1895, he had started to practise on his own in New York, including audits of a mortgage company, cotton plantations in Mississippi and Alabama, and railway companies.

In 1897, *JM* met Roger Simpson Mitchell in New York. They had previously met at the University of Glasgow. Mitchell had a textile business in Massachusetts. They formed the public accountancy firm of MMC in 1897 and became naturalised citizens. The practise prospered although, by 1903, there was open antagonism with the firm of CPAs of HS over professional practises, including navy yards work and accusations of low-balling to obtain clients. However, there was cooperation with CA Arthur Lowes Dickinson of PWC. *JM* became a CPA in Illinois (1907), Ohio (1908), Minnesota (1909), and Missouri (1911). However, he was never involved in the administration of bodies such as the AAPA (where he was a Fellow-at-Large from 1912) and the AIA. He was involved in the formation of the School of Commerce of Northwestern University in Chicago. In 1911, he met Sir William Peat and they formed the American firm of MMPC (later PMMC). He retired in 1917 although he remained on the look out for new business and regularly visited Scotland. His retirement was spent at Braemar Ranch at Santa Barbara in California, valued at $25,000 ($280,000 in 2004 terms) in 1930 when his occupation was stated as broker. He died of pneumonia in 1936 in Edinburgh while on a visit to Scotland. He was married three times – to Gwynevere from Minnesota, Sally Brewster, and Alice Emily Lawley (who was 21 years younger) from Nebraska. He had one step-daughter. His death was eventually recorded in the records of the IAAG in 1939 and there was an obituary in *The Accountant's Magazine* of August 1939. Details of *JM*'s life and career are contained briefly in T. A. Wise, *Peat, Marwick, Mitchell & Company: 85 Years* (Peat, Marwick, Mitchell & Company: New York, NY, 1982). Despite his high profile, he wrote only two publications – on the municipal ownership and accounting for tramways in *The Accountant* in 1905 and cost accounting in the *Engineering Record* in 1906.

MATTHEW, Alfred Alexander (1876–1906)   SAE (1898)

William Matthew, an Edinburgh bank agent (manager) from the county town of Cupar in Fife, and his wife Mary Millicent Watson, from the coastal village of Prestonpans on the River Forth in East Lothian, had three sons and two daughters. His father, Alexander Crombie Matthew, was a member of the Royal College of Surgeons in England (1828) and the Aberdeen Medico-Chirurgical Society, and a medical practitioner in Aberdeen, Kinross, and Cupar. The paternal grandparents were William Matthew, a farmer at Cupar, and Ann Millar, and the maternal grandparents were Hamilton Watson, a master potter, and Mary Wilson. A brother of William Matthew, Alexander Matthew, was a farmer in Cupar of more than 300 acres employing seven individuals. A nephew was a commercial clerk in Cupar.

William Matthew's sons included Alfred Alexander Matthew (*AAM*) who was born in Edinburgh in 1876. Other sons were William Hamilton Matthew, who became a bank agent, and Alexander Matthew, who was admitted as a SSC in 1909. *AAM* was educated at Daniel Stewart's College and apprenticed to CAs Bringloe & Maxtone Graham. He joined the SAE in 1898. He remained with the firm for three years before immigrating to New York and employment with public accountants PTD. He remained there for four years before ill health forced his return to Edinburgh in 1905. He died there in 1906. He was single and death was due to Banti's disease. An obituary appeared in *The Accountant's Magazine* of November 1906. *AAM* did not belong to any American public accountancy body.

MEDLOCK, Arthur (1890–1969)   IAAG (1914)

Arthur Medlock (*AM*) was born in the shipbuilding district of Govan in Glasgow in 1890. His father was James Medlock, an ironmonger in Govan who originated from the farming village of Cockpen in Midlothian and was the husband of Euphemia Bryce. His grandparents were John Medlock, a butler and domestic servant, and Grace Monoak, and David Bryce, a master grocer, and Mary Mackay. His brother, John Medlock, was fellow CA and immigrant, and he had two sisters and an uncle, John Medlock, who was a joiner and husband of Annie Chalmers from Lasswade in Midlothian. The latter was a daughter of Alexander Chalmers, a carpet weaver, and Jane McNeil of the village of Rosslin in Midlothian to the south of Edinburgh.

AM was apprenticed to Glasgow CAs William Boyd, Dunn & Todd and admitted to the IAAG in 1914. A year previously, he had joined his elder brother, John Medlock, who had just transferred to the Chicago office of CAs PWC. He was given a full-time contract of employment. His arrival in Chicago appears to have been from the PWC office in Winnipeg in Canada that opened in 1912. *AM* audited the accounts of the Province of Manitoba and was publicly critical of its accounting failures. In 1916, he joined the AIA and the IAPA. He also joined the AIA's Committee on the Earned Surplus in 1916. In 1929, *AM* was transferred to take charge of the PWC office in Pittsburg in Pennsylvania and became a Pennsylvania CPA. He was involved in fraud investigations in the accounting systems of the City of Pittsburg that was insolvent in 1931. He had a talent for staff relations and was well respected by younger employees. *AM* was married and had two sons and a daughter. His home in Pittsburg in 1930 was valued at $10,000 ($112,000 in 2004 terms). He retired to Florida in 1949 and died there at Vero Beach in 1969. He was never a PWC partner although his career with the firm is covered in C. W. DeMond, *Price, Waterhouse & Company in America: A History of a Public Accounting Firm* (Comet Press: New York, NY, 1951). Unlike his brother, John Medlock, no obituary appeared in *The Accountant's Magazine*.

MEDLOCK, John (1874–1940)   IAAG (1914)

John Medlock (*JM*) was born in Govan in Glasgow in 1874. He was the brother of Arthur Medlock (above). *JM* was educated at the University of Glasgow where he graduated as a Master of Arts in 1901. He was apprenticed to CA John Munn Ross (IAAG 1883) in Glasgow and immigrated to New York in 1903. He worked for CAs PWC in New York, Chicago, and Seattle by 1906. In fact, he opened the Seattle office in 1906. In 1905, he became an Illinois CPA. He was also a member of the AAPA (1909), and a CPA in New York, Wisconsin, Louisiana, and other states. He transferred to Chicago from Seattle in 1913 and was admitted to the PWC partnership in 1914 and the AIA in 1916. He joined the IAAG in 1914. Professional service included the AIA's Committee on the Earned Surplus and an Illinois State Board of Accountancy examinership (both in 1929–30). He chaired the State Board in 1931 and retired from practise in 1936. *JM* died in Chicago in 1940. According to the obituary written by his brother, Arthur Medlock, in the February 1941 issue of *The Accountant's Magazine*, he was depressed and suffering from sinus problems. He had opened a window and fallen out in December 1940. His career is detailed in C. W. DeMond, *Price, Waterhouse & Company in America: A History of a Public Accounting Firm* (Comet Press: New York, NY, 1951) in which he is described as sturdy, hearty, forthright and honest.

MELLIS, Thomas Crombie (1879–1936)   SAA (1909)

Thomas Crombie Mellis (*TCM*) was born in Aberdeen in 1879. He was the son of an Aberdeen innkeeper and refined spirit dealer, Thomas Mellis, and Mary Ann Herd. His grandparents were Thomas Mellis, an Aberdeen innkeeper and vintner, and Isabella Eckford, and William Herd, a fisherman from Ruthven in Banffshire, and Mary Bruce. The Eckford family appears to have come from Dundee and Fife and been involved as workers in the jute industry. *TCM* was apprenticed to an unrecorded Aberdeen firm of CAs before transferring to the Glasgow firm of Thomson McLintock & Company. He joined the SAA in 1909 and immigrated in

1910 to form a practise, Mellis, Pirie & Company in Minneapolis in Minnesota. His partner was fellow immigrant and CA, John Pirie, from Glasgow whose family came from Aberdeenshire. By 1923, *TCM* was working in Glasgow for the National Light Castings Association. Six years later, he was living in Saltcoats in Ayrshire. Later moves were made to Glasgow in 1933 and the farming village of Laurencekirk south of Aberdeen in 1935. He died there in 1936.

MILNE, John Robertson (1881–1962)   SAE (1904)

John Robertson Milne (*JRM*) was born in the farming village of Stobbo in Peebles-shire in 1881 as the son of a music hall caretaker and former butler in Edinburgh, John Milne. The latter was the son of John Milne, a domestic servant in Pimlico in London, and Catherine Robertson, a housekeeper. *JRM*'s mother was Elizabeth Robertson, the daughter of William Robertson, a butler, and Catherine Campbell. He was educated in Edinburgh at the Normal Private School and George Heriot's School before starting a CA apprenticeship with John McKerrell Brown of Romanes & Aitchison. Brown was a grandson of James Brown, one of the principal founders of the SAE in 1853–4 who became its first President. *JRM* joined the SAE in 1904. One year later, he was employed as an auditor by immigrant CAs MRC of New York. A year later, he moved to CAs MMC also in New York. He remained with this firm for seven years before transferring to BWGC where he was employed for a year.

  JRM left the US in 1915 to return to London and enlist in the British Army. He was a lance corporal in the London Scottish Regiment before returning in 1919 to BWGC in Boston. He had been made a Member of the Order of the British Empire for his war service. He then transferred to Santa Barbara in California. In 1924, further employment continued with MMC in New York and lasted until 1938 when he retired to Massachusetts and then to Yorkshire, London and Shropshire where he died in 1962. He had a wife from New York and a daughter. *JRM* was never a member of an American public accountancy body or a partner in any firm in which he was employed. An obituary notice appeared in *The Accountant's Magazine* of December 1962.

MITCHELL, Simpson Rodger (1860–1936)   UQ

The American national firm of public accountants MMC was founded by fellow Glaswegians, James Marwick and Simpson Rodger Mitchell (*SRM*). Rodger Mitchell was born in 1860 in the farming village of Milton in Dumbartonshire near Glasgow. He was the son of Alexander Mitchell, a power loom cloth manufacturer in Glasgow employing 245 individuals and son of Alexander Mitchell, a Glasgow jeweller, and Jane Simpson. *SRM*'s mother, Joan Cameron Campbell, was from the crofting village of Dalmally in Argyllshire and the daughter of Captain Alexander Campbell of the Royal Marines, a local landowner at Auchendarroch and a Deputy Lieutenant of Argyleshire, and Helen Turner. The Campbell family was reputed to be related to successive royal families of Scotland.

SRM had 12 siblings of whom several died young. His brothers included Alexander A. Mitchell, a cloth manufacturer; William Alexander Mitchell, a calico printer salesman, John James Mitchell, a dress goods manufacturer, and Ewan Henderson Mitchell, a ship builder at Liverpool in England. The Mitchell family business in Glasgow was cotton weaving at the Rockvilla Weaving Factory. *SRM* was educated in Glasgow at the Western Academy and Park School followed by the Gaillard College at Lausanne in Switzerland and the University of Glasgow (although he did not graduate) where he met James Marwick. After employment as a cashier in his father's business, *SRM* immigrated in 1890 to the US to open a branch of the family clothing business at Fitchburg in Massachusetts. This was a profitable venture until the imposition of cotton tariffs by the UK government. In 1896, *SRM* changed occupations and formed a firm of public accountants, Hopkins, Mitchell & Company, in New York. His partner was Seldon Hopkins, an Illinois CPA and the author of *Manual of Exhibition Accounting* (1879). At some time during his management venture in Fitchburg, he met James Marwick whom he knew from his university days in Glasgow. Marwick was auditing the Fitchburg Railroad Company and they agreed the need to expand public accountancy services in the US. *SRM* ceased his partnership with Seldon after a year and, with Marwick, formed MMC in New York in 1897. The partnership was to last until his retirement in 1925.

Also in 1897, *SRM* became a New York CPA. He also became a CPA in Illinois (1908), Ohio (1908), Minnesota (1909), Louisiana (1916), California (1921, revoked in 1931), and Michigan (1925). 1908 was the year in which he was a guarantor of the Northwestern University's School of Commerce in Chicago. In 1910, *SRM* was recorded in the US Census as living in Queens in New York, married with two daughters (his wife was from New York and 21 years his junior) and three servants, and a "member of a private family". He became the senior partner in MMC in 1917 when James Marwick retired. He adopted a backroom role and retired in 1925 to enjoy his rose collection. From 1919 to 1927, *SRM* was a member of the AIA's Endowment Committee. He was also a Canadian CA and a member of the ASCPA. He published "What Does an Accountant's Certified Statement Represent?" in the *Banker's Magazine* in 1916. By 1930, *SRM* had changed his name to Rodger Simpson Mitchell and was living with his wife in Westchester County in New York. He is recorded as a nurseryman and his residence was valued at $40,000 (£447,000 in 2004 terms). He died a widower in 1936 and his career is outlined in T. A. Wise, *Peat, Marwick, Mitchell & Company: 85 Years* (Peat, Marwick, Mitchell & Company: New York, NY, 1982).

MORRISON, Robert Miller (1891–1938)   IAAG (1914)

Born in Glasgow in 1891, Robert Miller Morrison (*RMM*) was the son of a tinsmith, William Morrison, and grandson of William Morrison, a carter, and Mary Prentice. His mother was Janet Stewart, a steam loom weaver and daughter of William Stewart, a gardener, and Isabella Walton. He was educated in Glasgow and apprenticed to CAs J. L. & T. L. Selkirk of Glasgow. He was admitted to the

IAAG in 1914. He left immediately for Chicago and worked there with English public accountants Ernest Reckitt & Company until 1936 when he was employed by the public accountancy firm of Scovell, Wellington & Company. He had a home in Chicago valued in 1930 at $20,000 ($224,000 in 2004 terms). His wife was from Illinois with Scottish parents, and he had a daughter. *RMM* died in Chicago in 1938. In the IAAG's records, he was described as a CPA although no record can be found of such a licence.

MUNRO, James (1875–1924)   IAAG (1913)

James Munro (*JM*) was born in 1875 in Glasgow to James Munro, a police sergeant. He had one brother and six sisters. His apprenticeship with CAs French & Hunter (later French & Cowan) resulted in a 1913 membership in the IAAG. He immigrated to the US in 1914 and worked for CAs BWGC in New York until 1918. By 1920, he was back in Glasgow and working for CAs Wilson & Stirling. In 1923, his address was in London and he died there in 1924.

MURPHY, Alexander (1889–1962)   IAAG (1913)

Alexander Murphy (*AM*) was born in Ayr in 1889, the son of John Hunter Murphy, a commercial clerk, and Margaret Bryden Wilson, a fruit merchant's assistant. His grandparents were Alexander Murphy, an upholsterer, and Flora Dunlop, and Margaret Wilson, a housekeeper. No maternal grandfather is registered. He was educated in Ayr and apprenticed to CAs Hardie & Macfarlane in Glasgow. He joined the IAAG in 1913 having been an audit clerk with Hardie & Macfarlane from 1911 to 1912. In 1913, *AM* was a recruit to the New York CAs MMC and became a New York CPA in 1915. However, in the same year, he returned to live in Glasgow and remained there until his death in 1962. He was mentally ill and resident in the Royal Mental Hospital in Glasgow since 1923 and the IAAG's Council waived his membership fee throughout this time. He was unmarried.

MYLES, James (1879–1967)   IAAG (1904)

James Myles (*JM*) is another immigrant about whom little is known prior to his US career. He was born in Glasgow in 1879. His father was James Myles, a Glasgow fish merchant and husband of Agnes Brownlie. A younger brother, George Alexander Mylne, was a Glasgow CA who immigrated to St Louis in Missouri and worked from 1916 to 1942 with PWC (and therefore not included in this study). *JM* was apprenticed to CAs Findlay, Kidston & Goff in Glasgow and admitted to the IAAG in 1904. He worked for several firms in Glasgow until 1906 when he became a partner in the firm of Wight, Wight, Myles & Fleming. This was a firm originally founded by an early Glasgow CA John Wight (IAAG 1861) from East Lothian, who trained in Edinburgh as a lawyer and specialised in local government audit services in Glasgow. The firm became Myles &

Fleming in 1911 but, a year later, *JM* immigrated to work for immigrant CA J. Gordon Steele in Minneapolis in Minnesota. He quickly moved to CAs Frame, Dougherty & Company in Minneapolis. Then, in 1915, he moved to PWC in St Louis in Missouri.

JM joined the AIA in 1916 and appears to have been a CPA in New Jersey and Minnesota. However, between 1917 and 1923, he had several addresses in New York and New Jersey without any sign of employment. In 1925, he was working for CAs BWGC in New York and became a partner in 1935. In 1930, he was living in New Jersey, owned a home valued at $14,000 ($157,000 in 2004 terms), and had a wife from Scotland and a son and two daughters. He retired in 1952 to Tenafly in New Jersey. He died there in 1967 as the fifth most senior member of ICAS. An obituary appeared in the June 1967 issue of *The Accountant's Magazine*.

NAPIER, John Stuart (1885–1952)   IAAG (1908)

John Stuart Napier (*JSN*) was born in the village of Ballater in Aberdeenshire near the royal residence at Balmoral in 1885. His parents were John Napier, a police constable from the village of Dunotter in Kincardineshire, and Catherine Ogilvie Milne from the village of Old Deer west of Peterhead in Aberdeenshire. The Napier family cannot be traced but the Milne family appears to have worked as farm labourers in Old Deer. *JSN* was apprenticed to Carswell, Murray & Landers, CAs of Glasgow, and admitted to the IAAG in 1908. He immigrated to the US in 1909 and was employed in New York by CAs MMC. Then, in 1910, he transferred to the MMC office in Butte, Montana. A year later, *JSN* was back in the New York office. He then worked for a local public accountant in Chicago from 1912 to 1914, and TNC in New York from 1914 to 1915, before founding his own practise as Napier, Jones & Company at Portland in Oregon. This remained his address until his death in 1952. He was unmarried and did not belong to any American public accountancy body. In the 1930 US Census, *JSN* was living in rented accommodation at a monthly rental of $45 ($500 in 2004 terms) in Portland and was reported as unemployed.

NELSON, Robert (1870–1913)   IAAG (1893)

Robert Nelson (*RN*) was born in 1870 in the village of Milton to the north of Glasgow to Gilbert Nelson, a wine merchant and church officer born at the south Ayrshire village of Colmonnell near Girvan, and Mary Manson, a domestic servant from Edinburgh. His grandparents were William Nelson, a boot and shoe maker, and Mary Haldane, and Adam Manson, a paper worker, and Jane Cross. He had three brothers, two of whom died in infancy, and his twin, Adam Nelson, Bachelor of Divinity and ordained in 1901, who became the Church of Scotland minister at Tyrie parish in Aberdeenshire. *RN* had uncles and cousins at Colmonnell. John Nelson was a public carter, David Nelson was a gamekeeper, and Alexander and Thomas Nelson were masons.

RN was educated at St Mungo's College in Glasgow prior to a CA apprentice-ship in Glasgow with J. Wylie Guild & Fisher from 1888 to 1893. He joined the IAAG in 1893 having been an associate member for three years. In 1895, he left for the US. No information about employment is available until 1899 when he joined the AAPA and was a partner in Nelson & Leith in Chicago. John Leith immigrated to Chicago from Scotland around 1895 and worked for Scottish accountants Stuart & Young prior to partnering *RN*. In 1902, the latter practised on his own in that city and, a year later, became an Illinois CPA. In 1912, he resigned from the AAPA and, in 1914, ceased to be a member of the IAAG because of non-payment of dues. A year later, the IAAG refused to reinstate him because of his poor financial state. In 1900, in response to an editorial invitation in *The Public Accountant* as to the definition of a public accountant, *RN* wrote "A man's books are the written history of his business. In them are recorded the experience of years. It is important that these records be correct. A public accountant is a specialist in accounts and in the varied and complex interests of our present business life he is a necessity". In the 1910 US census of Chicago, *RN* was living with his Scottish wife and a brother-in-law who was a clerk in a real estate office. There were no children present. No further information is available about the career or life of *RN* although he is recorded as dying about 1913. A brief biography appears in N. E. Webster, *The American Association of Public Accountants: Its First Twenty Years 1886–1906* (American Institute of Accountants: New York, NY, 1954).

NIVEN, John Ballantine (1872–1954)   SAE (1893)

John Ballantine Niven (*JBN*) was a significant figure in the early development of the public accountancy profession in the US. Not only did he co-found the firm of TNC that is now part of the international firm of Deloitte & Touche, he also was very active in the administration of various public accountancy bodies including the AIA of which he was President in 1924.

JBN was born in Edinburgh in 1872. He was descended from a family of farm-ers and merchants located in Ayrshire by mid-eighteenth century. His great grand-father, Alexander Niven, was Church of Scotland minister at the cathedral and farming town of Dunkeld in Perthshire from 1793. His children included two sur-geons with the Honorable East India Company and several relatives on the mater-nal side of the family held military, legal and administrative positions in India at approximately that time. This suggests that emigration would not have been unknown to the Niven family by the time of *JBN*'s immigration to the US in 1898. His grandfather was also a Church of Scotland minister. Alexander Niven entered the ministry after graduating from the University of St Andrews and was ordained at the weaving and farming town of Balfron in Stirlingshire in 1825. He married Eliza Brown, a daughter of the Reverend Dr Thomas Brown, minister of St John's Parish Church in Glasgow and one of the architects of the Disruption in the Church of Scotland in 1843 that led to the foundation of the Free Church of Scotland. The couple had three sons and a daughter. The eldest son was

Alexander Thomas Niven who was a leading Edinburgh public accountant, exceedingly active in the affairs of the Church of Scotland, and one of the founders in 1853–4 of the SAE. He was also *JBN*'s father. His brother, Thomas Brown William Niven, was a leading minister in the Church of Scotland at Polockshields (ordained 1859) and Moderator of the General Assembly of the Church of Scotland in 1906. He had six children, three of whom migrated from Scotland.

Alexander Thomas Niven married a second cousin, Agnes Howie Ballantine, daughter of John Ballantine, an Ayr banker. The couple had two sons and six daughters, including Janet Ballantine Niven who married Henry Moir, a close friend of *JBN* who qualified as a Fellow of the Faculty of Actuaries in 1893 and was employed by the Scottish Life Assurance Company in Edinburgh. He immigrated to the US in 1901 and became an internationally prominent actuary in the insurance world as President of the Actuarial Society of America, President of the United States Life Insurance Company, and one of the most prolific authors on actuarial matters of his time. Alexander Thomas Niven had several links to the US that may have prompted *JBN*'s migration there. He was the Edinburgh agent for the Liverpool & London Fire & Life Assurance Company that was one of the major British insurance companies in the US in the second half of the nineteenth century and a major investor in American property during the same period. He also founded and managed the American Mortgage Company with the objective of lending to property developers in North America. One of the other subscribers was Austin Corbin of Corbin's Bank in New York. This suggests that Alexander Thomas Niven had at least one business connection to the US before *JBN* migrated there. The American Mortgage Company lent to clients in Alabama, the Dakotas, Georgia, Iowa, Mississippi, Missouri, Oregon, and Washington. Its eventual parent company, the Scottish American Mortgage Company, was one of the most successful property trusts investing in the US, and had 65 per cent of its loans in the southern part of that country by 1890.

JBN was educated at Ariad House School and George Watson's College in Edinburgh. He excelled at school as a singer and at mathematics. He was then apprenticed to CA David Pearson of C. & D. Pearson in Edinburgh and admitted to the SAE in 1893. David Pearson was the son of Charles Pearson, one of the founders of the SAE in 1853–4. He was an Edinburgh CA (SAE 1862) and member of the Faculty of Actuaries (1862). He was SAE President between 1898 and 1901. *JBN* worked in his father's firm until 1897 and lectured on bookkeeping and accounting for the SAE. He immigrated to Chicago a year later and worked on a non-contract basis for CAs JCC. Why he migrated is unknown but it could have been due to the influence of a boyhood friend and apprentice of his father's, George Alexander Touche, who was significantly involved in British investment in the US by the end of the nineteenth century. Touche had left for the London firm of CAs Broads, Paterson & May, after joining the SAE in 1883. He became heavily involved in the investment management movement, particularly as it related to investment in the US. His strategy included audits of the financial records and statements of potential investments and he held numerous directorships in American companies funded with British capital. Touche frequently traveled to the US to advise British investors on American companies and met many influential American businessmen. He founded the public accountancy firm of George Touche & Company in London in 1899 and lack of public accountancy services in the US resulted in his founding TNC with *JBN* in 1900 in New York. The firm was formed initially as an agency of George Touche & Company in London and incorporated as a corporation with limited liability. Its partners held shares in it until 1913 when professional pressure from other American public accountancy firms forced it to revert to the customary partnership structure. The firm's first audit report was issued in 1900 to the directors of the North American Transportation & Trading Company. Its first audit engagement was the International Steam Pump Company. In 1902, *JBN* was responsible for the disclosure by the International Steam Pump Company of a consolidated balance sheet, preceding that of the US Steel Corporation.

JBN became a New York CPA by examination in 1901, and joined the AAPA in 1904. By means of examination waiver through reciprocation, he was licensed in the states of Illinois, New Jersey, Ohio, Louisiana, and Michigan, and was also a Canadian CA. He became an American citizen in 1905. In 1908, he was one of the first public accountants in the US to be appointed as a corporate receiver. He also provided accounting assistance in a federal investigation of the financial practises of life assurance companies in New York. TNC expanded rapidly into Chicago, Minneapolis, St Louis, Cleveland, Los Angeles, Atlanta, and Detroit on the basis of a need to provide services for a major client. Early TNC employees included several UK immigrants.

By 1936, TNC had 19 partners and was auditing major corporations such as H. J. Heinz & Company and R. H. Macy & Company. This success, however, exposed the firm to the possibility of lawsuits as its audit opinions were increasingly relied on in the public domain. In 1931, it defended the landmark civil court case of *Ultramares Corporation v. Touche* in which it had given a clean opinion to fraudulently prepared financial statements. Each partner in the firm was charged with intent to defraud and professional negligence. The fraud charge was dismissed and, following two appeals, the New York Court of Appeals unanimously decided that, due to no specific contract between the firm and Ultramares, there was no basis for a negligence claim. The judge, however, stated that Ultramares could have made a case on the basis that audit partners had closed their eyes to the obvious nature of the fraud. The case concerned the still-debated issues of third party liability by auditors and the nature of fraud in cases of auditor negligence. *JBN* was the partner exclusively involved in the successful defence of the case over two years.

Despite the tribulations of the *Ultramares* case, the professional success of *JBN* as an American public accountant and TNC as a national public accountancy firm is evident from several organisational mergers in which the firm was later involved – with George Bailey & Company of Detroit and A. R. Smart & Company of Chicago to form Touche, Niven, Bailey & Smart (TNBS) in 1947. George Bailey was an American CPA who was a partner in Ernst & Ernst in

Detroit before forming George Bailey & Company after an irreconcilable dispute with the senior Ernst partner. Allen Richard Smart was a UQ public accountant working for his brother John Richard Smart, an English CA in Peterborough in England from 1885. He came to the US to work on an assignment from his brother in 1890. He remained there to work for immigrant accountant James Anyon of BWGC in New York in 1891 and became BWGC manager in Chicago in 1895 and a partner in 1911. Smart formed Smart, Gore & Company with fellow BWGC partner Edward Everitt Gore in 1922. Gore was an American-born CPA. Smart's younger brother, John English Smart (ICAEW 1909) migrated to Chicago in 1910 to join BWGC, formed his own firm in 1924 in Dayton Ohio, but had a relatively unsuccessful career thereafter. *JBN* was senior partner of TNBS shortly before his death in 1954. TBNS eventually became Deloitte & Touche when it merged with the successor firm of DDGC in 1989. Although he was a migrant to the US, *JBN* did not rely heavily on British immigrant accountants for the early development and growth of TNC. There were only 14 British accounting immigrants employed prior to 1915. Three remained with the firm for significant periods of time.

JBN contributed greatly to the institutional aspects of American public accountancy. He was deeply involved in the management of professional bodies. The offices he held, for example, included Vice-President of the AAPA (1914–17), President of the NJSCPA (1915–21), President of the New Jersey State Board of Accountancy (1915–21), member of the AIA's Council (1917–26), Executive Committee (1917–49), Board member of the NYSSCPA (1918), and AIA President (1924–5). *JBN* was a moderating voice in the disputes of the early 1900s concerning the relative merits of federal and state regulation of the profession and was a major influence in the introduction of the uniform CPA Exam and in the development of the *Journal of Accountancy*. He was also one of the pioneers of tax accounting in the US and wrote the income tax department of the *Journal* from 1913 to 1920.

According to his obituary in the *New York Herald Tribune* in November 1954, *JBN* contributed greatly to his local community. He was active in public service as a director of the New York Chamber of Commerce, and as a trustee and Mayor of Mill Neck, Long Island where he lived for most of his professional life. He married Susan Wallace Ogden Gordon in New York in 1905. She was a Canadian lawyer's daughter. *JBN* and his wife initially lived in Montclair, New Jersey and, in 1915, moved to Oyster Bay overlooking Long Island Sound. They had no issue but adopted William Seton Duys (renamed Dwyer), a nephew and the son of a brother-in-law and German migrant merchant in New York. William Niven was a graduate of Princeton and Harvard Universities, trained with his father's firm, a New York CPA (1945), and a partner in PMMC in New York until 1975.

In 1930, the Niven property at Mill Neck was valued at the then very large sum of $145,000 ($1,620,000 in 2004 terms) and had two resident servants. Its neighbouring property was that of then Governor of New York Franklin Delano Roosevelt, later 32nd President of the US. *JBN* died as an Episcopalian despite the strong Presbyterian background of the Niven family through two centuries.

He was a member, vestryman, and former Treasurer of St John's of Lattingtown Church near Oyster Bay. He alternated as Treasurer with his friend and the Church's senior warden, John Pierpont Morgan, head of bankers J. P. Morgan & Company from 1913 until 1963. The friendship resulted from the business relationship originating between Morgan and George Alexander Touche in London and New York at the turn of the century. The life and family of *JBN* are researched in T. A. Lee, "A Genealogy of Professional and Public Service: the Contributions of Alexander Thomas Niven and John Ballantine Niven", *Accounting and Business Research*, 2002, 32 (2), 79–92. Obituaries about *JBN* in 1954 were published in the *New York Herald Tribune* (November), *Journal of Accountancy* (December), *The Accountant's Magazine* (December), and *The Scotsman* (November).

NOBLE, Eric Mackay (1847–92)   SAE (1875)

As far as can be ascertained, Eric Mackay Noble (*EMN*) was the first CA from the UK to migrate permanently to the US. He did so in 1875 at the age of 28, having joined the SAE in the same year. He only remained a member for several months as he is recorded as having resigned at some time in 1875. *EMN* was born in the farming village of Muckhart in Perthshire in 1847. He was the son of the Reverend Andrew Noble (ordained 1841) from the village of Stobbo near Peebles in Peebles-shire and a Free Church of Scotland minister at Muckhart who became minister at the village of Newmills in the parish of Loudoun in Ayrshire, east of Kilmarnock. His mother was Wilhelmina Mackay and he had an uncle, James Noble, who farmed 220 acres at Livingston in Linlithgowshire. His unmarried brother, Kenneth David Noble, was an engineer and chief draughtsman at a marine engine factory near Loudoun. An uncle, John Dobbie, was a corn merchant in Edinburgh who was born at the village of Symington in Lanarkshire.

EMN was educated at Newmills and apprenticed from 1871 with Edinburgh CA Richard Wilson. Wilson was from Fife and an early CA (SAE 1855) who was a member of its Council (1876) and of Edinburgh Town Council for several years. *EMN* immigrated to the US as soon as he qualified as a CA and appears to have formed a public accountancy firm in Washington, District of Columbia which existed until his death there in 1892. He was a member of the AAPA from 1888 to 1892 and a Commissioner of the US Court of Claims. He died in Washington in 1892 and a brief biography appears in N. E. Webster, *The American Association of Public Accountants: Its First Twenty Years 1886–1906* (American Institute of Accountants: New York, NY, 1954). He does not appear to have married.

OGG, William Alexander (1884–1955)   SAA (1907)

William Alexander Ogg (*WAO*) was the son of John Orr, an Aberdeen granite merchant and bank agent (manager) who was born in Banchory in Aberdeenshire, and Janet Simpson from Glenmurick also in Aberdeenshire. The Ogg family originated at the farming village of Kincardine O'Neil in Aberdeenshire, near to

Banchory. Grandfather William Ogg was a wood sawyer there as were his sons, George and William Ogg. Great uncle Alexander Ogg was a farmer of 66 acres at Kincardine and employed four individuals in addition to his sons, John and James Ogg. Uncle William Ogg was a farmer of 75 acres in Banchory. *WAO* was born in the district of Old Machar in Aberdeen in 1884. His brother, John Simpson Ogg, was educated at Aberdeen Grammar School and served a CA apprenticeship with local firm Flockhart & Jamieson. He did not qualify and left for Chicago in 1913 where he was employed by PWC. He was transferred to Milwaukee in 1914 before being appointed as Comptroller of the Aetna Explosives Company in New York in 1916, the Air Reduction Company in 1919, and the National Aniline & Chemical Company in 1920.

WAO was educated between 1897 and 1900 also at Aberdeen Grammar School. He was then apprenticed to Aberdeen CA Harvey Hall and passed his examinations with distinction. Hall joined the SAA in 1877 after graduation as a Master of Arts from the University of Aberdeen. He practised as a lawyer and public accountant, being a member of the Faculty of Advocates in Aberdeen, and was SAA President from 1885 to 1887. *WAO* joined the SAA in 1907 and immigrated to Boston in the same year. He was employed first by the US Coal & Oil Company and then by the US Smelting, Refining & Mining Company. He was successively, the Internal Auditor, Comptroller, and President of the American Zinc, Lead & Smelting Company. These companies were largely involved in mining copper, lead, and zinc in at Midvale in Utah. They became UV Industries in 1908 and this company ceased operations in 1971 and conveyed its mining assets to Sharon Steel Corporation in 1979. The latter company defended and settled federal lawsuits as a result of environmental contamination at Midvale and legal arguments about the insurance settlement continue to the present day.

Later positions held by *WAO* included Appalachian Coals Incorporated in Cincinnati, Ohio in 1934 and the Island Creek Coal Company at Huntington in West Virginia in 1948. The Island Creek Coal Company continues to own several of the largest coal mines in West Virginia in the 1990s and has successfully defended against lawsuits by the United Mine Workers of America for infractions of mine safety regulations in the late 1990s. *WAO* was married to a woman from Scotland, lived in a home in Massachusetts in 1930 valued at $15,000 ($168,000 in 2004 terms), and had three daughters and a son. He retired to Cincinnati in 1954 and died there a year later. His obituary appeared in the October 1955 issue of *The Accountant's Magazine*. *WAO* was one of a few immigrants who did not work in public accountancy at any time in the US.

OGILVY-RAMSAY, Alexander Henderson (1866–1957) SAE (1890)

Alexander Henderson Ogilvy-Ramsay (*AHO*) was educated at Wallace Hall Academy in the village of Closeburn in Dumfries-shire, north of Dumfries. He was born in 1866 as the son of a Church of Scotland minister, the Reverend Doctor David G. D. Ogilvy-Ramsay (ordained 1855), and Sarah Mary Maxwell (who died before 1881), and had two brothers, David and Maxwell Ogilvy-

Ramsay, and two sisters. The Reverend Ogilvy-Ramsay was born in Alyth in Perthshire and had a brother-in-law, James A Scott, a landed proprietor and farmer of 700 acres with 13 workers at St Andrews in Fife. The Ogilvy-Ramsay siblings were born in Kirriemuir in Angus. David Ogilvy-Ramsay died in 1925 of a broken skull. He was unmarried and had been the Registrar of Births in Dumfries. There is no further record of Maxwell Ogilvy-Ramsay. *AHO*'s father was the son of the Reverend William Ramsay, the Church of Scotland minister at Guthrie in Angus-shire (ordained 1844), and Mary Nicol, and held ministries at Kirriemuir and then Closeburn. *AHO*'s mother's parents were James Maxwell, a Doctor of Medicine, and Ann Gilmour.

AHO was apprenticed to one of the founders of the SAE, Alexander Thomas Niven, and father of John Ballantine Niven (above). He was admitted to the SAE in 1890 and then worked for CAs Moncrieff & Horsburgh in Edinburgh for three years. In 1894, he was resident in Portland, Oregon in the US and, one year later, was working for a lawyer, E. H. Dickson, in Waco, Texas, 90 miles south of Dallas. It is probable that these work locations were connected to *AHO*'s earlier employment with Alexander Thomas Niven and Moncrieff & Horsburgh who may have had property clients in Portland and Texas. The 1880s and 1890s were periods in which there were numerous investment syndicates and companies formed in Scotland to provide mortgage loans in the US. *AHO*'s job in Waco was as a negotiator of mortgage loans and, in 1905, he became area manager for the Waco Loan & Trust Company. He remained in this position for the next twenty-five years until retiring back to Scotland at Thornhill in the county of Dumfries. This is the village next to Closeburn where he was brought up as a boy. He died there in 1957 and an obituary appeared in *The Accountant's Magazine* of April 1957. He was never a member of any American public accountancy body and does not appear to have married.

PARKER, Angus McColl (1881–1938)   IAAG (1906)

Andrew Parker, a master cabinet maker, and Mary McColl, a vest maker, had a son born in Glasgow in 1881. His name was Angus McColl Parker (*AMP*) and he had a brother James. Andrew Parker was from the small and remote village of Sorbie in Wigtonshire. His parents were James Parker, a farm labourer, and Jane Milroy. His wife's parents were Angus McColl, a farm labourer, and Catherine Forrest. Both grandparents were from Wigtonshire. An uncle, Alexander Parker, was a labourer in a saw mill at Sorbie.

Nothing is known of *AMP*'s education. He was apprenticed to Thomson, Jackson, Gourlay & Taylor CAs of Glasgow. Following his apprenticeship in 1903, he worked as a cashier for A. Ferguson and J. J. Brown, Writers (lawyers) in Glasgow. In 1904, his address was Westwood Farm in Ontario in Canada and he joined the IAAG in 1906. A year later, the address changed to Andrew Parker & Sons in Ontario which suggests that a family relative had a business in Canada. However, in 1908, *AMP* was employed by Canadian CAs F. H. McPherson & Company in Detroit and, from 1909 to 1912, by John Mackay & Company in

Toronto. A year later, his employer was BWGC in New York. This was followed in 1914 by employment with MMC in Toronto that lasted until 1927 when *AMP* was appointed as the Accountant at Toronto General Hospital. Three years later, he was working in the audit department of the City of Toronto. He died there in 1938.

PATE, William (1867–1928)   IAAG (1912)

William Pate (*WP*) was a member of an extensive farming family in several Scottish counties. The family origins were at the cotton manufacturing, coal mining, and farming town of Lesmahagow south of Glasgow in Lanarkshire (population 8,700 in 1871), but Pates also farmed in Fife and Midlothian. The earliest recorded Pate (Pait) was Thomas Pait who was born in 1728 at Townhead in Lesmahagow and married Isobel Meikle in 1756. His parents were Thomas Pait and Margaret Donald. Meikles and Donalds were also Lesmahagow farmers. *WP* was born at his grandfather's farm at Lesmahagow in 1867. His father was Thomas Pate and his mother was Marion McGowan, the only child of William McGowan and Mary Torrance. The McGowans were Lesmahagow farmers and *WP*'s uncles, John and Thomas McGowan, were farming 150 acres there during his early life. There were several McGowan farms of similar size. *WP* had one brother, Robert Pate, who became a farmer, and two sisters. The Pate farm comprised 225 acres and employed five individuals when managed by Thomas Pate, *WP*'s grandfather. Great uncle Robert Pate was a farmer of 136 acres in the village of Glencorse near Edinburgh, and uncle Robert Pate farmed more than 200 acres at Lesmahagow. *WP*'s father, Thomas Pate, became a farmer near Newburgh in Fife and was married there to his second wife Jessie Meikle.

WP was educated in Lesmahagow and then Newburgh and apprenticed to CAs MIC in Dundee across the River Tay. He was admitted to the IAAG in 1912 and became a CPA in Ohio in the same year. This was the time when he worked for his Dundee firm in its office in New York. In 1914, however, he was employed by a small firm in New York for a year before transferring to PWC as a contract staff member. He moved with this firm to Chicago in 1917 and joined the AIA in 1916. *WP* joined the US Navy in 1917 and served in it for a year before founding his own practise in New York in 1918. This lasted until 1920 when he became a partner in the immigrant CA firm of David Elder & Company in New York. Four years later, he became the Treasurer and a director of the Kerr Steamship Company in New York. This company remains in operation at Chesapeake in Virginia as part of K Line America. In 1928, while on holiday in Scotland with his wife Louise Hall, *WP* died of a heart attack on his father's farm at Newburgh in Fife. An obituary was published in the November 1928 issue of *The Accountant's Magazine*.

PHILP, Andrew Campbell (1876–1947)   IAAG (1904)

Andrew Campbell Philp (*ACP*) was born in the seaside village of Saltcoats north of Irvine in Ayrshire in 1876. He was the son of the Reverend George

Philp (ordained 1864), the United Presbyterian minister at East Church in Saltcoats, and Annie Campbell. George Philp was one of seven children of John Philp, a farmer in the farming village of Ballingry near Loch Leven in Fife, and Ellen Birrell, and his brothers had varied occupations. Thomas Philp was a labourer in Abbotsford in Fife and William Philp was a farmer of 63 acres in the village of Saline in the same county. His sister, Helen Philp, married a labourer. *ACP*'s maternal grandparents were Alexander Campbell, a farmer, and Jane Kirkwood from the port of Ardrossan in Ayrshire. He had two brothers, John Philp who also immigrated to the US as a CA, and George Philp, about whom nothing is known.

ACP was educated in Saltcoats and apprenticed to James Wyllie Guild, a leading CA in Glasgow. He was admitted to the IAAG in 1904 and worked for two years with CAs Grahams & Company. Then, in 1905, he immigrated to the US and worked for CAs MMC in New York until 1907. His next employer was the CA firm of BWGC in New York. He remained with this firm until 1909 when he returned to Scotland and his own practise in the towns of Dunfermline and Kirkcaldy in Fife. By 1920, the firm had expanded and was titled Philp, Dalgleish & Murray in Dunfermline. This appears to have been a short-term partnership founded in 1919 with two Edinburgh CAs, John Erskine Dalgleish (SAE 1908) and Adam George Murray (SAE 1919) who practised as Dalgleish & Murray in Edinburgh from 1919 to 1949. Both Dalgleish and Murray were Editors of *The Accountant's Magazine* and leading lecturers in accounting. By 1920, *ACP*'s firm title had reverted to A. C. Philp & Company.

ACP died in Dunfermline in 1947 of heart problems. He had been a member of Dunfermline Town Council, a Baillie, Secretary of the West of Fife Agricultural Society, auditor of the burghs of Alloa and Perth, and associated with the Dunfermline District Savings Bank and the Dunfermline Building Society. He was Treasurer of Erskine Church in Dunfermline for many years and served on the Presbytery of Dunfermline and Kinross. An obituary appeared in *The Accountant's Magazine* of December 1947.

PHILP, John (1875–1947)   IAAG (1910)

John Philp (*JP*) was the elder brother of Alexander Campbell Philp and was born in Saltcoats in Ayrshire in 1875. He was educated in Saltcoats and apprenticed to Glasgow CAs Finlay, Kidston & Goff. He joined the IAAG in 1910, at which time he immigrated to Rhode Island in New York. Nothing is known of his employment until 1914 when he started to work on a casual basis for CAs PWC. This continued until 1920 when his employer became the Consolidated Pneumatic Tool Company in London. This was and remains a subsidiary company of the Chicago Pneumatic Tool Company and suggests that *JP* was associated with the latter during his residence in the US. The Chicago Pneumatic Tool Company is currently part of the Swedish industrial power tool group, Atlas Copco AB. It is not known whether *JP* served in the forces during the First World War. However, in 1925, he was a director and Secretary of the Consolidated

Pneumatic Power Tool Company. He retired in 1943 and died in 1947. He was married and had a son. His obituary appeared in the August 1947 issue of *The Accountant's Magazine*.

PIRIE, John (1873–1964)   IAAG (1909)

The family of John Pirie (*JP*) originated in the farming and fishing communities of Ross & Cromarty and the Shetland Islands. His parents were John Pirie, a physician and surgeon in the ship building town of Govan in Glasgow, and Jane Harvey. John Pirie senior was from Ross & Cromarty and the son of John Pirie, a land factor and farmer, and Mary McLellan. He was a Doctor of Medicine (1851) from the University of Aberdeen, a Licenciate of the Royal College of Surgeons of Edinburgh (1851), and a Fellow of and Examiner in Arts for the Faculty of Physicians of Glasgow. He had previously been a surgeon in Campbelltown, Argyleshire (including its prison) in the 1860s. Jane Harvey was his second wife and the daughter of Robert Harvey, a surgeon, and Janette Kirkpatrick. *JP* was born in Govan in 1873 and had four brothers and two sisters. Robert Harvey Pirie, Master of Arts and Bachelor of Laws, was a Glasgow Solicitor. George Pirie was a student at university who died young, as did Archibald A. Harvey Pirie.

JP was educated in Glasgow, graduated with a Bachelor of Laws degree from the University of Glasgow, and initially trained as a stockbroker. However, he entered a CA apprenticeship with Davidson & Workman, Davidson, Workman & Gilchrist, and Wilson & Nelson in Glasgow before admission to the IAAG in 1909. He immediately immigrated to the US and, a year later, was a partner in Mellis Pirie & Company in Minneapolis in Minnesota. His partner was fellow immigrant CA Thomas Crombie Mellis from Aberdeen. The partnership lasted until 1923 when *JP* was appointed as assistant Secretary and Treasurer of the Purity Bakeries Corporation in, first, St Paul in Minnesota and then in Chicago. He was promoted to Secretary in 1929. The company has been part of American Bakeries of New York from 1925 to the present day. *JP* was living at Evanston in Illinois by 1930 with a wife from Minnesota and a daughter. In the 1930 Census, he is recorded as having been born in Scotland in 1886 instead of 1873. Assuming birth was in 1886, he was 18 years older than his wife. He retired from American Bakeries in 1951 and died at the Homestead Hotel in Evanston in 1964. An obituary appeared in the May 1964 issue of *The Accountant's Magazine*.

POOLE, Joseph (1889–1935)   IAAG (1913)

Born in Kelvin in Glasgow in 1889, Joseph Poole (*JP*) was the son of Joseph Molleson Poole, a watchmaker from the fishing town of Arbroath in Angus-shire, and Christina Taylor, a domestic servant. His grandparents were Robert Poole, a flax dresser in Arbroath, and Isabella Morrison, and John Taylor, a Glasgow coal manager, and Mary Kirkland. An uncle, James Poole, was a soft leather cutter in

Arbroath. Prior to his marriage, *JP*'s father was employed at the county town of Alloa in Clackmannanshire (population 1,300 in 1881) and boarded with John Breingan, a carrier there. This name is contained in the title of a company in which *JP* later worked in the US.

JP was apprenticed to CAs McAuslin & Tait and Kidson, Goff & Findlay in Glasgow. He joined the IAAG in 1913 and immediately left to work for CAs MMC in Chicago. This employment lasted for a year before he worked for the Breingan Seaman Company in Chicago. This company was a wholesale paper firm and appears to have been his employer until 1935 when he died in Chicago. He was never a member of an American public accountancy body. In 1930, he was living in Evanston in a property valued at $20,000 ($224,000 in 2004 terms) with his wife from Wisconsin and two sons.

PRINGLE, William Black (1872–1968)   IAAG (1912)

William Black Pringle (*WBP*) was born in the Gorbals district of Glasgow in 1872. His father, William Pringle, was a tinsmith who later became a boiler inspector in Glasgow. He originated from the university and golf town of St Andrews in Fife and was the son of John Pringle, a private in the 60th Regiment of Foot, and Janet Mackay. *WBP*'s mother was Mary Ann Black, a factory worker and daughter of John Black, a tailor, and Helen Hume. He had three sisters and two brothers, including James Pringle, a Glasgow office boy. Despite his birth in Glasgow, he appears to have been educated in Dundee and was apprenticed there to CA James Murdoch of A. Tosh & Son. He joined the IAAG in 1912 and worked for his apprenticeship masters in Dundee until 1914 when he immigrated to the US. He was employed in New York by CAs TNC until 1917 when he returned to Dundee and founded the firm of Pringle & Watt. He remained its senior partner until his death in 1968 which was reported in *The Accountant's Magazine* of March 1968.

PRITCHARD, Robert Todd (1887–1951)   IAAG (1910)

Thomas Cuthbertson Pritchard was a CA (IAAG 1891) and partner (1899–1918) with the Glasgow firm of CAs D. & A. Cuthbertson & Provan. He was also the father of Richard Todd Pritchard (*RTP*) who was born in Glasgow in 1887. His mother, Thomas Pritchard's second wife, was Margaret Lang Leithead, a saleswoman in her father Thomas Leithead's umbrella manufacturing business that employed 13 individuals in Glasgow. Her mother was Ann Lang. The Leitheads appear to have originated from the farming and market town of Melrose in Roxburghshire and to have been farmers there. *RTP*'s paternal grandparents were Robert Pritchard, a muslin manufacturer, and Agnes Todd. He had a brother who was a Glasgow music teacher and church organist.

RTP was apprenticed to the Glasgow firm of CAs Kerr, Anderson & McLeod and admitted to the IAAG in 1910. A year later, he was employed by CAs AYC in Chicago. In 1917, he opened his own public practise at Riverside in Illinois and remained there until 1930 when it relocated to Chicago. His home at Riverside in 1930 was valued at $15,000 ($168,000 in 2004 terms) and he had a German-born wife and two daughters. By 1935, he was a member of the AIA and by 1951 the practise was named Pritchard & Rasmussen. This was the year of his death in Chicago.

RENNIE, Thomas (1885–1954)   SAA (1912)

Born in 1885 in the fishing town of Arbroath in Angus-shire (population 22,000 in 1881), Thomas Rennie (*TR*) was the son of Thomas Rennie, a wood finisher, and Jessie Liddel. His paternal grandfather was Thomas Rennie, an Arbroath fish dealer married to Mary Morrison. His maternal grandparents were Peter Liddel, a cooper, and Mary McIntosh. An aunt, Catherine Rennie, was a fish dealer in Arbroath. In Forfar, his uncle, David Liddel, was a cabinet maker who employed his wife as a saleswoman. Another uncle, Grindlay Liddel, was a picture frame maker employing two people in Dundee.

Following school in Arbroath, *TR* moved in 1905 to Aberdeen and a CA apprenticeship with James Meston & Company (one of the founding SAA firms in 1867). He finished his contract in 1910 and was admitted to the SAA in 1912. He immigrated to Chicago and worked for CAs MMC in this year. By 1914, his address was at Chevy Chase in Washington, followed by an address in Aberdeen in 1915. Two years later, he was working with F. W. Barker & Company in Singapore and, by 1923, with the Anglo-Persian Oil Company in Persia (a company that was later renamed British Petroleum). The latter employment lasted until 1927 when he set up practise on his own in Aberdeen as T. Rennie & Son. This suggests he was married and had a son. The practise continued until his death in 1954 (with an obituary in the July 1954 issue of *The Accountant's Magazine*).

RETTIE, Henry Blyth (1877–1934)   SAE (1902)

The family of Henry Blyth Rettie (*HBR*) came from Aberdeen. His father was Middleton Rettie who was born in Aberdeen, educated at Aberdeen Grammar School, and admitted to the Faculty of Advocates in 1855. He was appointed a King's Counsel in 1904 and married Isabella Kerr, thus acquiring the estate of Dunearn in Fife. Middleton Rettie received an honorary doctorate from the University of Aberdeen and was Editor of *Law Reports* from 1865. He wrote with others *Cases Decided in the Court of Session 1821–2* (1822 and 1824). *HBR*'s mother was the daughter of John Kerr, an engineer and landowner from Dundee. He had four brothers and a sister. William John Kerr Rettie was educated at Edinburgh Institution and became a Lieutenant-Colonel in the Royal Field Artillery who served in France and Gallipoli during the First World War and was awarded the Distinguished Service Order. Theodore Rettie was also educated at Edinburgh Institution and became an engineer who received a Doctorate of Science. Archibald C. Rettie died young. Norman Rettie was educated at the

Edinburgh Academy prior to immigrating to farm sheep in New Zealand and plant tea in Ceylon, where he died in 1902. *WBR*'s grandfather, William Rettie, was a jeweller in Aberdeen employing four people. He was also the Secretary and Treasurer of the East Free Church of Scotland, Auditor of the Aberdeen Bible Society, and husband of Ann Campbell. He had four unmarried daughters, one daughter who married a minister, and one who married a bank accountant David Easton. *WBR*'s uncle, James Rettie, was a jeweller and goldsmith in Aberdeen employing nine individuals.

WBR was born in Edinburgh in 1877, educated at the Edinburgh Academy from 1889 to 1895, and Dux of the school in 1894. He was apprenticed to Edinburgh CAs Lindsay Jamieson & Haldane and admitted to the SAE in 1902. He then became the Cashier of the General Accident Assurance Company formed in 1885 in Perth. He left Edinburgh in 1905 to represent that company in the US and entered in 1906. By 1907, however, he was working for CAs DDGC in New York. He remained with this firm for less than three years before moving to TNC in Chicago. This job did not last long. In the 1910 US Census, he is recorded as an accountant with a brokerage firm, single, and boarding in Chicago. By 1912, he was employed by another public accountancy firm in Chicago LBC. He appears to have returned to Scotland for a short time in the early 1920s. He served in the US military during the First World War and had returned to New York by 1928 to work for BWGC. He transferred with this firm to its office in Texas in 1930. Also in that year, he was lodging at Hot Springs in Arizona. He died unmarried at New Gulf in Texas in 1934. He was never a partner in any of his employers and did not join any American accountancy body despite working as an auditor throughout his career in the US. An obituary appeared in *The Accountant's Magazine* of June 1934.

RITCHIE, Alfred Alexander (1880–1964)   IAAG (1905)

Alfred Alexander Ritchie (*AAR*) was born in Dundee in 1880 as the second child of George Ritchie, a wholesale grocer from the county town of Forfar (population 13,000 in 1881) who employed four men in Dundee, and Agnes Ritchie from Dundee. He had a brother William. His paternal grandfather was Alexander Ritchie, a quarry worker in Forfar. Great grandfather George Ritchie was a mason's labourer in Forfar. An uncle, John Ritchie, was a master mason in Forfar employing seven men. His son and *AAR*'s cousin, Peter, worked as a grocer's assistant for George Ritchie *AAR* was apprenticed to CAs Mackay & Ness (later MIC) in Dundee, joined the IAAG in 1905, and immigrated to New York and BWGC in 1906. He rapidly progressed and was appointed as a partner in 1908, the year in which he became a CPA in Ohio. *AAR* practised on his own as a CA in New Jersey and resided there in 1910 with a wife from Scotland and a Scottish maid. In 1914, he joined the AAPA and, in 1916, the AIA. He was admitted to the NYSSCPA in 1931. Retirement came in 1952 at the Hotel Suburban at East Orange in New Jersey. *AAR* died in 1964 and an obituary appeared in the June 1964 issue of *The Accountant's Magazine*.

RITCHIE, Robert Bowes (1886–1956)   SAE (1910)

Robert Bowes Ritchie (*RBR*) was born in 1886 in the farming village of Creich in north-east Fife. He was the son of the Church of Scotland minister at Creich, the Reverend John Ritchie, Master of Arts, from Longforgen in Perthshire (ordained 1875). John Ritchie was the son of the Longforgen minister (ordained 1838), William Ritchie, Doctor of Divinity, and Margaret Bowes. William Ritchie was the son of a shoemaker and crofter, and had been a minister in Edinburgh from 1836 to 1843. *RBR*'s mother was Andrewina Bell Clark, a daughter of Andrew Clark, a Fife farmer, and Christine Carstairs. He had three brothers and three sisters. William Andrew, John, and Frederick John Ritchie died at Creich as teenagers. *RBR* was educated at Bell Baxter School in Cupar in Fife. He was then apprenticed to CA Frederick Walter Carter (SAE 1868 and the son of an SAE founder) of Carter, Greig & Company in Edinburgh and admitted to the SAE in 1910. He appears to have been unemployed since that date and resided at his father's manse until 1913 when he immigrated to the US.

RBR was employed by CAs MMC in New York until 1922 when he worked for George E. Merrill & Company in Salt Lake City, Utah. This remained his employment address until 1935 when he started to work for the Western Savings & Loan Company in Salt Lake City. He appears to have been the company's Secretary and Treasurer for some years before taking a similar position with a lumber company. He died in 1956. The company exists today as the Crossland Mortgage Company in Salt Lake City. His home in Utah in 1930 was valued at $7,000 ($78,000 in 2004 terms) and he had a wife from Ohio and a son and daughter. *RBR* was a member of the AIA and a CPA of Utah. His obituary appeared in *The Accountant's Magazine* of June 1956.

ROBERTSON, David Binny (1877–1953)   IAAG (1903)

David Binny Robertson (*DBR*) was born in Dundee in 1877 to William Morrison Robertson, a jute merchant of Dundee, and Agnes Laing Binny from Forfar. His brother was William Binny Robertson, an insurance manager in Toronto in Canada, who married Isabella Lennox before dying of a lung abscess while staying with his father on a family visit. His sister, Barbara Robertson, was unmarried. Grandparents were Alexander Robertson, a schoolmaster in Dundee, and Ann Morrison, and David and Agnes Binny from the farming village of Tannadice near Forfar who were cattle dealers. A Binny uncle, David, was a bank agent and a great uncle, James Binny, was a life insurance collector in Forfar and married to Binnie W. Binny. Their children included three jute weavers and a steam loom mechanic.

DBR was educated in Dundee and apprenticed to CA James Drummond of Honeyman & Drummond in Glasgow. He was admitted to the IAAG in 1903 and worked as an audit clerk in Glasgow for Alfred Tongue & Company. In 1905, he immigrated to New York and worked for CAs BWGC until 1909 when he moved to Montreal in Canada and practised there on his own. Three years later, he became a partner in the firm of CAs MacIntosh, Cole & Robertson in Montreal. The partnership lasted until his retirement in 1948. *DBR* died there in 1953 and an obituary appeared in the June 1953 issue of *The Accountant's Magazine*.

ROBERTSON, James Roderick (1845–1901)   UQ

James Roderick Robertson (*JRR*) was born in Scotland in 1845 but no details of his birth or family can be discovered. He immigrated to the US in 1880 following an accountancy apprenticeship in Scotland and was a Fellow of the AAPA from 1886 until death in 1901, being at the organising meeting of the Association. He practised in New York from 1880 until his retirement in 1891 when he moved to Victoria in British Columbia. He then died from an accident in New York in 1901. A brief biography appears in N. E. Webster, *The American Association of Public Accountants: Its First Twenty Years 1886–1906* (American Institute of Accountants: New York, NY, 1954).

ROBERTSON, John Hussey (1870–1900)   SAE (1893)

John Hussey Robertson (*JHR*) was born in North Leith in 1870. His father, John William Robertson, was the captain of a fishing boat, and his mother was Charlotte Barron Hunter, a domestic servant from Aberdeen. His grandparents were Thomas Charles Robertson, a mason, and Catherine Youngson, and James Hunter, a fisherman, and Agnes Duncan. *JHR* had two brothers, Alexander and Francis Robertson, who died very young, and three sisters. He was educated at Mr Oliphant's School and George Watson's College in Edinburgh, and Morrison's Academy at Crieff in Perthshire. He was then apprenticed to Edinburgh CAs Moncrieff & Horsburgh and admitted to the SAE in 1893. He worked for Moncrieff & Horsburgh and was in partnership in Edinburgh with CA Alexander A. Gordon (SAE 1889), a Member of the Victorian Order, until 1896 when he left to work in San Pablo in Brazil. He remained there until 1900 when he immigrated to New York, worked as a non-contract member of staff for PWC, and then formed the firm of MRC with an English migrant accountant, Frederick William Menzies, who was a member of the SIAA. He died in New York in the same year and an obituary was published in the October 1900 issue of *The Accountant's Magazine*. He does not appear to have married.

ROBERTSON, Percy Douglas Macbeth (1883–1913)   SAE (1911)

Andrew Macbeth Robertson was a commercial traveller from the fishing town of Lerwick in Shetland. He was originally a watchmaker and the son of William Robertson, a general merchant in Lerwick, and Jane McBeth. He and his wife, Jane Fairbairn, from Glasgow (a daughter of Robert Fairbairn, wine merchant, and Elizabeth Robertson) had five sons and four daughters. They were living in Dumfries (population 17,000 in 1881) in 1883 when Percy Douglas Macbeth Robertson (*PDMR*) was born. *PDMR* was educated at Dumfries Academy before proceeding to Edinburgh to start an accountancy career. His brothers were William Macbeth Robertson (who trained but did not qualify as a lawyer), Victor J. Macbeth Robertson (who became a banker), and Andrew Macbeth and Eric H. Macbeth Robertson about whom there is no information.

PDMR was trained by Edinburgh CA James Andrew Smith (SAE 1881) and joined the SAE in 1911. He left for the US almost immediately and was working with CAs TNC in New York in 1912. He died at Phoenix in Arizona in 1913, presumably working on a mining client of TNC. An obituary appeared in *The Accountant* of February 1914. He did not belong to an American public accountancy body and was unmarried.

ROLLO, David (1847–1914)   UQ

David Rollo (*DR*) was born in the county and market town of Perth (population 20,000) in 1847. His father was David Rollo, a master baker, son of John Rollo, a vintner, and Ann McNaughton of the village of Kinnoull in Perthshire, and husband of Margaret Greig. His brothers were John Rollo, a ship's joiner at Govan in Lanarkshire, and James Rollo, a messenger at arms in the High Court and a sheriff's officer at the Sheriff's Court in Perth. He had a sister, Ann Rollo. *DR* married Annie Tees from Glasgow and the couple had no children. His wife was the daughter of James Tees, a commercial traveller, and Ann Jack, granddaughter of Joseph Tees, a foreman cotton dyer, and niece of Hamilton Jack, a tobacco pipe manufacturer.

DR was educated at Perth Academy and apprenticed to local accountants James and Robert Morison from 1873 to 1877. James Morison was the father of one of the founders of the SAE in 1854, Peter Morison, and partnered his brother Robert in Perth. Robert Morison was also a stockbroker there. *DR* moved to Edinburgh in 1877 to work for the leading firm of CAs Lindsay, Jamieson & Haldane until 1881. He then worked for Edinburgh CAs A & A. Paterson until 1887. However, there is no record of *DR* having an indentured apprenticeship with the SAE or having sat any of its examinations. Instead, in the 1881 *Census*, he is described as a managing clerk with a firm of accountants and has a boarder, David Walker, who was an accountant's clerk from Perth. Walker did not become a CA.

The above details contradict *DR*'s biography in N. E. Webster, *The American Association of Public Accountants: Its First Twenty Years 1886–1906* (American Institute of Accountants: New York, NY, 1954). It states that he was an Edinburgh CA and a lawyer, having studied law at the University of Edinburgh and then been called to the bar. Trade directories for Edinburgh show that *DR* was a partner in the firm of Rollo & Stuart from 1888 to 1890 and practised on his own in London and then Manchester from 1890 to 1892. James J. Stuart was the son of an Edinburgh merchant, served a CA apprenticeship, but did not become a CA. In 1892, *DR* immigrated to the US and worked for a year with the New Jersey accountants Boaker & Chapman. Frank Broaker was an American public accountant from Millersburg in Pennsylvania who was reported as training with a "Scots" accountant, John Roundy, in the 1880s and becoming the first New York CPA in 1896 (Roundy was, in fact, an "expert accountant" in New Jersey and born in Massachusetts). His partner, Richard Marvin Chapman from New York, received the second certificate. Boaker was AAPA Secretary in 1892 and President in 1897. Chapman was AAPA Treasurer in 1892. *DR* was employed from 1892 to 1893 with the New York CAs BWGC. He became a Fellow of the AAPA in 1893. *DR* practised on his own in New York and New Jersey from 1894 to 1907 and became a New York CPA in 1896. He held several offices in public accountancy. From 1896, he was a Trustee of the AAPA, becoming its Vice-President in 1898 and President in 1899 when the membership stood at 87. He was also a member of the ASCPA from 1897. In 1907, *DR* left public accountancy and became the treasurer of a company in Philadelphia. He remained there until his death in 1914.

ROSE, James (1874–1953)   SAE (1906)

James Rose (*JR*) was born in the village of Rathen near Peterhead in Banffshire in 1874. His father, John Rose, was the schoolmaster there and was a native of Aberdeen. His paternal grandparents were John Rose, a master tailor in Aberdeen, and Jane Gavin. His mother, Jessie Thomson, was a domestic servant from Edinkillen in the county of Elgin, and the daughter of a painter and decorator, and Jane Lawson. Other relatives in Edinburgh were an uncle and railway guard, Alexander Rose, and a great uncle and colliery engine keeper, Alexander Thomson. *JR*'s brothers were John A. Rose and Charles G. Rose (about whom nothing is known), and he had one sister. He was educated at the public school at the village of Cultercullen west of Aberdeen in Aberdeenshire where his father was employed as the schoolmaster, and apprenticed to the Edinburgh CAs Romanes & Munro. He was admitted to the SAE in 1906 and immigrated at about the same time to work for TNC in New York.

JR remained with this firm until 1921 when he began to practise on his own at Clarks Summit in Pennsylvania. He had become an Ohio CPA in 1913. In 1925 he was a member of the AIA and the NYSSCPA. By this time, he was practicing as a CPA in Buffalo in the state of New York. He remained in practise on his own in Buffalo until his death there in 1953. He had an English wife and a son who was unemployed in 1930.

ROWBOTHAM, Geoffrey Guthrie (1884–1958)   IAAG (1908)

It was difficult to find information about the family of Geoffrey Guthrie Rowbotham (*GGR*) because of his birth in 1884 in India. His father, Daniel Hugh McIntosh Rowbotham, was a merchant there and originally came from Edinburgh where his father was David Booth Rowbotham, quartermaster sergeant of the 12th Regiment of Foot and husband of Catherine McIntosh. Daniel Rowbotham was married to Janet Jeffrey White, daughter of John White, a seaman, and Elizabeth McArthur. By 1891, at the age of seven, *GGR* was attending a small school in Glasgow for the children of parents in India. By 1901, he was residing in Glasgow with his mother Janet Jeffrey Rowbotham who was born in Glasgow, widowed, and a schoolteacher. He appears to have been an only child.

School in Glasgow was followed by a CA apprenticeship with McOmish & Arthur in Glasgow and admission to the IAAG in 1908. A year earlier, *GGR* had immigrated to Montreal in Canada and moved to CAs PWC in New York in 1908. He stayed there until 1917 when he moved back to Canada and the city of Toronto. From then until 1921, he was manager there for PWC and his clients included the Grand Transcontinental Railway. In 1921, he joined the NYSSCPA and worked in the New York office of PWC. Five years later, he became a partner and remained as such until 1940. He was a CPA in Louisiana, Ohio, and Wisconsin, and joined the AIA in 1932. In 1930, he was seconded to Chile to work with PWC clients in nitrate mining. *GGR* joined the PWC Executive Committee in 1935. He was a member of the AIA's Budget Committee (1932–3) and Committee on Cooperation with the Stock Exchange (1936–9). He died unmarried in 1958. An obituary was published in the December issue of *The Accountant's Magazine*. *GGR*' main claim to fame as a public accountant in the US was as the engagement partner involved in the Securities Exchange Commission (SEC) case of *McKesson & Robbins* in 1937. McKesson & Robbins Inc was a wholesale drug company in the US that, by 1937, had grown into one of the largest businesses of its type in the country. However, its senior executives were convicted fraudsters and created a Canadian subsidiary company that contributed one-half of McKesson's sales and profits. However, these were fictitious and the auditors failed to detect the fictional accounting entries in the company's records. *GGR* claimed his firm was using current audit methods. Following a critical report by the SEC in which *GGR* was described as complacent, the public accountancy profession in the US immediately changed its audit methods to include debtor confirmations and physical inspections of inventory. McKesson & Robbins survived as a company and today exists as a major public corporation, Foremost-McKesson.

SALVESEN, Edgar Christian (1884–1959)   IAAG (1907)

The Salvesen family originated from Tveden in Sor Undal in Norway, settled in Scotland in the first half of the nineteenth century, and was involved in timber, coal exporting, and shipping. Several family businesses evolved over several decades into the current Christian Salvesen international transportation group. Edgar Christian Salvesen (*ECS*) was descended from these early generations of Scottish Salvesens. His father was Henrik Emil Salvesen, a coal exporter, who was born in Norway and later became a shipbroker in Glasgow and husband of Louise Mathilde Wolff. *ECS* was born at the family home at the small village of Inverkip west of Greenock in Renfrewshire in 1884. He had two brothers and three sisters. Frank H. W. Salvesen was employed in the family business of shipping but no further information is available of his career or that of his brother Alfred Salvesen.

The Salvesen family origins can be traced to the birth of Ole Salvesen at Tveden in 1765. He was a farmer's son who trained as a glazier before starting a timber exporting business in Mandal. In 1810, this business was destroyed by a fire and Ole Salvesen moved to Christiansund and became a merchant and tobacco manufacturer. He returned to Mandal in 1824 and became a shipbroker. He had three sons including Thomas Salvesen who entered his father's business and married in 1811 Johanna Ross, daughter of Hans Ross. The couple had nine children including Hans Edward Ross Salvesen, a Doctor of Medicine, who married Marion Christine Nielsen. These were *ECS*'s paternal grandparents. His maternal grandparents were Carl Wolff, a wine merchant in Leith, and Mathilde Meusel.

There were numerous other Salvesen relations in Scotland who originated from the 1811 marriage of Thomas Salvesen and Johanne Ross of Sor Audenal in Vest Agder in Norway. Johan Theodore Salvesen was a great uncle who traded as a shipbroker in Germany before moving to Glasgow and then forming a business as a ship owner and timber merchant in Grangemouth on the Firth of Forth. He also formed a business partnership in Leith with his brother Salve Christian Frederick Salvesen who was married to Amelie Georgine Salome. Johan Theodore Salvesen had several children including Edward Theodore Salvesen, an Advocate and King's Counsel who became Sheriff of Berwick in 1901 and Solicitor General of Scotland in 1905. In 1922, he was admitted as a law Lord and member of the Privy Council. He wrote several books including *The Medico-Legal Aspect of Cremation* (1926), *The Futility of Local Option* (1930), and *Memoirs of Lord Salvesen* (1949). Theodore Emil Salvesen was also a ship owner in Edinburgh and the father of Noel Graham Salvesen who was Dux at the Edinburgh Academy in 1910 and 1911 and played rugby for the University of Oxford. He graduated as a Bachelor of Arts and was a Captain in the Royal Scots when injured in the same railway accident as his brother. Theodore Salvesen was educated at the Edinburgh Institution, President of the Edinburgh Institution Club, a director of the Commercial Bank of Scotland, Fellow of the Royal Society of Edinburgh, Consul to Finland in Edinburgh during the First World War, and a Lieutenant-Colonel in the City of Edinburgh Royal Artillery.

ECS had several cousins who were educated at Edinburgh Academy and served during the First World War. Charles Emil Salvesen was a stockbroker who served as a Major in the Royal Artillery in France. Christian Raymond Salvesen was a Lieutenant in the Royal Scots when he was killed in a railway accident at Gretna in Scotland. Eric Thomas Somervell Salvesen was killed in action in France as a Lieutenant in the Royal Scots. Harold Keith Salvesen was trained at the Royal Military College at Sandhurst and served as a Captain in Mesopotamia before joining a military mission to Siberia in 1919.

ECS was educated in Glasgow and apprenticed to Glasgow CA S. Easton Simmers. He was admitted to the IAAG in 1907 and immigrated to Calcutta in India to work for accountants McKinnon, Mackenzie & Company. He remained there for a year and entered the US in 1909. He quickly became the Secretary and Treasurer of the Minnesota Society of Certified Public Accountants (MNSCPA) in 1909 and a Minnesota CPA in 1910. By this time, he was employed by the immigrant Scottish CA firm of J. Gordon Steele & Company in Minneapolis. However, in 1912, he opened his own practise in Tampa in Florida and married Minnie Armour in Glasgow. She was the daughter of Robert Armour, an engineer, and Annie Wolf. The Florida practise does not appear to have worked out and *ECS* returned to Minneapolis to work for CAs TNC. In the same year, he became a member of the AAPA and joined the AIA in 1916. He was the resident manager of TNC in Minneapolis by 1917. Then, for three years, he was employed by PWC before working for the Longacre Engineering & Construction Company in New York. This company was responsible for building many skyscraper buildings in New York in the 1920s and remains in operation in that city. In 1933, *ECS* was practicing in New Jersey and continued in this capacity until his retirement in 1948 to Vermont. He wrote a 1914 paper in the *Journal of Accountancy* entitled "Advertising as an Asset on the Balance Sheet". He died in New York in 1959. His obituary was published in *The Accountant's Magazine* of April 1960. The Salvesen family history is contained in W. Vamplew, *Salvesen of Leith* (Scottish Academic Press: Edinburgh, 1975).

SANDERSON, Walter (1879–1961) SAE (1906)

The son of John Sanderson, a master joiner and builder in Edinburgh, and grandson of James Sanderson, also a joiner and builder, and Jacobina Blair, Walter Sanderson (*WS*) was born in Edinburgh in 1879. His mother was Helen Scott from Ladhope near Melrose in Roxburghshire where her father, Walter Scott, was a tailor and clothier and married to Alice Walker. *WS* had one brother, James Sanderson, a cabinet maker, and three sisters. The brothers were educated at Clarehall Academy in the Newington district of Edinburgh.

WS was apprenticed to Edinburgh CA W. G. Walker (SAE 1887) of Walker & White, and joined the SAE in 1906. He does not appear to have been employed between 1907 and 1909 when he immigrated to Chicago to work for CAs MMC. He remained in this employment for two years before moving to Kansas City in Missouri in 1911 to work for AYC. He remained with AYC until 1928 when he began to work for the firm of CPAs founded by Edinburgh CA Edward Fraser, Fraser, Dell & Company. It is not known if he became a partner but he retired from the firm in 1946. He was not a member of the AAPA or the AIA but was a CPA in Wisconsin. He died in Kansas City in 1961. He had a wife from Maine who was 15 years his junior.

SANGSTER, Andrew (1880–1965) SAE (1906)

Andrew Sangster (*AS*) was born in 1880 at Edinburgh to insurance clerk and inspector, Andrew Sangster. His paternal grandparents were Andrew Sangster, a gardener, and Margaret Innes. His mother was Margaret Cobban, a domestic servant from the county town of Elgin in Morayshire (population 7,000). She was the daughter of George Cobban, a horse dealer, and Elizabeth Forsyth, the former wife of Thomas Robb, a shipping superintendent. *AS* had one sister and an uncle, George Sangster, who was a commercial traveller in tea. He was educated at the public school in the district of Gorgie and later at James Gillespie's School. He then entered a CA apprenticeship with the Edinburgh firm of Tait & Elgin, joining the SAE in 1906. He remained with Tait & Elgin until 1912 when he immigrated to Chicago and employment with the CA firm of MMC. He remained in this position until 1915 when he transferred to Washington, District of Columbia – presumably to work with federal government departments. In 1926, *AS* founded his own practise in New York and continued with this until 1942, except for a period between 1936 and 1941 again in Washington. In 1942, he became Director of Accounting for the New York State Department of Public Service and held this position until his retirement in the early 1950s. The Department is now called the Public Service Commission and regulates all utilities in the State of New York. *AS* died in New York in 1965. There is no record of *AS* being a member of an American public accountancy body or of being married.

SANGSTER, John (1884–1962)   SAA (1910)

John Sangster (*JS*) was born in the western suburb of Summerhill in Aberdeen in 1884. He was the son of John Sangster, secretary and cashier of a shipping company in Aberdeen, and Georgina Cooper Jamieson, daughter of John Jamieson, a ship's master, and Mary Henry. The paternal grandparents were John Sangster, a shoemaker, and Isabella Singer. *JS* had two sisters. From 1896 to 1900, *JS* attended the Aberdeen Grammar School and was then apprenticed to CAs Whyte & Williamson of Aberdeen. He joined the SAA in 1910, having resided in Glasgow in 1908 and London in 1909. A year later, he was the manager of a firm of accountants, Stirling & Rankine, at Moose Jaw in Canada. In the same year, he relocated to New York and employment with CAs MMC in New York. He transferred to the Chicago office in 1913. He then enlisted as a private in the 196th Overseas Battalion of the Canadian forces. He remained on service until 1918. *JS*'s next employment appears to have been with CAs George A. Touche & Company at Calgary in Canada in 1926. By 1943, however, he was residing in Winnipeg in Manitoba. This remained his address until 1952 when he moved to East Croydon in Surrey. By 1962, he was living in Edinburgh. He died there in that year and an obituary appeared in *The Accountant's Magazine* of January 1963.

SCOBIE, John Crockert (1878–1944)   SAE (1902)

John Crockert Scobie (*JCS*) became a leading American practitioner in the first half of the twentieth century and was active in the affairs of the AIA. He was educated at George Heriot's School in Edinburgh. He was the son of a carpenter, George Scobie, from the farming village of Abernethy to the east of Perth in Perthshire. His paternal grandparents were William Scobie, a mason, and Isabella Colville. His mother was Martha Crockert from the village of Scoonie in the same county, a domestic servant and daughter of John Crockert, a ship's master, and

Elizabeth Gordon. *JCS* was born in 1878 and had a brother William and three sisters. His maternal grandmother was an annuitant living in the fishing village of Newburgh on the River Tay in Fife (the nearest village to Abernethy).

JCS's apprenticeship as a CA was served with the Edinburgh firm of Romanes & Aitchison. He joined the SAE in 1902 and appears to have worked for a short period in 1903 prior to immigrating to New York. There he worked for PWC and became a CPA in Illinois. He had been recruited by English CA Arthur Lowes Dickinson. *JCS* became a CPA in Pennsylvania in 1909 and New York pre 1916, and a member of the AAPA in 1910. Later, he was licenced in Michigan (1925) and Louisiana (1929). By 1910, he was working for PWC at Pittsburgh in Pennsylvania. In 1915, he transferred back to New York to a partnership in the firm. *JCS* became an AIA member in 1916 and was on its Board of Examiners from 1919 to 1922, chaired its By-Laws Committee in 1927–8, and was on the Committee on Publications from 1929 to 1935. In 1939, *JCS* was senior partner in PWC when it was investigated by the SEC following the sub-standard audit of McKesson & Robbins. He was largely responsible for managing improvements to the firm's audit procedures as a result of this case – particularly with respect to evaluating internal controls. *JCS* specialised in factory cost accounting and was Treasurer of a major American subsidiary of a Canadian arms manufacturer. He also produced his firm's manual on balance sheet audits that was also adopted by the AIA as a result of the approval of English CA migrant and PWC senior partner George Oliver May. May was the son of a Devon grocer and wine merchant who joined the ICAEW and PWC in London in 1897. A year later, he was sent to New York to assist in the development of the JCC and PWC arrangement. He became a PWC partner in 1902, senior partner in 1911, and one of the most influential American accountants in the 1930s as convener of the AIA Committee on the Development of Accounting Principles. He was also a prolific writer on accounting and auditing issues.

JCS was a freemason, member of the St Andrew's Society, Union League Club, City Midday, Blind Brook Country Club, Round Hill Club and Indian Harbour Yacht Club. He was also a trustee of the General Theological Seminary in New York and a vestryman at Christ Episcopal Church in Greenwich. He was married to a woman from Pennsylvania and had a daughter and two sons. His recreations included boxing as a younger man and golf, and he is reported as having a dry sense of humour coupled with stubbornness in his professional activities. He died in New York in 1944 and his obituary appeared in *The Accountant's Magazine* of November 1944. His career is covered in C. W. DeMond, *Price, Waterhouse & Company in America* (Comet Press: New York, NY, 1951), and D. G. Allen & K. McDermott, *Accounting for Success: a History of Price Waterhouse in America 1890–1990* (Harvard Business School Press: Boston, MA, 1993).

SIMMERS, John Alexander (1877–1963)   IAAG (1895)

John Alexander Simmers (*JAS*) was born in Dundee in 1877 to Adam Simmers, a master ironmonger from the village of Strathmartine on the outskirts of Dundee in Forfarshire, and Jessie Saunders from the farming village of Kirriemuir in Perthshire (near Forfar), a house servant. The Simmers were originally yarn bleachers at Strathmartine. Paternal grandparents were William Simmers, a master tailor, and Mary Alexander, and the maternal grandparents were David Saunders, a crofter, and Janet Keay. *JAS* has two sisters and three brothers, about whom nothing can be found. He was educated in Dundee and apprenticed to Glasgow CAs Abercrombie & Cadell. He joined the IAAG in 1895 and was a partner from 1896 to 1899 in Cadell & Simmers of Glasgow and Paisley. In 1900, he left for London and worked there as a secretary of a public company for three years before immigrating to Las Cruces in Mexico by 1904. He then moved in 1905 to El Paso in Texas. By 1914, *JAS* was resident in Los Angeles in California. It appears he was working for a small firm of accountants or on his own and, in 1917, joined the AIA. He became a CPA in California in 1923. In 1925, he was a partner in Simmers, Mills & Adsit in Los Angeles and, by 1934, was in practise on his own as John A. Simmers & Company. The firm expanded to Simmers, Davidson & Caves at Pasadena in California in 1955. Seven years later and at the age of 85, *JAS* retired. He died in Los Angeles in 1963. He had a wife who was French and 17 years his junior. The family home in Los Angeles in 1930 was valued at $45,000 ($503,000 in 2004 terms).

SKINNER, William Henry Kirk (1856–1927)   SAE (1881)

William Henry Kirk Skinner (*WHKS*) was the son of a well-known Edinburgh lawyer. He was born in 1856 in George Square in Edinburgh to William Skinner of Corra. The latter was the son of John Robert Skinner, a WS (1813) and Clerk to the Signet, and Ann Black, daughter of William Black, a Writer (lawyer), of the market town of Brechin in Forfarshire. John Skinner was the son of Colonel James Skinner, an Edinburgh Writer. William Skinner's wife was Johann Farish Kirk, the only daughter of a landed gentleman in Kirkudbrightshire, Robert Kirk of Drumstinchnell. William Skinner was educated at Edinburgh Academy, qualified as a WS (1848), and became the Town Clerk of Edinburgh from 1874 to 1895. He was also Moderator of the High Constables of Edinburgh from 1861 to 1863 and a Fellow of the Royal Society of Edinburgh (1876). He authored *Edinburgh Municipal and Police Act 1879* (1879 and 1883). *WHKS*'s uncle, Hercules Skinner, was educated at Edinburgh Academy and a Captain with the 14th Bengal Irregular Cavalry of the Honorable East India Company Service (1852). Uncle David Skinner was educated at Edinburgh Academy and cannot be traced. *WHKS* had three brothers. Robert Riddell Kirk Skinner was educated at Edinburgh Academy and the Universities of Cambridge and Edinburgh before developing a career as a rancher in Kansas in the US. Percy Alexander Warren Skinner was educated at Edinburgh Academy and graduated as a Master of Arts from the University of Cambridge before ordination in the Church of England as a Curate in Carlisle (1908) and then Chester (1911). Charles Edward Kirk Skinner became a manager with the trading firm of Jardine, Skinner & Company at Bombay in the North West Province of India.

A sister, Jane Ann Kirk Skinner, married Thomas Wilson of Hill of Beath, a Fife landowner.

WHKS was apprenticed to Edinburgh CA Adam Gillies Smith (SAE 1855) and became a member of the SAE in 1881. Smith was one of the earliest Edinburgh CAs – educated in Aberdeen, trained in Edinburgh, and practicing in Glasgow for a short period. He was Manager of the North British & Mercantile Insurance Company at the time of *WHKS*'s apprenticeship and had retired from full-time public accountancy practise in 1880. *WHKS* remained with Smith until 1883 when he immigrated to Kansas to join his brother as a rancher. In 1886, he was removed from the SAE membership when he refused to pay the dues that were outstanding. He appears to have returned to Scotland because there are two later marriages recorded. The first in 1902 was to Elizabeth Miller, a china saleswoman from Partick in Glasgow and the daughter of Thomas Miller, a china merchant there, and Elizabeth Dewar. His occupation at that time was a clerk in the Town Clerk's office in Glasgow. In 1904, his second marriage was to Jessie McLean McLennan, the daughter of Grant McLennan, an auctioneer, and Mary Quinn. *WHKS* died of heart disease in Glasgow in 1927. His occupation was described as commercial clerk and he does not appear to have had any children.

SMITH, Arthur John (1883–1941)   IAAG (1907)

Arthur John Smith (*AJS*) was born in Dundee in 1883. His father, William Clark Smith, was variously described as a mercantile accountant and jute manufacturer's clerk, and became the company Secretary for a firm of jute spinners and manufacturers in Dundee. This was possibly a family business as *AJS*'s grandfather was James Smith, a jute manufacturer. His mother was Letitia Browne from Ireland whose father was John Browne, a farmer, and he had three brothers, Robert Browne Smith, William Smith, and Edwin Smith, and two sisters. His uncle James Smith was an optician in Dundee.

Following school in Dundee, *AJS* was apprenticed to the local firm of CAs MIC and remained employed by them for a further two years. He was admitted to the IAAG in 1907 and transferred to his firm's New York office in 1908. He became an Ohio CPA in the same year and an Arizona equivalent in 1920. By this time, he was employed by the Dundee-Arizona Copper Company in Phoenix in Arizona. In 1934, his employer was the Belmont Copper Mining Company and the Queen Creek Copper Company in Phoenix for which he was Secretary and Treasurer. He retired in 1940 and died in Phoenix in 1941. His obituary in the August 1942 issue of *The Accountant's Magazine* stated that he was a gifted musician and organist of the Trinity Episcopal Cathedral in Phoenix. He had been the organist at St Luke's Parish Church in Dundee at the age of 15. His wife was originally from Massachusetts and there was a daughter. The family home in 1930 was valued at $10,000. Environmentalists in Arizona are currently protesting proposed mining by a British company, Rio Tinto Zinc, of copper in areas previously abandoned by the companies for which *AJS* worked.

SPENCE, Alexander Pyott (1872–1931)   IAAG (1897)

Another son of Dundee immigrated to the US in 1899. Alexander Pyott Spence (*APS*) was born in Dundee in 1872. He was the son of George Clark Spence of Dundee, a mercantile clerk, and later a linen merchant and accountant, and Jessie Williamson. His paternal grandparents were Alexander Spence, a Dundee house factor (real estate agent), and Mary Pyott who came from England. The other grandparents were Alexander Williamson, a master builder in Aberdeen, and Isabella Hutton. He had one brother, George William Spence, a mercantile clerk, and four sisters. School at Dundee was followed by a CA apprenticeship with David Myles in Dundee. He joined the IAAG in 1897 and was employed by Dundee CAs Moody, Stuart & Robertson from 1893 to 1899 when he left for New York. His employer there was the firm of English CAs BWGC.

By 1903, *APS* was a partner in BWGC, an Illinois CPA (1903), and member of the IAPA and AAPA (1905). However, in 1905, his business address in New York changed to that of the immigrant accountants Cuthbert & Menzies. Then, a year later and until 1920, he is recorded as a partner in the London firm of Lever, Anyon & Spence. Samuel Lever was an English CA who immigrated to New York in 1892 and was a partner in BWGC in New York and London from 1898 to 1922. He was knighted in 1917 and became a baronet in 1920 for his UK government work in Australia and Canada. James Thornley Anyon was also an English CA (ICAEW 1886) and immigrant, senior partner with BWGC in the US from 1890 to 1916, and a founder of the AAPA in 1886 (calling its first meeting and proposing its name).

It must be assumed that *APS* continued to be a partner in BWGC in the US as his recorded addresses were in New York and London. He became a member of the AIA in 1916 and was a member of its Interest & Cost Committee in 1917. He became senior partner in BWGC in 1929 but retired in 1930 due to ill health. He visited his mother in Dundee in that year. His wife was from Scotland and 16 years younger, and they had three sons, two daughters and two servants in 1930 when the New Jersey home was valued at $75,000 ($839,000 in 2004 terms). *APS* died in New York in 1931.

STEELE, John Gordon Anderson (1880–1932)   IAAG (1905)

John Gordon Anderson Steele (*JGAS*) also came from Dundee. He was born there in 1880 to master draper and warehouseman James Steele, the son of John Steele (a woollen manufacturer and husband of Mary Anderson), and Euphemia Ogilvie, the daughter of Thomas Ogilvie (an Aberdeen hat manufacturer from Edinburgh and husband of Margaret Finlayson from Aberdeen). His uncle, also Thomas Ogilvie, was a hat manufacturer's assistant.

Following school in Dundee, *JGAS* was apprenticed to CAs Hodge & Smith in Glasgow and joined the IAAG in 1905. By this time, he had been a contract staff member of CAs PWC for two years in New York, San Francisco, Winnipeg and Chicago. Then, in 1905, he moved to CAs MMC in St Louis and, in 1906, Minneapolis. In 1909, he became a Minnesota CPA and, two years later, left MMC to form his own firm in Minneapolis as J. Gordon Steele & Company. Membership of the AAPA followed in 1912. *JGAS* ceased his practise in 1914 when he rejoined PWC as a contract staff member. He quickly became Comptroller-General of Manitoba in Canada in 1915. However, he continued his public accountancy career at a later date with memberships expanded to include the AIA in 1921, and CPA licences in Arizona (1923), Missouri (1929), and Wisconsin (1923). At some time prior to 1921 he joined the partnership of AYC at Milwaukee in Wisconsin and was responsible with English accountant Frederick George Colley for an investigation of the Union Oil Company of Delaware prior to its acquisition in 1922 by the Royal Dutch Shell Company. Colley was born in Crewe in Cheshire and a railway engineer before becoming private secretary to Nicholas Waterhouse, one of the founders of PWC in London. In 1892, he immigrated to the US to join JCC in New York. Following experience as an industrial accountant, Colley was a partner with TNC (1913) and AYC (1919). He specialised in accounting systems. *JGAS* transferred to the Kansas City office of AYC in 1929 and became a Vice-President of the MSCPA in 1932. He was a member of the AIA Committee on Meetings in 1931. He died in Kansas City in 1932. He is remembered in T. G. Higgins, *Thomas G Higgins, CPA: An Autobiography* (Comet Press: New York, NY, 1965) as burly, boisterous and a chain smoker. His wife was from Minnesota and he had one son.

STEVEN, James Angus (1876–1966)   IAAG (1903)

James Angus Steven (*JAS*) was born in the district of Kelvin in Glasgow in 1876. His father, Roderick Steven, was an engine fitter and mechanical engineer who originated from Inverness. Roderick Steven was the son of James Steven, a carter, and Ann Chisholm, and his brother was also a carter in Inverness. A cousin was a plasterer there. *JAS*'s mother was Marjory Fraser from Inverness, a domestic servant and daughter of John Fraser, a handloom weaver, and Catherine Fraser. He had two sisters and two brothers, both of whom became medical practitioners. John Fraser Steven was an army surgeon who died in 1919 at Gartnavel Royal Lunatic Asylum of a general paralysis that had lasted since 1917 and was presumably wounded during the First World War. His widow, Gladys Fraser, was a cousin. Roderick Alexander Steven was a medical practitioner in Glasgow who died aged 48 from chronic bronchitis. His widow was Jane White.

JAS was educated in Glasgow, apprenticed to CAs J. & G. Moffatt and joined the IAAG in 1903. He was employed by the Moffatts from 1890 to 1902 and there is no information regarding his employment until 1906 when he appears in Atlanta in Georgia as a contract staff member of PWC. He remained in that position until 1918, moving to New York in 1907 and Chicago in 1908. In 1910, he became a CPA in Minnesota followed by Illinois in 1913, the AAPA in 1914, and the AIA in 1916. In 1914, he married Margaret Drever, the daughter of John Barry

Stewart Drever and Janet Ross. He therefore became the brother-in-law of fellow Scottish CA and immigrant Thomas Drever. There is no information about *JAS*'s career during the period of the First World War and it has to be assumed he served with the armed forces as his address was an accommodation one in Chicago until 1923 when he formed his own practise there as Angus Steven & Company. He remained in this position until his death at Wilmette in Illinois in 1966. He was a Vice-President of the IAPA in 1925. An obituary appeared in *The Accountant's Magazine* of 1966. *JAS* was the fourth most senior member of ICAS at the time of his death. He had a Scottish wife and his home in 1930 was valued at $25,000 ($280,000 in 2004 terms).

STEWART, Andrew (1888–1971)   IAAG (1910)

Andrew Stewart (*AS*) had a distinguished career as a public accountancy practitioner in the US although he appears to have come from very humble beginnings. He was born in Perth in 1888. His father was Daniel Stewart from the farming village of Blairgowrie in Perthshire, a Perth joiner and husband of Elizabeth Stewart from Perth. His paternal grandparents were Peter Stewart, a mill overseer, and Jane Holme. His parents' marriage was not registered in Scottish parish records and it has therefore been impossible to identify the maternal grandparents. *AS* had three brothers, James, William S., and Henry Stewart. James Stewart was a bank agent (manager) and Deputy Sheriff Clerk at Thurso in Ross & Cromarty and had a son, Charles Holme Stewart. The latter was Dux of Thurso High School, graduated with first class honours from the University of Edinburgh, was a prisoner of war during the Second World War, and became Secretary to the University of Edinburgh from 1947 to 1978. He was also a CA in Glasgow (IAAG 1945).

Despite his working class origins, *AS* was educated at Glasgow Academy and the University of Glasgow where he graduated with the degrees of Master of Arts and Bachelor of Law. He served a CA apprenticeship with James William Stewart & Company in Glasgow and joined the IAAG in 1910. James William Stewart appears to have had an unusual beginning to his accountancy career. He was born at the village of Killin in Perthshire in 1857 and, in the 1881 *Census*, was working as a bookkeeper in a sewing machine factory in Govan near Glasgow. This was probably the factory set up by the American Singer Manufacturing Company in 1867 that moved to larger premises at Clydebank in 1882. It may be that James William Stewart was a relative of *AS*.

Although *AS* became a CA in 1910, he was recruited by fellow Scottish immigrant, James Marwick (founder of MMC) earlier than that. He was a Massachusetts CPA in 1906 and Manager of the MMC office at Winnipeg in Canada in 1907 – where he was summonsed by the MICA and requested not to employ American accountants on Canadian government audits and to use British accountants instead. This was a time of considerable anti-American sentiment in Canada. He moved to MMC in New York in 1910 and, in 1919, he joined the AIA and became a partner in MMC. A year later, he was a New York CPA and served on several committees of the NYSSCPA. For example, he was chairman of the Committee of Complaints (1925), member of the Board of Directors (1926), and President (1941). He joined the ASCPA in 1923 and became the Auditor of the AIA a year later. His other AIA appointments included Board of Examiners (1927), Treasurer (1928–30), Endowment Committee (1934), Committee on Cooperation with the Stock Exchange (1934 and 1942) and the Securities & Exchange Commission (1935–8), Committee on Accounting Procedure (1936, chairman), Committee on the Development of Accounting Principles (1936), Committee on Stockbroker Accounting (1939), Council (1941), and Committee on Cooperation with Investment Bankers (1941), *AS* was a CPA in Michigan (1925), Pennsylvania (1925), Louisiana (1926), Washington (1927), and Tennessee. He was also very active in the American Red Cross during the 1920s.

In 1932 *AS* left MMC for Wall Street and investment banking. However, unsuccessful because of the stock market crash, he tried to return to his former firm as second in command in 1934. This was not agreed and, instead, he became an influential partner in the public accountancy firm of Haskins & Sells (HS) in New York. HS was founded in 1895 in New York by Charles Waldo Haskins and Elijah Watt Sells. It was the first major non-British public accountancy firm in the US. It eventually joined with DPGC to form Deloitte, Haskins & Sells and then Deloitte Touche. Haskins was a New Yorker and one of the principal founders and first President of the NYSSCPA in 1897. Sells was from Iowa and specialised in railway accounting prior to joining Haskins. He was AIA President in 1906–8 and a well-known writer on accounting matters.

In 1941, the US Secretary of War appointed Arthur H. Carter, senior partner of HS, to be Fiscal Director in the Office of the Fiscal Director for the Army Service Forces and responsible for accounting, auditing, payments, contracts, and training in the Office based in Washington. Carter became a Major-General in 1943 and received an Oak Leaf Cluster in 1948 for his service. *AS* was appointed as Deputy Director to Carter. He was commissioned as a Lieutenant-Colonel in 1942 and Colonel in the same year. He became inactive as an officer in 1945 and remained with HS until his retirement in the early 1960s – which was spent predominantly at the Marine Hotel at Troon in Ayrshire with his wife and daughter. He had a son who cannot be traced. In 1948, *AS* was awarded the Legion of Merit for his wartime service which included a complete modernisation of accounting and auditing services in the US War Department. He died in 1971 in New York. His obituary was published in *The Accountant's Magazine* of June 1971. *AS* was wrongly described as having a doctorate in T. A. Wise, *Peat, Marwick, Mitchell & Co.: 85 Years* (Peat, Marwick, Mitchell & Company: New York, NY, 1981). A brief biography appeared in *The American Accountant* of September 1929 with regard to his involvement in the administration of the International Congress of Accountants of that year. He was also present at the next Congress in London in 1933. The Stewart home in New York in 1930 was valued at $60,000 ($671,000 in 2004 terms). His wife was from Scotland and his two daughters were born in Canada.

STRACHAN, Douglas Hunter (1889–1953)   IAAG (1913)

Douglas Hunter Strachan (*DHS*) was born in Dundee in 1889 where his father, Alexander McDonald Strachan, was a master draper in the firm of William Gunter & Company and married to Anne Salmond, who was from England and a teacher. His father was born in nearby Arbroath. His grandfather, Thomas Strachan, came from Arbroath and was a draper and clothier in Dundee. His grandmother, Jean Hosie, was born in the farming village of Arbirlot near Arbroath in Forfarshire. Thomas and Jean Strachan had six sons and three daughters in addition to Alexander Strachan and they all appear to have worked in the family business. *DHS*'s maternal grandparents were James Salmond, a master joiner from the Lochee district of Dundee, and Elizabeth Hunter. His maternal aunt, Helen Salmond, was an unmarried dressmaker.

A CA apprenticeship with MIC followed schooling in Dundee. *DHS* joined the IAAG in 1913 and soon left Dundee to migrate to New York and employment with CAs AYC. He then may have served in the armed forces during the First World War because his address was an accommodation one with MIC in New York during this period. However, by 1920, he was in practise there as Strachan & Rains. Then, in 1921, he was admitted to a partnership in MIC. This remained the case until 1932 when he was practicing on his own in New York as David Strachan. *DHS* died in New York in 1953 and does not appear to have joined any American body of public accountants. His obituary appeared in *The Accountant's Magazine* in May of 1953. The family home in 1930 in New Jersey was valued at $18,000 ($201,000 in 2004 terms) and he had a wife from Ireland and a married daughter.

STUART, John McKerrell (1882–1926)   IAAG (1905)

John McKerrell Stuart (*JMS*) was born in 1882 in Glasgow to Robert Stuart, a master ironmonger, and Elizabeth Baird Anderson. His parental grandfather was Archibald Stuart, a labourer, and Jane Liddell. Maternal grandparents were John Anderson, a stock taker, and Jane Birkett. By 1891, the family had moved to the village of Rhue in Dumbartonshire and, in 1901, *JMS* was working in the fishing town of Montrose in Forfarshire as an apprentice CA. He had a sister and brother, neither of whom can be traced. The apprenticeship was with Glasgow CAs Walter & W. B. Galbraith from 1888 to 1903. *JMS* was employed for a further two years with this firm until 1905 when he joined the IAAG. Also in 1905, *JMS* immigrated to New York to work for CAs MMC. He became a Minnesota CPA in 1910. In 1918, he was working for the Canadian Western Lumber Company at Vancouver in Canada. *JMS* died there in 1926. The Canadian Western Lumber Company was formed in 1899 as the Ross, McLaren Mill and continued in production until 1992. The mill was built at Millside in British Columbia for $350,000 and became the largest facility in the Pacific Northwest. It was acquired in 1954 by Crown Zellerbach. Details of the company are contained in M. Hardbattle, *Canadian Western Lumber Company Limited*, University of British Columbia Library (2002).

SUTHERLAND, Donald Finlayson (1874–1949)   SAE (1898)

Donald Finlayson Sutherland (*DFS*) was born in Edinburgh in 1874. He was the son of the cashier in the Edinburgh firm of CAs Lindsay, Jamieson & Haldane. Donald Sutherland senior was the son of Donald Sutherland, a shoemaker in the fishing port of Thurso in Sutherland, and Christian Finlayson. His mother was Margaret Trotter Johnston, the daughter of William Johnston, a commission agent in the farming village of Ecclefechan to the east of Dumfries in Dumfriesshire, and Jane Trotter. A Sutherland uncle was a tailor in Glasgow and an aunt was a lodging housekeeper there. His mother's siblings included a clog-maker and joiner in the mill and farm town of Langholm and a farmer at Hoddam, both in Dumfriesshire.

DFS was educated at George Watson's College in Edinburgh. He was then apprenticed to his father's employers and joined the SAE in 1898. A year later, he immigrated to New York and employment with CAs TNC. This lasted no more than a year and his next employer was DDGC in New York. In 1903, however, he returned to Edinburgh with health problems. He then partnered CA Alexander Thomas Niven as Niven & Sutherland in Edinburgh. Niven was an SAE founder in 1853–4 and the father of John Ballantine Niven, a fellow Edinburgh CA immigrant and co-founder of TNC. The partnership was dissolved in 1909 and *DFS* practised singly until 1916. At this time, he moved to London to work as an accountant with the precious metals firm of Johnson, Mathey & Company in Hatton Gardens. Eight years later, he became a London partner in Lindsay, Jamieson & Haldane and was senior partner there until his death in 1949 at Hampton-on-Thames. He was married with a son and two daughters, a keen golfer and fisher, and Secretary of the Cammo Golf Club in Edinburgh for some years. His obituary appeared in *The Scotsman* of June 1949 and *The Accountant's Magazine* of November 1949.

SUTHERLAND, William (1878–1973)   UQ

William Sutherland (*WS*) was Arthur Young's right-hand man in the American public accountancy firm of AYC. The firm's partnership agreement stated he was to replace Young as senior partner – although he did not hold that position. He was the administrative partner and never joined the firm's Management Committee formed by Young in 1933 because the latter and *WS* were designated as consultants to it. Nevertheless, *WS* was a key figure in the early history of AYC.

WS was born in Glasgow in 1878 to John Sutherland, a bookkeeper from the iron and steel manufacturing town of Coatbridge in Lanarkshire, and Jane Stirling from nearby Airdrie. His maternal grandparents were James Stirling, a master baker, and Jane Baird. His paternal grandparents were John Sutherland, an iron-stone contractor, and Bethia Muir. He had three brothers and four sisters, including John Sutherland, a mechanical engineer, James Sutherland, a clerk, Robert Sutherland, a mining engineer, Jane Sutherland, an elementary schoolteacher, and Janet Sutherland, a housekeeper.

Following schooling in Glasgow, *WS* was apprenticed from 1893 to 1897 to Glasgow CAs Thomson, Jackson, Gourlay & Taylor. In 1897, he became an associate member of the IAAG but did not complete his apprenticeship or examinations. Instead, in 1903, he immigrated to Chicago at about the time of the Illinois CPA law and the formation of the IAPA. He had been recruited by Arthur Young. He became a partner in AYC in New York in 1915 and was a national partner from 1921 to 1945. He was an Illinois CPA, a member of the ASCPA, and a member of the AIA Committee on Cooperation with Bankers from 1927. He died in 1966. His home in Illinois in 1930 was valued at $100,000 ($1,119,000 in 2004 terms) and he had a wife from Ohio, 3 daughters, a son, and two servants. He retired to Pinehurst in North Carolina where he died in 1973 aged 95 years. In 1968, he recounted some of his personal experiences in practise and an extract was published as W. Sutherland "Early Days of the Firm and the Profession", *The Arthur Young Journal*, Spring-Summer 1969, 32–3. He reports on the poor quality of American public accountancy in the early twentieth century, the rarity of corporate audits, and the difficulties of ensuring fair disclosure in financial statements.

TAIT, William Kerr (1889–1956)   IAAG (1913)

Born in Glasgow in 1889, William Kerr Tait (*WKT*) was the son of William Tait, a mercantile bookkeeper, and grandson of John Connor Tait, a mercantile clerk, and Helen Thomson. His mother was Mary Kerr, an English teacher and daughter of William Kerr, a railway station master, and Janet Brown. He was educated in Glasgow and, from 1906 to 1911, apprenticed to CAs Thomson, Jackson, Gourlay & Taylor in Glasgow. He joined the IAAG in 1913 and immigrated to MMC in Philadelphia in 1914. He remained there until 1915 when his address was in Maxwell Park in Glasgow. His next address was Surbiton in London in 1920 and it must be presumed these changes were due to military service during the First World War. By 1927, he had returned to Pollokshields in Glasgow and, in 1934, was in Kampala in Uganda in East Africa where he practised as William K. Tait & Company until his retirement in 1955. His partner was a member of the SIAA. *WKT* died in 1956 at the St Germaine Nursing Home at Bournemouth in Hampshire. He was married but had no children. Obituary notices appeared in the May 1956 issue of *The Accountant's Magazine* and *The Glasgow Herald*.

TANNOCK, Thomas White (1872–1941)   IAAG (1894)

Thomas White Tannock (*TWT*) was born in 1872 in the textile manufacturing town of Renfrew (population 5,000 in 1871) in Renfrewshire to Hugh Dreghorn Tannock, a commercial traveller in drapery from Kilmarnock in Ayrshire, and Agnes White from Liverpool in England. His paternal grandfather was James Tannock, an Ayrshire carpet weaver and husband of Margaret Cunningham. He had two brothers and a sister, none of whom can be traced. Educated in Renfrew, *TWT* was apprenticed from 1889 to 1893 to Glasgow CA William Hart Junior. He was an associate member of the IAAG from 1893 until he joined it in 1894. Two years later, he was in New York and resided there until 1907 without disclosure of employment. However, in 1908, he was working for CAs MMC and an Ohio CPA. Then, in 1910, his employment was with a public accounting firm, Ladenburg, Tannock & Company in New York. The last record with the IAAG was in 1939 and he appears to have died in 1941. He was married with no children.

TAYLOR, Herbert Dryden (1887–1972)   IAAG (1911)

James Taylor was a grocer in the village of Cambusnethan on the outskirts of Motherwell in Lanarkshire and husband of Margaret Dryden, a domestic servant in the area. The couple had a son in 1887. His name was Herbert Dryden Taylor (*HDT*) and his grandparents were David Taylor, a contractor, and Isabella Walker, and Herbert Dryden, a corn miller, and Jane Arthur from England. He was apprenticed to the well-known Glasgow firm of CAs D. & A. Cuthbertson, Provan & Strong, joining the IAAG in 1911. He soon immigrated to work for the Scottish immigrant CA firm of J. Gordon Steele & Company in Minneapolis in Minnesota and became a Minnesota CPA in 1912.

A year later, *HDT* was working for TNC in New York and an associate member of the AAPA. In 1913, he was employed by CPAs Harris, Allan & Company in New York and a full member of the AAPA. This membership transferred to the AIA in 1916. By 1920, employment was with AYC in New York followed by the Union Petroleum Company in Philadelphia in 1923 (an AYC client to be later acquired by Royal Dutch Shell), and BWGC in New York in 1927. The BWGC address changed to New Jersey in 1932 and, in 1948, to Gannett Newspapers at Rochester in New York. This newspaper group exists today and has publications in 44 US states as well as in several European countries, including the UK. Its main newspaper is *USA Today* and employees total 45,000 individuals. The company remained the place of employment for *HDT* until retirement in 1960. He died in Rochester in 1972. An obituary appeared in *The Accountant's Magazine* of February 1973. His home in New Jersey in 1930 was valued at $8,500 ($95,000 in 2004 terms) and he had a wife from New York and two daughters.

TAYLOR, Matthew Gibson (1880–1948)   IAAG (1902)

Matthew Gibson Taylor (*MGT*) was born in the Gorbals district of Glasgow in 1880. His father, Edward Graham Taylor, was a wine and spirit merchant there and from Neilston in Renfrewshire, and his mother was Edward Taylor's second wife, Agnes Lang McDonald. His first wife was Jessie Shaw. The paternal grandparents were William Taylor, a goods carrier, and Mary Holland from Kilmarnock in Ayrshire, and the maternal grandparents were Matthew Gibson McDonald, a boot and shoemaker, and Agnes Lang also from Ayrshire. Edward Graham Taylor had several siblings including William (a Glasgow coachman), Hamilton (who died young), and John Taylor (a shopman in the Glasgow spirit trade), and four sisters. *MGT* had four brothers and a sister, including Johnston Taylor Taylor, a spirit merchant in Govan, Henry Taylor, also a spirit merchant, and Edward Graham Taylor, a Glasgow medical practitioner who died young due to bronchitis and was married to a sister of *MGT*'s wife.

MGT was educated in Govan and apprenticed to Ferguson & Vost, CAs of Glasgow. He was admitted to the IAAG in 1902 and worked for several years in the city (including Thomson, Jackson & Son, CAs) until 1906 when he immigrated to New York to work for CAs DDGC. This lasted until 1909 when he returned to Glasgow to practise as Taylor & Gilmour. This appears to have been *MGT*'s occupation until 1940 when he retired to Campsie in Stirlingshire. He died there in 1948 of a coronary thrombosis. He married Georgina Tribe Stewart in 1910. She was from Cathcart in Glasgow and the daughter of Archibald Stewart, a builder's contractor, and Jane Anderson Walker. Archibald Stewart was the son of Archibald Stewart, a mason, and Elizabeth Tribe. Jane Walker was the daughter of William Walker, a forester, and Ann Jackson. *MGT* had three sons, including a medical practitioner, and his nearest descendants live in England.

THOMSON, William Garth (1875–1941)   IAAG (1898)

Born in Rutherglen near Glasgow in 1875, William Garth Thomson (*WGT*) was the son of William Garth Thomson, the manager of a chemical manufacturing facility, and Jane Brown Pinkerton, William Thomson's second wife. His grandparents were John Thomson, a Glasgow seed merchant, and Margaret Garth, and John Pinkerton, a farmer, and Jane Brown. He had a brother, Charles Pinkerton Thomson, and two sisters. Margaret Garth was the daughter of William Garth, a carter, and Margaret Taylor. *WGT* also had a brother-in-law, Robert Aitken Rennie, a Glasgow Writer (lawyer) and son of James Rennie, a Glasgow schoolmaster. In 1906, he married Mabel Violet Wright of Partick, the daughter of James Wright, a brewer's agent, and Nelly Mitchell.

WGT was educated in Glasgow and apprenticed there to CA Thomas A. Craig (IAAG 1877) from 1893 to 1898 when he was admitted to the IAAG. He remained with Craig until 1899 when he was employed by CAs Thomson & Jackson in Glasgow. This lasted until 1912 when he immigrated at the age of 37 to New York and CAs MMC. In 1922, he transferred to MMC's office at Montreal in Canada and became a partner there until his death in 1941. He was a friend from his Glasgow days of William M. Black who was senior partner of MMC in the US from 1947 to 1965. In 1916, he wrote a paper on bank audits in the *Canadian Chartered Accountant*.

TOD, Andrew Kinnaird (1871–1945)   SAE (1895)

Born in 1871 in the village of Lasswade south of Edinburgh in Midlothian, Andrew Kinnaird Tod (*AKT*) was the son of Andrew Tod and Jane Crawford Russell. His father owned a papermaking mill at Lasswade that employed more than 200 individuals and his mother was from the village of Airth in Stirlingshire. She had been a domestic servant before her marriage to Andrew Tod. Her mother was Ann Crawford, a dressmaker, and her two brothers were, respectively, a pattern maker and a railway clerk. *AKT* had several siblings. William Leonard Tod was a student at the University of Edinburgh before joining his father's firm. Brothers Russell, Logan Millar, and Herbert Noble Tod, however, cannot be traced. Stuart Tod, on the other hand, was educated at the Edinburgh Academy where he was Dux of the school in 1894 and 1895, Regimental Sergeant Major in the army cadet corps, and a member of the school rugby and rowing teams. He became an associate member of the Royal School of Mines in 1898 and immigrated to Boston in the US. There was one Tod sister.

AKT was educated at George Watson's College and apprenticed to Edinburgh CAs A. & J. Robertson. He was admitted to the SAE in 1895. He remained with A. & J. Robertson until 1899 when he formed a partnership with fellow CA David Callender (SAE 1892). Callender became an SAE Council member. Three years later, in 1902, the partnership ended and *AKT* went to New York to work for CAs DDGC. A year later, he was employed by CAs MRC and, in 1906, became a CPA in Illinois. In 1908, he was employed by CAs MMC, certified as a public accountant in Ohio and Minnesota, and joined the AAPA. However, by 1910, he was back in New York with MMC, unmarried, and boarding in Manhattan. He remained with MMC and became a partner in New York in 1922. He retired to Palm Beach in Florida in 1933 where he died in 1945. There is no record of a marriage.

TOLLETH, William Robertson (1867–1957) UQ

Edinburgh provided several public accountancy immigrants. Most were members of the SAE. One of the exceptions was William Robertson Tolleth (*WRT*). He was born in 1867 in Edinburgh. His father was Thomas E. Tolleth from the village of Luncarty in Perthshire. Thomas Tolleth was an engineer in Edinburgh who became a master grocer. He was the son of James Tolleth, a cloth lapper, and Margaret Robertson of Edinburgh. *WRT*'s mother was Helen Hay Lowson from the village of Dysart in Fife, the daughter of George Lowson, a spirit merchant, and Jane Hay. He had a sister, Margaret D. Tolleth.

Following school in Edinburgh, *WRT* was employed by one of the founders of the SAE, Alexander Thomas Niven who was father of TNC co-founder John Ballantine Niven. He worked for Niven from 1882 and 1889 but there does not appear to have been an indenture contract although *WRT* applied to sit the SAE preliminary examination in 1884. He does not appear to have sat or passed it and immigrated to Norfolk in Virginia in 1889 to hold a number of accounting-related positions including Secretary and Treasurer of Duke & Smith, and Auditor in the Treasurer's Department of the Jamestown Exposition Company. This organisation was formed in 1901 to prepare for an exposition at Norfolk in 1907 to celebrate the 300th anniversary of the first permanent settlement in Virginia. Funding for the series of events came from private sources and Federal funds under the direction of President Theodore Roosevelt.

WRT formed his own practise and, in 1908, was one of eight Virginia accountants who founded the Tidewater Society of Accountants & Bookkeepers at

Norfolk. In 1909, he became a charter member of the Virginia Society of Public Accountants (VSPA, later VSCPA) and chairman of its Membership Committee. The VSPA had 85 members but only one was a public accountant, *WRT*. He joined the AAPA in 1910, was Secretary of the VSPA in 1913, and became its President in 1916. He wrote a paper on expert testimony by accountants in the *Journal of Accountancy* in 1917. It was reproduced in *The Accountant* (1918), the *South African Accountant* (1918), and the *Canadian Chartered Accountant* (1918).

WRT held various appointments in the AIA. He was a member of its Committee on Meetings (1917), Auditor (1919), and Council member (1921–5 and 1934–9). He was also on the Development Committee. *WRT* died at Norfolk in 1957. A brief biography appears in W. P. Hilton, *The Growth of Public Accountancy in the State of Virginia to December 1950* (Virginia Society of Public Accountants: Norfolk, VA, 1953). A photograph of accountants' wives in this publication at an annual conference reveals that he was married.

URQUHART, Charles Rodger (1889–1961)   SAE (1913)

Charles Rodger Urquhart (*CRU*) was born in Edinburgh in 1889. He was the son of a Glasgow commercial traveller, Charles Rodger Urquhart, and the grandson of John Urquhart, a warehouseman, and Eliza Roger. His mother was Jemima Torbain from the port of Leith, the daughter of Alexander Torbain, a carter and Town Officer for South Leith, and Agnes Annan, the daughter of gardener Thomas Annan. Torbain relatives in South Leith included Alexander Torbain, a cab proprietor, and John W. Torbain, a postman. *CRU* had one brother and two sisters. His father married a second wife in 1909. She was Christina Bell, the daughter of James Bell, a master tailor, and Christina Fraser.

CRU was educated at George Watson's College in Edinburgh and apprenticed to CAs Romanes & Aitchison. He joined the SAE in 1913. As soon as he qualified as a CA, *CRU* immigrated to CAs MMC in New York. He remained for two years before transferring to the firm's Toronto office in Canada. He was employed there until 1921 when he returned to New York to work for the British Ministry of Food in the US. Then, in 1924, he moved to MMC in London for three years before becoming a partner with the firm in Liverpool in 1930. Further moves with the firm occurred in 1934 to Manchester and in 1946 to Sheffield. He retired in 1955 to Horley in Surrey where he died in 1961.

WATSON, Albert John (1879–1970)   IAAG (1908)

Dundee immigrants included Albert John Watson (*AJW*). He was born in the rural parish of Liff & Benvie on the outskirts of Dundee in Forfarshire in 1879 to George Watson, a printer and compositer from the coastal village of Boyndie near Banff in Banffshire, and Margaret Innes Paton, a domestic servant from Banff. His aunt, Emily Paton, was a lady's maid. *AJW*'s grandparents were John Watson, a ship's carpenter at Banff who came from Boyndie, and Helen Watson, and

Thomas Paton, a blacksmith, and Jane Innes. Great uncle Henry Watson was a plumber. *AJW* had eight siblings including Robert Innes Watson who became an electrical engineer in Edinburgh and married Catherine Cree Law, a daughter of William Law, a French polisher. Brother David McEwan Watson was an SAA member and a Virginian CPA who followed his brother to the US and MMC in 1929 and became a senior partner in the firm from 1947 to 1960.

The Watson family moved to Dundee after his birth and *AJW* was educated and apprenticed there to CA Daniel McIntyre of McIntyre & Grant and then with Welsh, Walker & MacPherson. He was awarded Distinction in his final examinations in 1907 and admitted to the IAAG in 1908. This was the year in which *AJW* immigrated to Missouri and opened a new office as audit manager for CAs MMC in Kansas City. He became a Minnesota CPA in 1909 and similar licences followed in Missouri (1910), California (1921), Oregon (1922), and Washington (1927). He joined the AAPA in 1911 and the AIA in 1916. State public accountancy positions held by *AJW* included the Missouri State Board of Accountancy (1912), Kansas State Board of Accountancy (1913), Missouri Board of Examiners (1917), and Vice-President (1927) and President (1928) of the CSCPA. His AIA appointments included the Committees on State Laws (1934), State Corporation Laws (1936), Inventories (1938), and Cooperation with Investment Bankers (1940) which he chaired in 1942 and 1943.

AJW worked in MMC in Kansas City for 12 years, during which time he is reported as having attempted to solicit a client from rivals HS. At this time there was a running battle on this issue between the two firms (T. A. Wise, *Peat, Marwick, Mitchell & Company: 85 Years*, Comet Publishing: New York, NY, 1981). In addition, during this period, he entered the US Navy and, by 1917, was a Captain. He did so after seeking the permission of James Marwick. In 1920, following his return from military service, *AJW* moved to the San Francisco office and was promoted to partner in 1923. In 1924, he became a member of the San Francisco Chamber of Commerce and, a year later, of the San Francisco City Council.

AJW retired in 1948 but remained involved with his Scottish public accountancy roots. In 1947 and 1955, he established and augmented a prize fund to award the two best candidates in part four of the examinations of ICAS. In 1961, he endowed a fund to provide a gold medal for the leading candidate in the ICAS final examinations. He also wrote from time to time in *The Accountant's Magazine* in which his obituary appeared in January 1971 following his death in 1970 in Burlinghame in California. He had a wife from Minnesota and three sons. The family home in 1930 was valued at $20,000 ($224,000 in 2004 terms).

WATSON, John Charles (1885–1955)   SAA (1910)

John Charles Watson (*JCW*) was born in Aberdeen in 1885. His father was Robert Caird Watson, an elementary schoolteacher from Aberdeen, and grandson of James Watson, an Aberdeen joiner, and Margaret Caird. His mother was Jane Law who was also born in Aberdeen. Her parents were James Law, a farmer, and

Jane Low. He had a brother who died as an infant and a sister. *JCW* was educated in Aberdeen and trained as an advocate's clerk there before an unrecorded CA apprenticeship and membership of the SAA in 1910. A year earlier, he was employed by CA Richard Brown in Edinburgh. *JCW* then moved in 1910 to English CAs Armitage & Norton, at Halifax in Yorkshire before immigrating in 1911 to MMC in New York. He appears to have served in the armed forces between 1914 and 1920 before joining the Vacuum Oil Company in London in 1927. He remained there until 1943 when he became an accountant with a motor car sales company at Orpington in Kent. He retired there in 1947 and died in 1955. *JCW*'s obituary appeared in the March 1955 issue of *The Accountant's Magazine*.

WEBSTER, George Rae (1873–1938)   IAAG (1896)

Born at Dundee in 1873 to James Forrest Webster, a ship's master, and Jessie Lawson Robertson, George Rae Webster (*GRW*) was the grandson of George Webster, a linen manufacturer in Dundee, and Isabella Rae, and William Robertson, a Dundee builder, and Isabella Grant. His brother Norman William Webster was a Dundee clerk who died unmarried at the village of Forgandenny in Perthshire at the age of 52. *GRW* was educated in Dundee and then apprenticed to CA David Myles. He joined the IAAG 1896. He appears to have worked briefly for CAs Lindsay, Jamieson & Haldane in Edinburgh and London before joining CAs JCC in New York in 1899. He became a Fellow of the Faculty of Actuaries during this time.

JCC became PWC and *GRW* was admitted as a partner in 1906. He had opened the firm's office in Pittsburg in 1902 and spent time working on railway audits in Mexico. Prior to 1906, he was one of two PWC managers receiving a share of the firm's profits. He opened the San Francisco office in 1904 and was present there during the great earthquake and fire of 1906 which caused relocation to Oakland. All the firm's records were destroyed in the earthquake. *GRW*'s clients in San Francisco included many large organisations recommended by the Bank of California. He was also largely responsible for the formation of the CSCPA in 1909. His contributions to public accountancy are recorded but not as well recognised as those of others because of his reluctance to publicise his efforts.

In 1903, *GRW* became an Illinois CPA and, in 1905, a member of the AAPA. Between 1907 and 1911, he worked in the San Francisco office before returning to New York. By 1914, he was a New York CPA and, in 1916, a member of the AIA. He was also a Pennsylvanian CPA. He was regarded as particularly strong on matters of accounting theory and assisted PWC's senior partner Arthur Lowes Dickinson in his development of group accounting practises. He was largely responsible for administering the New York office. He joined the Executive Committee of the firm in 1920 but had to retire due to a breakdown at the age of 48 in 1923. His retirement was spent in Paris in France where he died unmarried in 1938. His career is covered in C. W. DeMond, *Price, Waterhouse & Company in America* (Comet Press, New York, NY, 1951). *GRW* published several papers including "Methods of Writing Off Discount on Bonds" in the *Journal of Accountancy* (1913), "Consolidated Accounts" in the *Journal of Accountancy* (1919), and an undated thirty-two page monograph "Theoretical Depreciation: A Menace to the Public and the Investor".

YOUNG, Alexander Norman (1878–1954)   SAA (1909)

The Reverend Alexander Young, Master of Arts from the University of Aberdeen, ordained in 1858, was born in the small farming village of Birse in Aberdeenshire. He was the Church of Scotland minister at the Chapel of Garioch and a farmer of 300 acres at the village of Pitcaple north-west of Aberdeen. His son, Alexander Norman Young (*ANY*), was born at Picaple in 1878. *ANY*'s father was a former colonial chaplain in Ceylon and the son of Charles Young, a farmer in Birse, and Christian Alexander. His mother was Helen Maitland Cook from the farming village of Tarland in central Aberdeenshire, the daughter of George Cook, Master of Arts, Church of Scotland minister at Bathgate in Linlithgowshire (ordained 1841), and Agnes Watson. His uncle George Young was also a farmer in Birse, managing 70 acres and two men. Other Birse Youngs included sawmillers and blacksmiths. Of *ANY*'s three brothers, Andrew Watson Cook Young was a Lieutenant-Colonel in the Indian Army Medical Service, married to Paulina Leonora McHardy, and died of severe burns from an accident aged 52. George Cook Young was a farm manager. There were two sisters.

ANY appears to have been a student of law at the University of Aberdeen by 1901. However, he was also apprenticed to CA A. S. Mitchell of Aberdeen and joined the SAA in 1909. He then appears to have been admitted to a partnership with Mitchell in that year and practised as Mitchell & Young until 1912. A year later, he migrated to New York and was employed by CAs MMC. He then transferred to the Dallas, Texas office of MMC in 1916 when he also applied and was rejected for membership of the TSCPA. In 1920, he transferred to the firm's office in Chicago and remained there until 1923 when he founded his own firm. Also in 1920, *ANY* was living in Chicago with his Scottish wife who migrated with him and their daughter in 1913. There were no other children of the marriage. The family's Chicago residence had a monthly rental of $100 ($1,100 in 2004 terms). *ANY* was removed from the records of the SAA in 1934 and he joined the AIA in 1948. He died in Chicago in 1954. A curiosity of *ANY*'s American Census records is that, in 1920, his birth date is recorded as 1881 and, in 1930, as 1885. In fact, he was born in 1878.

YOUNG, Arthur (1863–1948)   UQ

Arthur Young (*AY*) was one of the most influential members of the early American public accountancy profession. He was different from almost all of the other immigrants in the sense that he was trained as a lawyer rather than as a public accountant. He was born in Glasgow in 1863. He was one of 11 children of Robert Young, a ship's broker and Chairman of the Glasgow Tramway Company.

Robert Young was from the town of Kirkintilloch (population 8,000) in Dumbartonshire to the north of Glasgow and initially had a career as a ship owner. However, he lost most of his capital as a shareholder of the City of Glasgow Bank when it failed in 1878. He had capital of £2,500 invested in the bank and the first call by the receiver amounted to £12,500. The City of Glasgow Bank was one of the most serious cases of fraud in the UK during the nineteenth century. It was a Glasgow-based bank that grew rapidly using deposits mainly from middle and working class families and used the money in bad lending and foreign investments. The directors and manager were all well-known and reputable men in the west of Scotland. They falsified the bank's balance sheet for several years in order to cover up overstated assets and loss making. After ship broking, Robert Young became a general merchant in Glasgow.

AY's mother was Ann Henderson Lusk from the farming community of Cumbernauld in Dumbartonshire to the north-east of Glasgow. His paternal grandfather was John Young, a lawyer and husband of Jessie Kirkwood. The maternal grandparents were Daniel Henderson Lusk, a paper manufacturer, and Isabella Corbett. Great grandparents were Robert Lusk, an underwriter, and Ann Henderson. *AY*'s eleven siblings reduced to six because of infant deaths. His brothers chose differing careers. Daniel Henderson Lusk Young was the eldest brother and was senior partner in James Templeton & Company, carpet manufacturers, when he died. He was a Commander of the Order of the British Empire. Alfred Alexander Young was a Glasgow surgeon and physician who was deaf, as was Frederick Henderson Young who succeeded Daniel Young as senior partner of the Templeton carpet mills in Glasgow. *AY*'s sister, Anna Lusk Young, married Frederick E. Dubs, a barrister and son of Henry Dubs, a locomotive engineer, and Agnes Sillars. Her brothers-in-law included Frank A. Dubs, an engineer, Henry J. S. Dubs, a locomotive engine builder, and Charles R. Dubs, also a locomotive engine builder. Other Lusk relatives included Andrew Lusk, a fire clay pipe maker at Cumbernauld. Nephews of *AY* included Sir Arthur Young, Member of Parliament and a junior Lord of the Treasury in Winston Churchill's government during the Second World War.

AY was born with a hearing defect. Despite this problem, he was educated at the Glasgow Academy where he was Dux in 1880 and, from 1880 to 1883, at the University of Glasgow where he graduated as a Master of Arts having won prizes in his mathematics classes. He was captain of the university rugby team, played for Glasgow against Edinburgh, and was a reserve player for Scotland. In 1883, he was apprenticed in Glasgow to the law firm of A. J. & A. Graham. He also studied law at the University of Glasgow from 1883 to 1887 and graduated as a Bachelor of Laws, having won first place in his Scots law class. He was then sent to Switzerland and Algiers in an attempt to resolve his hearing problem and worked as a teacher and part-time journalist. However, from 1887 to 1890 he continued to work for Grahams but had to abandon his career intention to be an Advocate because of his deafness.

With a legal career not an option, *AY* immigrated to New York in 1890 to work, first, in the carpet industry and, second, for an old school friend in a firm of investment bankers, Kennedy Tod & Company. The Kennedy family was originally from Glasgow. This employment lasted for three years until *AY* went to Chicago in 1893 to work on liquidating several companies. There he met Charles Urquhart Stuart who had an accounting training and was the Comptroller of a Boston-based copper company in Montana. He had also audited the newspaper company owning the *Chicago Tribune* and was almost alone at that time in recognising the potential of the emerging audit services market. Stuart and *AY* agreed in 1894 to form a firm of public accountants, Stuart & Young, and concentrated on clients who were Scottish and English investment trusts whose directors they knew. Several of these trusts had been financially damaged by a market panic in 1893. Each partner contributed 250 dollars of capital and the partnership lasted until 1906 when *AY* split with Stuart because of the latter's inabilities as a public accountant. Stuart was a member of the AAPA from 1894 to 1896 and an Illinois CPA (1902). He was believed to have been born and trained in Scotland although no record can be found either of the birth or training. It is more likely he was born in the US of Scottish parents. Stuart continued to practise on his own in Chicago after the partnership dissolution.

In 1903, *AY* became an Illinois CPA and three years later formed AYC with his brother Frank Stanley Young. He frequently returned to Glasgow to recruit public accountants and one of his greatest successes was William Sutherland whom he hired as an UQ accountant for $100 a month. Other recruits were less successful. Many lost their jobs with AYC because of drink problems. This was a continuation of a problem that started in the UK. According to *AY* in his memoirs, many accounting immigrants had left Scotland or England because of drink-related issues. He also had the problem of expanding the firm because few American companies hired auditors. In 1906, he moved to New York with one accountant, leaving his brother in charge of the Chicago office. His total fee income for many years was less than $100,000 and he managed his firm in New York by entering into arrangements with local firms such as those of Scottish immigrant CA Robert Cuthbert (1909–11) and SIAA member Alexander James Baxter (1911–20). Cuthbert's biography is related earlier. Baxter was born, educated and trained in London where his Scottish father, Alexander Baxter, was a banker. In 1912, *AY* became a Wisconsin CPA and President of the IAPA. A year later, he was a Vice-President of the AAPA and of the IAPA. In 1914, he joined the AAPA Committee on Federal Legislation. At this time, *AY* was a horseman and lost an eye in a riding accident when a horse kicked him in 1915. By 1930, he was living in rented accommodation in Manhattan with a monthly rental of $500 ($5,600 in 2004 terms) and two servants.

Further public accountancy appointments with the AIA continued for *AY* despite his disabilities. For example, he was a member of the Council and Board of Examiners (1916–20), Committee on a National Charter (1921), Committee on Nominations (1923), and Endowment Committee (1927). He was particularly active in the endeavour to establish generally accepted accounting principles by the Institute's Committee of Accounting Principles. He became a CPA in Michigan (1925) and New York (1930). *AY*'s audits included the accounting records of the New York bankers, J. P. Morgan & Company, in connection with its purchases of munitions for the British and French governments during the First World War. He also audited the Midvale Steel & Ordinance Company that manufactured Enfield rifles for the British government. The audit of the Atlantic Fruit Company led to the recruitment as a partner of Scottish immigrant CA Andrew Craig in 1918. Other AYC clients included the Atlas Portland Cement Company. He died in retirement in 1948 at "Crossways" in Aiken in South Carolina. He is buried in the Bethany Cemetery. *AY* never married and was succeeded by his nephews and nieces. He was remembered in a social setting for his loose fitting tweed clothes from Whitaker & Company in London, pipe smoking and martinis, elaborate meals at Aiken with his cook Margaret Beckford, and his many dogs. He always wore a cravat rather than a tie and had a passion for golf although he played it badly. His close friends included Charles Deering of Chicago who was the President of the International Harvester Company, and John Pierpoint Morgan, the New York banker. He was regarded as kind, intelligent, enthusiastic, and of good judgment. His career is covered in T. G. Higgins "Arthur Young (1863–1948)" a biography prepared for the NYSSCPA Committee on History and published in the *New York Certified Public Accountant* in November 1968. His memoirs were privately published in 1948 by J. C. Burton, *Arthur Young and the Business he Founded* (Merrymount Press: Boston, MA).

YOUNG, David (1883–1955)   SAE (1906)

Educated at the public school at the farming village of Kinross on Loch Leven in Fife and George Heriot's School in Edinburgh, David Young (*DY*) was the son of Kinross master grocer and wine and spirit merchant David Young from Kinross and Euphemia Ballingall Storrar from the farming village of Kingskettle in the same county. His parents were married in Glasgow in 1864 and he had three brothers, Robert Young (who cannot be traced), John Storrar Young (a Bible Society manager in Edinburgh who died in 1938 and was married to Elizabeth Mary Ranson), Edward McKillop Young (a medical missionary who died overseas at the age of 68), and four sisters. His grandfather, also David Young, was a packer. An uncle, John Storrar of Kingskettle was a farmer there, working more than 500 acres with 9 employees. His brother, George Storrar, was also a farmer in Kingskettle. Cousins included Alexander Storrar, an engineer at the village of Collesie in Fife.

DY was born in 1883 in Kinross and apprenticed to CA Frederick Marshall (SAE 1893) in Edinburgh. He joined the SAE in 1906 and immigrating in the same year to San Francisco in California. He was employed by CAs PWC at various times from 1906 to 1924, during which time he became a CPA in Minnesota. In 1910, however, he was single, residing as a boarder, and working as an accountant in a dry goods store in San Francisco in California. In 1912, he transferred to the Toronto office of MMC and remained with the firm in Canada for the remainder of his career. In 1921, he moved to the Winnipeg office and, in 1928, became a partner in the Montreal office until his retirement to West Mount in Quebec in 1946. He died there in 1955 leaving a widow and a daughter.

DY was a CPA in California and member of the AAPA prior to 1916 when he became a member of the AIA. He was also a member of the CICA and served on its Council during his career in Montreal. His obituary appeared in *The Accountant's Magazine* of April 1955.

YOUNG, Frank Stanley (1871–1914)   UQ

Frank Stanley Young (*FSY*) was a younger brother of Arthur Young (above). He was born in Glasgow in 1871, educated at Glasgow Academy, and graduated as a Master of Arts from the University of Glasgow. He immigrated to the US in 1896 and proceeded to Kansas City in Missouri where he opened an office of the public accountancy firm of Stuart & Young in which he was a partner. Then, in 1907 with the dissolution of Stuart & Young, he joined his brother as AYC in Chicago. A year later, he opened the firm's Kansas City office and was also Manager of the Kansas City Clearing House Association. In 1909, *FSY* became a Missouri CPA and the first President of the MSCPA. He was also President from 1913 to 1914, during which time the Society publicly challenged the practise of "stealing" clients from other public accountants. In 1913, *FSY* was appointed a Vice-President of the AAPA. A year later, he died in Kansas City of a brain tumour. His career is mentioned in D. E. Breimeier, *A History of the CPA Profession in Missouri* (Missouri State Society of Certified Public Accountants: St Louis, MO). He does not appear to have married.

Bibliography

The following publications provide detailed support for the introductory essay and biographies in this book. Data for the research were found in these and various public records (including school and university registers, professional and trade directories, journals and newspapers, and births, deaths, marriages and census files).

Migration

These texts provide considerable detail regarding the various migrations from the UK to North America and several focus on the specifics of Scottish migration to the US and Canada.

Aspinwall, B. (1985), "The Scots in the United States", in Cage, R. A. (editor), *The Scots Abroad: Labour, Capital, Enterprise, 1750–1914*, London: Croom Helm, 80–110.

Berthoff, R. T. (1953), *British Immigrants in Industrial America 1790–1950*, Boston, MA: Harvard University Press.

Brander, M. (1982), *The Emigrant Scots*, London: Constable.

Devine, T. M. (1992), "The Paradox of Scottish Emigration", in Devine, T. M. (editor), *Scottish Emigration and Scottish Society*, Edinburgh: John Donald Publishers, 1–15.

Erickson, C. (1972), *Invisible Immigrants: the Adaptation of English and Scottish Immigrants in Nineteenth Century America*, London: Weidenfeld & Nicolson.

Harper, M. (2003), *Adventurers and Exiles: the Great Scottish Exodus*, London: Profile Books.

Jackson, W. T. (1968), *The Enterprising Scot: Investors in the American West After 1873*, Edinburgh: Edinburgh University Press.

Musgrave, F. (1963), *The Migratory Elite*, London: Heinemann.

Nugent, W. (1992), *Crossings: the Great Transatlantic Migrations, 1870–1914*, Bloomington, IN: Indiana University Press.

Public accountancy history

There are many sources relating to the early modern history of institutionalised public history. The following relate to such a history in both the UK and the US.

Anyon, J. T. (1925), *Recollections of the Early Days of American Accountancy 1883–1893*, New York, NY: privately published.

Brown, R. (1905) (editor), *A History of Accounting and Accountants*, Edinburgh: T. C. & E. C. Jack.

Carey, J. L. (1969), *The Rise of the Accountancy Profession from Technician to Professional 1896–1936*, New York, NY: American Institute of Certified Public Accountants.

Edwards, J. D. (1960), *History of Public Accountancy in the United States*, Lansing: MI: Michigan State University.

Littleton, A. C. (1942), *Dictionary of Early American Accountants*, Urbana-Champagne: IL, University of Illinois.

Miranti, P. J. (1990), *The Development of an American Profession 1886–1940*, Chapel Hill, NC: University of North Carolina Press.

Previts, G. J. & Merino, B. D. (1998). *A History of Accounting in America: the Cultural Significance of Accounting*, Columbus, OH: Ohio State University Press.

Reckitt, E. (1953), *Reminiscences of Early Days of the Accounting Profession in Illinois*, Chicago: IL, Illinois Society of Certified Public Accountants.

Sutherland, W. (1969), "Early Days of the Firm and the Profession", *The Arthur Young Journal*, Spring-Summer, 32–3.

Zeff, S. A. (1988), *The US Accounting Profession in the 1890s and Early 1900s*, New York, NY: Garland Publishing.

Public accountancy firms

There are surprisingly few histories of specific public accountancy firms in the US and the following are the main sources for this text.

Allen, D. G. & McDermott, K. (1993), *Accounting for Success: a History of Price Waterhouse in America 1890–1990*, Boston, MA: Harvard Business School Press.

Andersen, Arthur & Company (1974), *Arthur Andersen & Company: the First Sixty Years 1913–73*, Chicago, IL: Arthur Andersen & Company.

Anyon, J. T. (1925), *Recollections of the Early Days of American Accountancy 1883–1893*, New York, NY: privately published.

Burton, J. C. (1948), *Arthur Young and the Business he Founded* (1948), New York, NY: privately published.

Cooper Brothers & Co. (1954), *A History of Cooper Brothers & Co. 1854 to 1954*, London: B. T. Batsford.

DeMond, C. W. (1951), *Price Waterhouse & Company in America: a History of a Public Accounting Firm*, New York, NY: privately published.

Ernst & Ernst (1960), *Ernst and Ernst: a History of the Firm*, Cleveland, OH: privately published.

Haskins & Sells (1947), *Haskins & Sells: the First Fifty Years: 1895–1945*, New York, NY: privately published.

Kettle, R. (1958), *Deloitte & Co. 1845–1956*, Oxford: Oxford University Press.

Lybrand, Ross Bros. & Montgomery (1948), *Fiftieth Anniversary 1898–1948*, New York, NY: privately published.

Reckitt, E. (1953), *Reminiscences of Early Days of the Accounting Profession in Illinois*, Chicago: IL, Illinois Society of Certified Public Accountants.

Richards, A. B. (1981), *Touche Ross & Co. 1899–1981*, London: privately published.

Sutherland, W. (1969), "Early Days of the Firm and the Profession", *The Arthur Young Journal*, Spring-Summer, 32–3.

Swanson, T. (1972), *Touche Ross: A Biography*, New York, NY: Touche Ross & Company

Wise, T. A. (1982), *Peat Marwick Mitchell & Co.: 85 Years*, New York, NY: privately published

Public accountancy and related bodies

Several US public accountancy bodies have published their histories, particularly as part of centenary celebrations. The following are the main ones that relate to this text. There are also studies of Scottish public accountancy and actuarial bodies.

Alkire, D. L. (1989), *The Accounting Profession in Washington State: One Hundred Years of Progress*, Seattle, WA: Kendall/Hunt Publishing.

Ancone Associates (1997), *A Centennial Chronicle: Pennsylvania Institute of Certified Public Accountants 1897–1997*, Philadelphia, PN: Pennsylvania Institute of Certified Public Accountants.

Anon (1954), *A History of the Chartered Accountants of Scotland From the Earliest Times to 1954*, Edinburgh: Institute of Chartered Accountants of Scotland.

Bruce, R. (2004), *ICAS: 150 Years and Still Counting. A Celebration*, Edinburgh: Institute of Chartered Accountants of Scotland.

Davidson, A. R. (1956), *The History of the Faculty of Actuaries in Scotland 1856–1956*, Edinburgh: Faculty of Actuaries.

Davis, J. W. (1977), *The History of Certified Public Accountants in Mississippi 1904–77*, Hattiesburg, MS: Mississippi Society of Certified Public Accountants.

Edwards, J. D. and Miranti, P.J. (1987), "The AICPA: a Professional Institution in a Dynamic Society", *Journal of Accountancy*, 163 (5), 22–38.

Ganz, D. R. (1983), *A History of the CPA Profession in Missouri*, St Louis, MO: Missouri Society of Certified Public Accountants.

Grant, J. (1995), *The New York State Society of Certified Public Accountants: Foundation for a Profession*, New York: NY, Garland Publishing.

Horne, H. A. (1947), *The History and Administration of Our Society: Fiftieth Anniversary of the Founding of the New York State Society of Certified Public Accountants*, New York, NY: New York State Society of Certified Public Accountants.

Kedslie, M. J. M. (1990), *Firm Foundations: the Development of Professional Accounting in Scotland 1850–1900*, Hull: Hull University Press.

New Jersey Society of Certified Public Accountants (1998), *A Centennial Chronicle*, Newark, NJ: New Jersey Society of Certified Public Accountants.

Stowe, N. J. & Luey, B. (1990), *Accountancy in Arizona: a History of the Profession*, Phoenix, AZ: Arizona Society of Certified Public Accountants.

Tinsley, J. A. (1983), *Texas Society of Certified Public Accountants: a History 1915–81*, College Station, TX: Texas A & M University Press.

Walker, S. P. (1988), *The Society of Accountants in Edinburgh: 1854–1914: a Study of Recruitment in a New Profession*, New York, NY: Garland Publishing.

Webster, N. E. (1954), *The American Association of Public Accountants: Its First Twenty Years 1886–1906*, New York, NY: American Association of Public Accountants.

Yeager, L. J. C. & Ford, G. (1968), *History of the Professional Practise of Accounting in Kentucky 1879–1965*, Louisville: KY: privately published.

Public accountancy migration publications

This text is part of a series of studies on the subject and several publications provide more detail about the general topic of the migration of UK Chartered Accountants to the US prior to the First World War. These are as follows:

T. A. Lee (1997), "The Influence of Scottish Accountants in the United States: the Early Case of the Society of Accountants in Edinburgh", *The Accounting Historians Journal*, June, 117–41.

T. A. Lee (2002a), "UK Immigrants and the Foundation of the US Public Accountancy Profession", *Accounting, Business & Financial History*, March, 12 (1), 73–94.

T. A. Lee (2002b), "US Public Accountancy Firms and the Recruitment of UK Immigrants: 1850–1914", *Accounting, Auditing and Accountability Journal*, 14 (5), 537–64.

T. A. Lee (2002c), "A Genealogy of Professional and Public Service: the Contributions of Alexander Thomas Niven and John Ballantine Niven", *Accounting and Business Research*, 32 (2), 79–92.

T. A. Lee (2004), "Economic Class, Social Status, and Early Scottish Chartered Accountants", *The Accounting Historians Journal*, 31 (2), 27–51.

T. A. Lee and S. P. Walker (1997) "Scottish Emigration and US Accountancy", *CPA Journal*, December, 46–9.

Other historical studies of early Scottish public accountants

There are numerous publications available for readers interested in further studies of the early history of Scottish public accountancy. The following are given as a selection only.

Briston, R. J. & Kedslie, M. J. M. (1986), "Professional Formation: the Case of Scottish Accountants – Some Corrections and Further Thoughts", *British Journal of Sociology*, 37 (1): 122–130.

Carnegie, G. D., Parker, R. H. & Wigg, R. (2000), "The Life and Career of John Spence Ogilvy (1805–71), the First Chartered Accountant to Emigrate to Australia", *Accounting, Business & Financial History*, 10 (3), 371–83.

Kedslie, M. J. M. (1977), "Accountants in Old Aberdeen", *The Accountant's Magazine*, 73 (12), 514–16.

Kedslie, M. J. M. (1990), "Mutual Self-Interest – A Unifying Force: the Dominance of Societal Closure Over Social Background in the Early Professional Accounting Bodies," *The Accounting Historians Journal*, 17 (2), 1–20.

Lee, T. A. (1996), "Identifying the Founding Fathers of Public Accountancy: the Formation of the Society of Accountants in Edinburgh", *Accounting, Business & Financial History*, 6 (3), 315–35.

Lee, T. A. (1996), "The Influence of the Individual in the Professionalisation of Accountancy: the Case of Richard Brown and The Society of Accountants in

Edinburgh", in Nobes, C. W. & Cooke, T. (editors), *The Development of Accounting in an International Context*, London: Routledge, 31–48.

Lee, T. A. (2000), "A Social Network Analysis of the Founders of Institutionalised Public Accountancy", *The Accounting Historians Journal*, 27 (2), 1–48.

Macdonald, K. M. (1984), "Professional Formation: the Case of Scottish Accountants", *British Journal of Sociology*, 35 (2), 174–89.

McKinstry, S. (2000), *Twenty Seven Queen Street, Edinburgh: Home of Scottish Chartered Accountants 1891–2000*, Edinburgh: Institute of Chartered Accountants of Scotland.

Mepham, M. J. (1988), "The Scottish Enlightenment and the Development of Accounting", *The Accounting Historians Journal*, 15 (2), 151–76.

Schmitz, C. (1990), "George Auldjo Jamieson", in Slaven, A. & Checkland, S. (editors), *Dictionary of Scottish Business Biography*, Aberdeen: Aberdeen University Press.

Shackleton, J. K. (1995), "Scottish Chartered Accountants: Internal and External Political Relations, 1853–1916", *Accounting, Auditing & Accountability Journal*, 8 (2), 18–46.

Shackleton, J. K. & Milner, M. (1996), "Alexander Sloan: a Glasgow Chartered Accountant", in Lee, T. A. (editor), *Shaping the Accountancy Profession: the Story of Three Scottish Pioneers*, New York: Garland Publishing, 83–151.

Shackleton K. & Walker, S. P. (1998), *Professional Reconstruction: the Co-Ordination of the Accountancy Bodies 1930–1957*, Edinburgh: Institute of Chartered Accountants of Scotland.

Shackleton, K. & Walker, S. P. (2001), *A Future for the Accountancy Profession: the Quest for Closure and Integration*, Edinburgh: Institute of Chartered Accountants of Scotland.

Stewart, J. C. (1975), "The Emergent Professionals", *The Accountant's Magazine*, 71 (3), 113–16.

Walker, S. P. (1991), "The Defense of Professional Monopoly: Scottish Chartered Accountants and 'Satellites in the Accountancy Firmament' 1854–1914", *Accounting, Organisations and Society*, 16 (3), 257–83.

Walker, S. P. (1993), "Anatomy of a Scottish CA Practise: Lindsay, Jamieson & Haldane 1818–1918", *Accounting, Business & Financial History*, 3 (2), 127–54.

Walker, S. P. (1995), "The Genesis of Professionalisation in Scotland: a Contextual Analysis", *Accounting, Organisations and Society*, 20 (4), 285–312.

Walker, S. P. (1996), "The Criminal Upperworld and the Emergence of a Disciplinary Code in the Early Chartered Accountancy Profession", *Accounting History*, 1 (2), 7–36.

Walker, S. P. (1996), "George Auldjo Jamieson: a Victorian 'Man of Affairs'", in Lee, T. A. (editor), *Shaping the Accountancy Profession: the Story of Three Scottish Pioneers*, New York: Garland Publishing, 1–79.

Walker, S. P. (2003) "Agents of Dispossession and Acculturation, Edinburgh Accountants and the Highland Clearances", *Critical Perspectives on Accounting*, 14 (8), 813–53.

Other historical studies of early American public accountants

Despite the availability of archival material, there has been relatively little historical research on the early days of the US public accountancy profession other than the material listed in previous sections above. The following items, however, are of relevance to a reader wishing to examine this history further:

McMillan, K. P. (1999), "The Institute of Accounts: a Community of the Competent", *Accounting, Business & Financial History*, 9 (1), 7–28.

Merino, B. D. (1975), "The Professionalisation of Accountancy in America: a Comparative Analysis of Selected Accounting Practitioners, 1900–1925", *PhD Dissertation*, Tuscaloosa, AL: University of Alabama.

Miranti, P. J. (1996), "Birth of a Profession", *The CPA Journal*, April, 14–20 & 72.

Romeo, G. C. and Kyj, L. S. (1998), "The Forgotten Accounting Association: the Institute of Accountants," *The Accounting Historians Journal*, 25 (1), 29–55.

Romeo, G. C. and Leauby, B. A. (2004), "The Bookkeepers' Beneficial Association of Philadelphia: an Early Signal in the United States for a Professional Organisation", *Accounting History*, 9 (2), 7–33.

Slocum, E. L. and Roberts, A. R. (1980), "The New York School of Accounts: a Beginning", *The Accounting Historians Journal*, 7 (2), 63–70.

Wilkinson, G. (1928), "The Genesis of the CPA Movement", *Certified Public Accountant*, September, 261–6 & 279.

Archival sources

The material for the biographies came from a variety of library and archival sources. These include:

- The institutional records of the IAAG, SAA, SAE, and ICAS held by the Scottish Records Office at Charlotte Square in Edinburgh.
- Member handbooks for various UK professional bodies held by the library of the Institute of Chartered Accountants in England and Wales at Moorgate Place in London.
- Sundry documents and texts held by the National Library of Scotland at George IV Bridge in Edinburgh.
- The family archive of John Ballantine Niven at Mill Neck in New York.
- Various documents and texts held in the archive of the Church of Jesus Christ of Latter Day Saints at Salt Lake City in Utah.

There were also sundry responses from staff of major public accountancy firms and bodies in the US (e.g. the AICPA and the NYSSCPA).

Notes

1 The first migrant

1 This court was formed about 1860 and continues to the current day as the Federal Court of Claims – deciding on monetary claims in areas such as property, tax, litigation and employment.

5 The US public accountancy profession

1 The AAPA was formed with advice and assistance from another founding member of the ICAEW, Edwin Guthrie. Guthrie was visiting New York and was also instrumental in forming the public accountancy firm of Barrow, Wade, Guthrie & Company (BWGC) in 1883.
2 JCC went through several name changes until 1920 when it was finally merged into PWC. For purposes of this text, the name PWC remains throughout unless it is more relevant to use JCC.
3 DDGC became Deloitte, Plender, Griffiths & Company in 1905. For purposes of this text, the name DDGC remains throughout.
4 MMC became Marwick, Mitchell, Peat & Company (MMPC) in 1911 and PMMC in 1925. For purposes of this text, the name MMC remains throughout.
5 These figures are explained in more detail in the next section. They differ from equivalent data reported earlier in Lee (2002a & 2002b) because of additional information since the earlier research and a clerical error in the data relating to return migrations between 1910 and 1914. None of the other results in these earlier papers is affected by these changes.

6 Overview of the Scottish Chartered Accountancy migrants

1 Their careers and misdemeanors can be found in Walker, S. P., "The Criminal Upperworld and the Emergence of a Disciplinary Code in the Early Chartered Accountancy Profession," *Accounting History*, 1 (2), 1996, 7–36.
2 It is possible that there were other UQ accountants from Scotland permanently resident in the US prior to the end of 1914. It is unlikely, however, that their public accountancy careers were high profile. Several of the biographical sources used in this study mention accountants in the US as Scots (e.g. born and educated in Scotland). However, further research of genealogical sources revealed they had been born in the US of Scots immigrant parents.
3 A study of these recruitment changes in the SAE between 1854 and 1914 can be found in Walker, S. P., *The Society of Accountants in Edinburgh 1854–1914: A Study of Recruitment to a New Profession*, New York, NY: Garland Publishing, 1988.

4 The AAPA reorganised itself into the AIA in 1916 as a result of concerns about the uneven quality of CPA state requirements. The AIA effectively became a body independent of state bodies and its membership requirements included the passing of a uniform examination and defined practical experience. In 1959, the AIA was renamed the AICPA.
5 The ASCPA was a rival body to the AIA and formed in 1921. It mainly represented CPAs outside the main financial centres and sought to preserve local state autonomy over CPA laws in contrast to the AIA's attempts to harmonise. The two bodies eventually merged in 1936.

Index

This index covers the entire text content but does not include the specific biographees. Their page references can be found in the contents pages at the beginning of the book.